BRING IN THE RIGHT-HANDER!

BRING IN THE
RIGHT-HANDER!

My Twenty-Two Years in the Major Leagues

JERRY REUSS

University of Nebraska Press
Lincoln and London

Library of Congress Cataloging-
in-Publication Data

2650499

Reuss, Jerry, 1949–
Bring in the right-hander! :
my twenty-two years in the
major leagues / Jerry Reuss.
pages cm
Includes bibliographi-
cal references.
ISBN 978-0-8032-4897-7
(cloth : alk. paper)—
ISBN 978-0-8032-5508-1 (pdf)
—ISBN 978-0-8032-5509-8 (epub)
—ISBN 978-0-8032-5510-4 (mobi)
1. Reuss, Jerry, 1949–
2. Baseball players—United
States—Biography. I. Title.
GV865.R4243A3 2014
796.357092—dc23 [B]
2013035021

Set in Lyon by
Laura Wellington.
Designed by Nathan Putens.

*To my wife, Chantal, whose encouragement
helped me through the rough times and who was
there to celebrate the good times, this book is
dedicated to you! You are the love of my life.*

Contents

Prologue

Who would've guessed the momentum of the 1981 World Series would shift in the space of five pitches? Ron Guidry, the Yankees starter in Game Five, had beaten the Dodgers in his last three World Series starts against them since 1977 and was cruising through the first six innings.

I wasn't at my best, allowing four hits, three walks, and the Yankees' only run in the second inning. I also dodged a huge bullet working out of a bases-loaded jam in the top of the fourth. Then I found my groove as I retired eight of the next nine Yankees from the fifth through the seventh.

When Guidry fanned Dusty Baker to lead off the home half of the seventh, it marked fifteen of the last sixteen Dodger batters retired as Pete Guerrero stepped to the plate. I sat on the bench and thought, "Just get me a run, and I'll hold them right there." Somebody listened. Pete hammered a hanging slider into the left-field bleachers that tied the game. The crowd of more than fifty-six thousand came alive. The electricity that filled the air at Dodger Stadium the past two days was back in full force. Steve Yeager, the next Dodger batter, fell behind in the count 1–2 on a couple of nasty sliders. Then Guidry tried to sneak a fastball past the veteran catcher. The pitch caught too much of the plate, as Yeager homered to give us a 2–1 lead. Maybe I should have asked for some runs earlier.

The Yankees were retired in order in the eighth. We had Davey Lopes on first base with two outs and Ron Cey batting against reliever Rich Gossage. On a 1-1 pitch Cey was hit square on his batting helmet. Suddenly, the importance of the game paled in comparison to the status of a man's life. The crowd was quiet as we all waited to see if Cey could get up. After a few minutes, Ron was helped to the clubhouse and then taken to a local hospital for X-rays. Talk about a peak and valley of emotions.

We still led 2-1 in the top of the ninth. Everybody in the house was on their feet. Like my teammates, I was riding that wave of momentum and the excitement that was just three outs away. Bob Watson grounded to short for the first out. Lou Piniella, with an RBI (run batted in) single in the second, bounced a single up the middle. I shook my head as the ball came back to the infield. "I should have known that it wouldn't be easy," I thought. The next batter, Rick Cerrone, lined my first offering to center for the second out. Aurelio Rodriguez, standing at the plate, was all that stood between me and taking a series lead of three games to two. Rodriguez lined the first pitch just foul down the third base line for strike one. He tapped the next pitch foul at the plate for strike two. Before I delivered my next pitch, I did something for the first time during a game. While rubbing the ball I walked around the mound and scanned Dodger Stadium from left field to right, drinking in all the excitement. This was the moment I dreamed of ever since I was a kid back in Overland, Missouri. Like anybody who has ever played the game, I lived this scene in my mind many times in different schoolyards and ball fields. My next pitch would make my dream a reality.

Acknowledgments

"Work hard . . . and play just as hard!" That was the mantra repeated by Willie Stargell regarding his baseball career as well as his life away from the game. For me, I was living my baseball life by this code long before we were teammates on the Pirates. In fact, as you read this book, you may think that I played much more than I worked. That was hardly the case. With all the workouts in gyms lifting free weights, sweating through the various Nautilus programs, jogging miles around the National League (NL) ballparks, and conditioning on a Versa-Climber later in my career, I did the work behind the scenes as well as the countless hours spent on the field. The "play" part of the equation presented an equilibrium that allowed me to play in twenty-two Major League seasons.

Of course, no player makes it to the big leagues much less plays as long as I did without the help of a huge supporting cast. The following groups and individuals were instrumental in creating the proper learning environment, while teaching, coaching, directing, or helping me on my life's path. My heartfelt thanks to the priests, nuns, and lay teachers at All Souls School in Overland, Missouri; the moms and dads who served as Little League coaches and chauffeurs; the administrators, teachers, and coaches at Overland's Ritenour High School (a special tip of the cap to baseball coaches Lee Engert and Pete Hensel); Thoman-Boothe, American Legion Post 338, including the veterans (thank you for your service), administrators, and coaches; the front-office personnel of Major and Minor League teams, including owners, general managers (GMs), scouts, managers, coaches, trainers, and clubhouse attendants; my teammates over the years, whom I credit for the wins as I take the blame for the losses; my parents, Melvin and Viola, who were there when I played my first Little League game and followed my career to my final professional game; my brothers, Jim, who introduced me to the game in the backyard, and John, who played in many of the neighborhood games while we were growing up; my children, Shawn, Jason, and Brittany, who experienced the middle and later parts of my career that included long stretches away from home; and my wife, Chantal, who was there for moral support through all of the good times, the bad times, and the times in between.

Special thanks are given to the number of people who helped with this book. There were a number of former players and teammates who gave me their time and recollections of many of the events mentioned in this book. They are Norm Miller, Jimmy Wynn, Larry Dierker, Steve Blass, Jim Rooker, Kurt Bevacqua, Bruce Kison, Phil Garner, Jim Fregosi, Steve Garvey, Jay Johnstone, Bill Madlock, Rick Monday, Wally Moon, Steve Rodgers, and Carl Erskine.

Many thanks to those employed by the Pittsburgh Pirates: director of baseball communications Jim Trdinich, team photographer Dave Arroyo, and the liaison for alumni affairs, Sally O'Leary.

Former and current members of the Los Angeles Dodgers front office were kind enough to provide guidance and their professional expertise: Peter O'Malley, Fred Claire, Toby Zwikel, Steve Brener, Chad Gunderson, and Mark Langill.

Many thanks to David Smith of retrosheet.org, whose website and answers to my personal requests provided many of the dates, places, and people that are included in this book; Jim Gates of the National Baseball Hall of Fame, who filled in many of the blanks with information on long-forgotten facts about my career; the people at baseball-reference.com for their stats and information regarding my early years in the Minor Leagues; John L. Smith, columnist for the *Las Vegas Review-Journal* and an author of numerous Las Vegas—related books for advice and direction; author of many books on baseball Doug Feldman for his thoughts on promotion and minute details of the St. Louis Cardinals; the Major League Baseball Players Association, especially the late Marvin Miller, Donald Fehr, Dick Moss, the late Mark Belanger, and all of the players who served as player representatives over the years; and Jack Sands and Joe Barinelli of Sports Advisors Group, who took care of the business side of baseball.

So, it's time now to grab a chair, kick back, and enjoy my life in baseball!

BRING IN THE RIGHT-HANDER!

CHAPTER ONE

The Early Years

It was my older brother, Jim (six years my senior), who took me out to the backyard to play ball that first time. Jim, being right-handed, was surprised that I batted and threw left-handed. There wasn't a problem with me using his bat (other than it was too big for a five- or six-year-old), but it was awkward using his glove to catch. Once Dad saw how I loved to play, he picked up a glove for me to use. When Jim started hanging with his high school buddies, I enlisted other kids in the neighborhood to play ball games in the backyard, the schoolyard, and the lot on Lackland Avenue between a church and Ortmann's Funeral Home. Today, a Walgreen's drugstore occupies the spot where the church and the lot once stood.

Because Jim was playing Little League at Overland's Legion Park, I wanted to play. Once I was old enough, I tried out for a team and didn't make the cut. As there were so many other kids my age who wanted to play, other teams were added, and I played my first year of Little League. I was a first baseman in those early years and pitched only because the coaches insisted. Because I was bigger than most of the other kids and could throw harder, I experienced early success as a pitcher. My dreams were to be a Major League Baseball (MLB) player. I once expressed that opinion to Jim. He told me, "That's a big dream. Do you know that the odds are one in a million of making it?" Jim made good grades in high school, so I figured he must know something. But I shot back at him, "Maybe so, but I'll be that one!" That's cocky for a second or third grader, but I knew what I wanted. And I wasn't about to let anybody or anything stand in the way of my dreams.

It might have been 1955 or 1956 when I attended my first Major League game. My two brothers (Jim and my younger brother by two years, John) and I jumped in the car with Dad on a picture-perfect early-summer afternoon. It took less than a half hour to get a few blocks from Sportsman's Park (renamed Busch Stadium in 1953) and maybe another half hour driving around the neighborhood, as street parking was at a premium.

We were on foot only a few blocks from the entrance on the third base side, and as we approached I could sense the electricity of activity surrounding the park. People rushed from all directions to the ballpark entrance. We turned our walk up a notch as we got in step with the rest of the crowd. We slowed down once we found our place in line, as Dad had the tickets in hand and we passed through the turnstiles.

All my senses were on high alert. The entry level was cool but humid, much like our basement. The pungent smell of cleaner couldn't wash away years of stale cigars and beer that was past its prime. There was the sight and sound of a nearby vendor, dressed in his red-and-white-striped jacket and straw hat, yelling, "Score-cards . . . get your scorecards here! Can't tell the players without a scorecard. Just a dime." It took all of just a few seconds to part with some of my allowance to buy my first souvenir scorecard. My next purchase happened just seconds later, when I had to shell out for a pencil. That took care of that week's allowance. It was a rookie mistake that never happened again.

Before we trekked to our seats, there was a bathroom stop. No way Dad was getting up from his seat once the game began. While waiting for one of my brothers to finish, we stood outside the men's room just a few feet from the concession stand. There were new smells and the sounds of fresh popcorn popping and hot dogs sizzling on the grill. Even though I was feeling the effects of a full stomach after Mom's breakfast that could have fed the neighborhood, it was there and then that I realized hot dogs at the ballpark always tasted better than those we ate at home.

Once all zippers were up, we walked up the ramp that took us to the "promised land" on the concourse level. As Dad showed the usher our ticket stubs, I gazed upon a sight that would be forever burned into my mind. Looking beyond the overlap of the upper deck, I saw the bluest sky ever, stopped only by the dark-green pavilion roof shading the right-field seats. Draped with a screen that ran from the right-field foul pole at the 310-foot mark to the 354-foot mark in right-center field and affixed at the bottom to the top of the right-field wall, the pavilion was the area that Harry Caray talked about when Stan Musial lofted a fly ball in that direction. "There's a drive . . . deep to right . . . It might be outta here . . . It could be . . . It is, a home run!" Harry said as the noise from the crowd in the background rose to a crescendo while we listened to his account on our radios. Now I was seeing it for the first time.

Directly in front of the wall was the warning track that bordered the outfield wall and the fence in front of the first row of seats around the perimeter of the playing field. On the other side of the track was the greenest grass I'd ever seen, with no bare spots or weeds!

We found our seats behind the Cardinals' third base dugout as I watched the spectacle in front of me in total amazement. It was batting practice (BP). Some players were hitting, others were fielding grounders, and the rest of the players were in the outfield, chasing fly balls. There was action on the field no matter where you looked.

Looking above the left-field wall, I saw the Budweiser scoreboard. Though basic by today's standard, that hand-operated scoreboard gave fans the current pitchers and the inning-by-inning score in games around the Major Leagues.

After the teams finished their infield practice, a group of men in work uniforms like the one Dad wore came on to the field, carrying rakes and a long hose. The grounds crew swept, raked, and watered everything, including the dirt!

The Cardinals took the field as the nearly full house stood and applauded. The noise stopped only when the organist played the national anthem. I took those moments to view the Cardinal players (Ken Boyer at third was the player closest to our seats) in their home whites, navy blue hats, and the red Cardinal logo on the front of their uniform that played perfectly against the green grass, the tan color of the dirt, the dark green of the right-field seats, and the bluest of skies.

If I had to pinpoint the exact moment I fell in love with the game of baseball, that was probably it. Coming to the ballpark as a fan was one thing. That wasn't enough for me. I wanted to be a ballplayer. I wanted to play on this field. I wanted to do it forever. Within a few years, that wish was granted.

Little League all-star teams from all over the St. Louis area descended on Busch Stadium on July 9, 1960, for a chance to play on these hallowed grounds. My Overland team made the pilgrimage to play three innings in one of the four games occurring simultaneously in the outfield grass at 1:00 p.m. When I found out our game was played in right field, I immediately envisioned blasting a homer on the roof. In my mind, I heard Harry, "It might be outta here . . . !" All I could manage was a single to left in my only at bat. But I had the thrill and memory of a lifetime.

Be True to Your School

Toward the end of my freshman year at Ritenour Junior High, in 1964, the gym teachers announced that the junior varsity (jv) baseball team was holding tryouts. There may have been six or seven of us from Ritenour Jr. that walked the mile or so to the high school field, toting our equipment for the big day. At one time or another, each of us played with or against each other in the local ABC league, which was the only Little League in our area. Once dressed, we met JV coach Pete Hensel on the field. After a brief meeting, he told us to get loose and take our positions with the sophomores already on the field. Being a lefty, there were only five positions on the field that I could play. Each of those positions was occupied with someone from ABC who played that position better than I did, with the exception of pitcher. I knew then that the only way I would make this team would be as a pitcher, especially as I could throw a curve better than I could hit one. My career as a pitcher was born that very minute.

Doing the Bunny Hop

I don't remember much about my performance during my freshman year. I know that it was good enough to impress John "Bunny" Ailworth, the head coach for the local American Legion team, Thoman-Boothe Post 338. Bunny watched many of our high school games because Thoman-Boothe drew their players from Ritenour. He knew me before I attended high school, as he coached Jim, while I was always around the park for the games.

When our season was over I tried out for the team, and to my surprise and the chagrin of my upperclassmen, I made it. No doubt, Bunny, a former Minor League player, caught some hell from some parents for the choice, but he had his reasons for choosing a raw fourteen-year-old. He pulled me aside and told me why I made the team: "You have a real chance for a baseball career."

Bunny watched over me that year. He made me sit near him in the dugout as he kept a running dialogue of the game. "Watch how he pitches this guy," he would tell me. Or, "What pitch would you throw in this situation?"

Bunny also included me on trips with his coaches and other players to scout our Legion opponents. Usually, I sat with the pitching coach, Harry Gurley, or one of the other players behind home plate, as I learned how to find a hitter's weakness or read his base-running tendencies.

Bunny was right about the invaluable experience. Playing against players four or five years older worked in my favor when basketball season rolled around during my sophomore year. I was called up to the varsity early in the season and started the rest of the games that year. This was a big deal, as Ritenour played deep into the state tournament the previous year. At just fifteen, I was playing with the big boys and holding my own.

More Than a Game

Our JV baseball team was a good one. Not only did the freshmen play in the ABC league, but we also competed in the same league against our sophomore teammates. By the time we freshmen were juniors, we won the 1966 Missouri State Baseball Championship. For good measure, Ritenour repeated as state champions in 1967, our senior year.

I don't remember many individual games, but I do remember how fundamentally sound we were as a high school team. The varsity coach, Lee Engert, was a stickler for practicing fundamentals. He coached in a classic manner. First he "chalked" the drill by writing it on a chalkboard, "talked" us through our individual responsibilities, and "walked" us through every aspect as the play was practiced. More important than the play on the field was his approach regarding the proper attitude to play the game. Preparation and execution in gamelike conditions were the order every day. Of course, he had his rules, which included a curfew, no drinking, and maintaining grades. Attitude for Coach Engert was more about responsibility as an athlete, a student, and a man. He made sure that his ideals were followed. He checked grades and talked with other teachers about his players. He made it a point to know their families. If there was a problem away from school, he was there for any of his players when it counted. In many cases, he was the father figure in the lives of many of his players when there was no one else around. The lessons we learned from Coach Engert were larger than the game of baseball.

After games I pitched, Lee would rub analgesic balm on my left arm and shoulder. Years later, I learned that ice applied to the elbow and shoulder would help recovery much quicker. But the conversations that centered on the game, the strategy he used, the key plays we made or didn't make, and how we would focus on them during our next practice were all building blocks that helped me during my years as a player and later as a coach and broadcaster. It turned out to be much more important than a bag of ice. To this day, whenever I get a whiff of that balm used in training rooms everywhere, I still think of those high school moments.

At the end of every practice, pitchers at Ritenour ran the hill beyond right field. Back in the '60s, I estimated the angle to be between thirty to forty-five degrees and the distance around sixty yards. (It's been graded a bit more level since then.) We ran up the hill and jogged down backward. After five or six of these sprints, we were gassed. Gradually, running the hill became a personal challenge. I hated running up and down the hill, but I wouldn't allow it to beat me. Six sprints became eight, then ten, then twelve. I ran the hill every day I didn't pitch. Sometimes, it caused me to miss a ride home. Once after a game on a miserable, cold, and rainy spring day, I was running my sprints when my buddies drove by. I looked over as one of them mooned me from the passing car. I could hear them laughing as they sped off. "That's okay," I laughed. "One day, you'll watch me pitch in the big leagues."

Watching the Pros

I attended a number of ball games at Busch Stadium (now referred to as Busch Stadium 1) over the years. Most of the time I sat behind the Cardinals' dugout, but I ventured out to the bleachers once or twice. When the Cardinals moved to Busch Stadium 2 downtown in May 1966, I still preferred to sit in the reserved section above the third base dugout. At the new ballpark the Cardinals moved from the third base dugout to the first base side. That was fine by me. I could look into the Cardinals' dugout and watch my favorite players, observing how professionals handled themselves at the best as well as the worst of times.

Now sixteen and seventeen, my friends and I were old enough to drive. The Cardinals instituted Teen Night, a Friday-night promotion that featured reserved-seat tickets for five dollars. That meant after our high school game, we changed, stopped home for a quick bite, picked up our dates, and headed to the ballpark. Sitting in our reserved seats along the third base line (where else?), we watched the Cardinals as we listened to the latest hits by local favorites Bob Kuban and the In-Men, between innings, as they were perched on the concourse near the foul pole in right field. Imagine . . . the Cardinals, Kuban, and my best girl on a warm Friday night. It didn't get any better than that! Or did it?

My Baseball Cards Came to Life

In July 1966, the visiting Atlanta Braves invited me to throw in the bullpen before a game against the Cardinals. By this time I'd become an accomplished high school pitcher and was drawing attention from scouts in the St. Louis area. I remember meeting the Atlanta scout in front of the double glass doors at Busch Stadium 2, the players' entrance. We made our way down the steps to the visitors' clubhouse and waited for the equipment manager to get me a uniform. There I was, just seventeen years old, staring at faces of players that I had seen only on baseball cards, only this time they were in various stages of preparation for that night's game. "This should fit," the man told me as he handed me a Major League uniform. "Go around the corner and take one of the open lockers there," he said. The scout said he'd meet me in the dugout.

There I was, with my high school gym bag, which carried my

shoes, glove, jock, and sweatshirt, as I walked into a Major League clubhouse for the first time. I tried to act as if I belonged. That was a tough act to pull off when my knees were knocking. There was only one open locker on the back side of the visitors' clubhouse. It was near the end of a row, between two lockers that were occupied by players' equipment. Because nobody was there, I dressed quickly and quietly and made my way to the field. I was seventeen, in a Braves uniform, as I walked down the ramp to the visitors' dugout, prepared for a tryout in Busch Stadium. I wasn't nervous . . . I was petrified!

I was ready in no time and cut loose with everything I had for a brief ten- or fifteen-minute session. Apparently, they liked what they saw, as they nodded when I threw a pitch. "Jerry, thanks for coming here to throw for us. We wish you the best, and we'll keep in touch," the scout said. I took a minute or two as I sat on the bench in the visitors' dugout and watched the Cardinals on the field. I recognized all of them. I had their baseball cards at home. On that day I dressed in a Major League uniform and walked on the same field they did.

Back in the clubhouse I found the equipment manager, reading a newspaper. "Where should I put my uniform?" I asked. He looked up and said, "Throw it in the basket in the middle of the floor." He went back to his newspaper. When I got to the locker, I saw the street clothes of the players who occupied the lockers on both sides of me. Both players were elsewhere.

Because I was in no hurry, I looked inside the locker to my left. There was the uniform top with the number 44 on it. My mouth dropped. I had a locker next to Hank Aaron! By the time I caught my breath, someone sat down on the stool in front of the locker to my right. I turned to see who it was and immediately recognized Eddie Matthews. In his shorts and sweatshirt, he grabbed his paperback and started reading. Not wanting to bother a future Hall of Famer, I got undressed, grabbed a towel, and headed for the shower. I hoped by the time I returned I could regain some composure and say hello.

Both Aaron and Matthews were at their respective lockers when I returned. Eddie was engrossed in his book, *Beau Geste*, the movie version playing at the local theaters. I was finally able to speak, so I asked him, "How's the book?" I thought, "That's a nice icebreaker." Without looking up, he said, "Horseshit!" Well, that's a word I never heard until that moment. If nothing else came from this tryout, I had added to my ever-increasing vocabulary. I didn't know how powerful this word was until I played professionally. This was one of those "magic words" that could get a player tossed from a game. Shout it loud enough in an umpire's direction, and it'll get you an early shower and probably a fifty-dollar fine.

"What brings you here, young man?" the voice to my left asked. I introduced myself and told Hank Aaron about the workout as I got dressed. After a few minutes he said with a smile, "I wish you all the best and good luck." I answered, "Mr. Aaron, thank you. I wish you the best as well." We didn't know then how our paths would cross in the future.

"Were you the kid warming up in the bullpen a little while ago?" asked Eddie Matthews, who closed his book and placed it in his locker to my right. I turned and answered, "Yes, sir, that was me," I said quietly. "I heard you were really bringing it," he said, looking me in the eye with a smile on his face. "Thank you" was all I could manage. I wanted to ask him why he was still reading a book if it was horseshit, but thought better of it.

As I gathered my gear and put it in my gym bag, I thanked both of them, wished them the best, and walked out of the clubhouse and back to reality. Years later, I met both Hank and Eddie on several occasions. I reminded them once that we met in St. Louis that July day. I can understand why they didn't remember. Me . . . I never forgot.

There's a postscript to this story. Whenever I played in St. Louis as a visiting player, I was always assigned one of those three lockers. On my last road trip as a player in 1990 with the Pirates, I dressed in that same middle locker. I thought about that first visit then, but haven't told the story until now.

College Scholarship or Professional Baseball?

*June 6, 1967: Drafted by the Cardinals
in the second round of the amateur draft*
Sometime during my junior year at Ritenour, Mom was sitting at the kitchen table, paying the bills. She stopped me as I entered the kitchen and said, "Sit down." She began in a businesslike tone. "Dad and I looked at our savings and realized that it won't be possible for us to send both you and John to college." She continued, "Even with Jim working, it cost us more than we budgeted. For both you and John to attend college, one of you will have to get a scholarship." She looked me straight in the eye and said, "You have the grades and athletic ability. I'm depending on you to make it happen." Because my focus throughout high school was to get a college scholarship or sign a baseball contract, this was something that had already crossed my mind. What surprised me was Mom's straightforward talk. Most of the time her approach to anything was to test the waters and ease into what was on her mind. This time, she just dove in. "Mom, it's already in the works," I told her.

Since the start of my sophomore year, I had received letters from different schools around the Midwest, inquiring about my college plans, with full-ride commitments from both Southern Illinois University and the University of Missouri coming during my senior year. During the spring of 1967 both Mom and Dad breathed a bit easier when I committed to SIU to play both baseball and basketball.

I was working at Boyd's in nearby Northwest Plaza, selling men's clothes, when Mom called me at work that day in early-June 1967 and told me that the Cardinals had drafted me. I was surprised it was the hometown Cardinals because their scouts had stayed in the background. George Silvey, the Cardinals' scouting and farm director, lived about a mile away from us, and his son, Tim, was a high school teammate. Maybe the Cardinals had decided a low-key approach best suited their interests when it came time to draft and sign me. For me, it was the first step toward a career as a Major League Baseball player.

CHAPTER TWO

Turning Pro

Being drafted by the Cardinals meant that I might have to rethink my commitment to SIU. Both Coach Engert and Bunny talked to me about my future. Coach spoke more about the right fit for me both academically and for sports. "Both are equally important," he started. "You don't know where a career in professional sports will take you. No matter where you go, however, you can take your education with you."

Bunny's approach was more pedestrian. I told him the scholarship offers were split between baseball and basketball. "Look, you're a good high school basketball player. But as far as major college material, you're too small and too slow. As a baseball player, you're one of the best pitching prospects I've seen in years. If you sign a contract, within a few years you will be pitching in the Major Leagues. You can attend school in the off-season."

I had two different opinions and two different points of view. Both were valid. Both were made with my best interests at heart. Before I made my decision, I wanted to hear what the Cardinals had to say.

My parents and I met with the Cardinals at Busch Stadium 2 on Sunday, June 25. While the Cardinals were playing the Phillies in a doubleheader, we met in the general manager's office with George Silvey and scouts George Hasser and Joe Monahan. The general manager in 1967 was Stan Musial, his only year at the helm.

We were at a definite disadvantage because none of us had any experience in negotiating baseball contracts. There was no information available to make any kind of valid judgment on what was or wasn't fair. The Cardinals, who did this every day and knew what kid got what and when they got it, weren't about to share anything. So we sat in Stan's office, admiring the pictures and citations on the wall and the trophies on his bookshelves, as the Cardinals put together a proposal.

This was what they offered: $15,000 cash, $7,500 payable upon contract approval and the other $7,500 payable in January 1968; a progressive bonus that paid $1,000 after ninety days on the Double A (AA) roster, $1,500 after ninety days on the Triple A (AAA) roster, and $5,000 after ninety days on the Major League roster; and a college scholarship of $1,000 a semester for eight semesters, with strings attached. If I met all the criteria, the signing bonus would be a maximum $30,500. That figure overwhelmed Mom and Dad. They had no idea that a Major League Baseball team would give a high school kid that kind of money just to sign a contract. Hell, it was more than they paid for the house!

Then, out of nowhere, Mom asked if there was any money for her and Dad to spend on a vacation. I sat there with my mouth wide open. I wasn't the only one. George and the scouts were speechless as they looked at one another. George cleared his throat and said, "Well, let's see what we can do about that." They needed some time to talk and invited us to sit in Stan's box and watch the ball game.

We walked from the glass doors of the reception area to Stan's seats behind the Cardinals' dugout. While sitting there for a few moments, I saw Orlando Cepeda miss a home run (HR) by a few feet as he drilled a Jim Bunning pitch foul off a window in the Stadium Club in left field. On the next pitch he hit another window of the Stadium Club; this time it was fair, as he connected for his tenth home run of the season.

As "ChaCha" rounded the bases, Dad finally spoke, "That's a

lot of money!" He paused and then said, "When I started working at eighteen, it took years before I earned what they offered you today." At least he had an idea. My thoughts were on the game. How I wanted to be out there. That first step on the road of opportunity awaited me on the other side of those glass doors.

I told Dad that I'd have to pass on the scholarship to SIU if I signed. Who knew what that scholarship was worth in terms of future dollars? Dad didn't. He never completed high school. The guidance counselors at Ritenour knew and explained the numbers to me in detail. They also told me the life experiences in college were as equally valuable and couldn't be measured by any metric.

There were other factors to consider. At the end of four years at twenty-two years old (a senior citizen in the eyes of an eighteen-year-old), would a pro baseball career opportunity still be there? What if I was hurt in college and couldn't play? However, if I signed, I could still attend college in the off-season, I rationalized. If I was hurt and couldn't play anymore as a professional, I could still get my education from the money included in the bonus and get on with my life. I was involved in an internal war and at a crossroads in my life. On one hand, there was a four-year college scholarship with the prospects of turning professional at twenty-two years old or the alternate universe of seizing the opportunity at eighteen and following my heart's desire. As we walked back to Stan's office, I didn't know what I would do, as Dad told me the decision was mine.

The Clincher

Once seated, George told us that the Cardinals would sweeten the deal by $2,000 for my parents' long-awaited vacation. At eighteen I had no business sense and didn't think to ask if we could improve on some of the other numbers. If they didn't, we could have still walked out with $32,500 on the table and time on our side. My freshman year in college didn't begin until late August or early September, at which point the Cardinals would lose their negotiating rights.

Instead, I got caught up in the emotion of the moment. I saw Mom's face light up. Remembering all the Little League, high school, and American Legion games they saw my brothers and me play as well as the other sacrifices parents make for their kids, this was the chance of a lifetime for me to repay them. Who knew if it would ever come again? I chose the opportunity of a lifetime and my heart's desire instead of the potential that a college degree could offer. The vacation money tipped the scales, and I signed my first professional contract that day.

To this day I don't regret the decision. My parents and John went on a cruise during the Christmas and New Year's holiday in 1967–68. I was invited to join them, but I declined. I was home during the holiday break from my freshman year at SIU. I had been living out of a suitcase since I signed the contract and needed the holidays to get my feet back on the ground. Besides, I had the house and the family car to myself for ten days!

CHAPTER THREE

Life in the Minors

After signing the contract there were a few people I had to contact. The coaches and players of Thoman-Booth Post 338 (my American Legion team), Coach Engert, and SIU head baseball coach Joe Lutz, with whom I had signed a letter of intent, were first on the list. Friends and relatives were next, as I packed what I needed for my first summer away from home. Everyone had wished me well.

I arrived in St. Petersburg, Florida, in late June, as workouts for the newly signed players were in the final days before the Rookie League season began in Sarasota. My first impression was that these guys looked like pretty good ballplayers. The pitchers could all throw hard, and the hitters were able to reach the fences in batting practice. The first few days were spent conditioning and transitioning to professional baseball.

The man in charge was George Kissell. George had already been in baseball since 1940 with the exception of three years of military service during World War II. During his baseball years he was a player, manager, scout, and roving instructor. Eventually, he spent seven years with the Major League club as a coach and field coordinator. By the time of his passing in 2008, he spent a total of sixty-nine years in service to the Cardinals.[1]

There wasn't much he didn't know about the game. He carried a legal pad on a clipboard and kept notes on everything we did.

Before workouts, he worked his way down the list compiled the day before, talked about it, and prepared us for that day's work. It was like Coach Engert and Bunny became one person and was wearing a Cardinals uniform.

Everybody who went through the Cardinals system had his own memory of George. I remember how he reminded us the correct height for every throw we would make. "Knock the bird off the chest!" he reminded us daily, referring to the stitching of two Cardinals perched on our threadbare uniform top. It didn't matter if the throw was a pitch from the mound to the catcher or a throw to an infielder from an outfielder. The correct height for every throw was chest high. He also advocated that pitchers purchase the heavy wool sweatshirts and wear them daily. It was the belief of George and other baseball people of that time that a pitcher had to keep his arm warm to prevent soreness, and the heavy wool sweatshirts did the job best. Never mind the fact that the wool in the sweatshirts caused them to shrink every time they were washed.

After a few days the team boarded a bus for Sarasota, as it was time to begin play for the first time as professionals. The fields we used were Payne Park for night games and a four-field complex that exists today behind Ed Smith Stadium.

On the day of my first start a huge thunderstorm chased us from one of the fields at the complex. I figured that was it for that day, especially after such a rainstorm. That's the way it was in St. Louis, but this was Florida in the summer. The field was ready within a half hour. My debut as a pro was a memorable one. I pitched four innings, striking out six, while allowing just one hit. My next start wasn't quite as impressive, as I surrendered my first pro home run to Darrel Evans, who played for the Kansas City A's rookie team. He would hit four more against me in eighty-four at bats during our Major League careers over the next twenty-plus years.[2]

Cedar Rapids, Iowa, Summer of 1967

In early July after two Rookie League appearances, I was sent to Class A Cedar Rapids in the Midwest League. Class A ball was a definite upgrade from the Rookie League, as we had uniforms (home and away) that fitted instead of hand-me-downs from the Major League club. At eighteen years old I saw the world . . . at least the world that included small cities in the upper Midwest. I loved the lifestyle and performed well. In nine starts I was 2–5, with a 1.86 ERA (earned run average), sixty-three strikeouts, and nineteen walks in fifty-nine innings. As I was ready to board the bus for our season-ending road trip, Jack Krol, the Cedar Rapids manager, pulled me aside and told me I was called up to the Pacific Coast League (PCL) in Tulsa, Oklahoma.

Tulsa, Oklahoma, Summer of 1967

In his first year as manager with the Tulsa Oilers when I joined them was future Hall of Famer Warren Spahn. I was in awe the first time I met him. He read it in my face and immediately put me at ease. "It's no different here than Cedar Rapids," he told me as we boarded a plane to Phoenix. "Just keep the ball down, throw strikes, and good things will happen."

My first Triple A game with the Oilers was at Westgate Park in San Diego, which was torn down in 1968 and replaced by Fashion Valley Shopping Center.[3] The date was August 28. I do remember a few things about the game. I threw my first pitch down the middle, and it was called a ball. The same thing happened on the next pitch. I walked the batter on four pitches and was behind 2–0 when Spahnnie came out to visit.

"Warren, if those pitches aren't strikes, then I can't pitch in this league," I told him. Later, Spahn was thrown out of the game for arguing a play at second base. Before the inning was over I gave up six runs and walked four, as Jim Gentile touched me for a grand slam.[4] Welcome to the PCL.

Little Rock, Arkansas, Summer of 1968

After the 1967 season ended I still hadn't registered for classes at SIU in Carbondale. Because I would have been eligible for the military draft had I not been a full-time student, I needed to be in school. Joe Lutz, the baseball coach, came to my rescue. He walked me through registration and secured an athletic waiver that allowed me to work out with the team during the school year. I took full advantage of the opportunity and never missed a practice. When spring break rolled around in March, the Cardinals flew me to Florida for ten days of Minor League spring training. When the Cardinals played in St. Louis on weekends during April and May, I drove home from Carbondale and worked out with them.

When school was finished in June, they assigned me to their Texas League AA club in Little Rock, Arkansas. Arriving in mid-June, I started sixteen games and pitched 112 innings, which was fewer than the 168 innings pitched by Santiago Guzman, who led the team.[5] I arrived at a crossroads regarding my career. If I continued as a full-time student, I could fall behind in my baseball development and watch other pitchers pass me by. If I played the whole season and picked up school when I could, I would lose my school draft deferment.

Another option was to join the U.S. Army Reserve, which allowed me a compromise. I joined a unit in Little Rock in August with a number of teammates, including pitcher Harry Parker. When the 1968 season was over I checked out a local army unit at the Records Center in St. Louis, just a few miles from where I grew up. Because they had an opening, I transferred to the St. Louis unit. It was a fortunate bit of luck, as Harry, who stayed in the Little Rock unit, was called into basic training in early-April 1969, thereby missing the entire 1969 season. Chances are I would have been there with him.

My First Spring Training, 1969

Over the winter of 1968 and 1969, baseball went through a number of changes. With the addition of the San Diego Padres and Montreal Expos in the National League and the Kansas City Royals and Seattle Pilots in the American League, each league of twelve teams was now divided into two divisions of six teams each. The winners of each division would compete against each other in a League Championship Series (LCS), then the best of five games, to determine the pennant winners that would face each other in the World Series.

There were some major rule changes for the upcoming year. In an effort to counteract a trend of low-scoring games, Major League Baseball adopted two measures during the Baseball Winter Meetings held in December 1968. The strike zone was reduced to the area over home plate between the armpits and the top of the knees of a batter. Also, the height of the pitching mound was reduced from fifteen inches to ten inches, and it was recommended that the slope be gradual and uniform in every park.[6]

There were also changes regarding the business of baseball. The first pension agreement between ownership and the players was set to expire in March 1969. Marvin Miller, the executive director of the Major League Baseball Players Association, had his pension proposals ready in mid-1968, which included an increase of the owners' contribution, a reduction in years to qualify from five to four, and retroactively including players from the previous ten years. In an effort to show that the players meant business, Marvin and the players devised a tactic that had players hold off on signing their 1969 contracts until an agreement could be reached.[7]

Baseball had a new commissioner. Bowie Kuhn was a compromise choice between the two leagues. Kuhn, who didn't want to start his term with labor problems, encouraged a new deal with the players. It took some arm-twisting on the part of Dick Meyer, vice president

(VP) of the Cardinals and chairman of the Players Relations Committee (PRC), to make it happen. The settlement included most of what the association wanted in pension contribution, the vesting requirement reduced to four years, and the retroactive application of benefits and vesting requirements.[8]

The players as a group scored a major victory, but some individual players paid a price. With spring training knocking at the door, there was little time to negotiate contracts, so many players were presented with take-it-or-leave-it offers. Joe Torre, then with the Braves, was one of those players. When Joe and Braves GM Paul Richards couldn't reach a contract accord, Joe was shipped to the Cardinals on March 17 in exchange for Orlando Cepeda, who slumped in 1968 to .248, with 16 HR and 73 RBI after batting .325, with 25 HR and leading the National League in RBI with 111 in 1967.[9]

August A. Busch Jr. Makes His Presence Known

Having his Cardinals play in three of the last five World Series and win World Championships in 1964 and 1967 should have put Cardinals owner August A. Busch Jr. on top of the world during the spring of 1969. He was anything but overjoyed. The game he bought into was changing. He liked to handle business his way without interference, much like he did when he purchased the Cardinals in 1953. It proved to be sports-marketing genius. Anheuser-Busch, also owned by Busch, went from second in the American brewing industry to first, where it stands today, because of the tie-in with the Cardinals.[10]

And Busch shared this good fortune with the Cardinal players. When he became aware of racial bias in St. Petersburg in 1961, he leased two of the best motels in the city so that in 1962 and for years after players could live in the same accommodations.[11]

Busch also helped set up Stan Musial in the restaurant business in St. Louis, awarded Roger Maris an Anheuser-Busch distributorship in Florida, and gave Lou Brock a yacht and Bob Gibson a motor home when they retired.[12]

In 1961 Busch intervened on Curt Flood's behalf and "asked" manager Johnny Keane to give Flood an opportunity to play regularly. Busch also provided the Flood family with financial help for their eldest son's medical bills and found Flood's wife a job as a print model for the brewery.[13]

When Curt painted Busch's portrait in 1967, the club owner was "tickled to death" with it and hung it on his yacht. Busch was so pleased with Flood's work that he commissioned him to paint his entire family. This made great newspaper copy, and once the story about the Busch painting came out, it led to exhibitions of Flood's paintings and for many paid commissions. Busch became a patron of Flood's art, and Curt took full advantage of it.[14]

Not only did Busch extend his benevolence to star players, but he extended it to all players in varying degrees. The Cardinals had baseball's first million-dollar payroll in 1968. On the road we enjoyed private rooms.

On my first trip with the Cardinals in September 1969, I unlocked the door to my room at the Pittsburgh Hilton to discover that I had a suite! I had only read about them. For this leg of the trip, I would stay in one.

Single rooms for players remained the custom for the Cardinals during my tenure. The rest of Major League Baseball still housed players two to a room, with the exception of some superstars.

When we returned from a road trip, each player received a "beer slip." That letter could be redeemed for a case of their favorite Anheuser-Busch beer. Being just twenty years old at the time, I couldn't use it. But Dad did and sure enjoyed having an extra case or two of beer every month.

While other clubs used both commercial airlines and charters for their transportation (the Dodgers with their own plane were the exception), the Cardinals chartered exclusively with United

Airlines, who stocked each flight with chilled cases of Budweiser for every trip.

There were numerous family picnics at Grant's Farm, Busch's estate, whose acreage housed many wild animals as well as the brewery's famed team of Clydesdales. The farm had tours open to the public, but during the team picnics it was closed for the enjoyment of Cardinal family members.

Yes, Mr. Busch could be a very generous man, as long as his generosity was on his terms.

Trouble Brewing in a Baseball Paradise

The divide between the Cardinal players and Busch had been growing since Marvin Miller became head of the Players Association in 1966. Marvin negotiated the first Basic Agreement with baseball owners in 1968 that called for a grievance procedure, a raise in the minimum salary from $7,000 to $10,000, and the development of an owners-players committee to study the reserve clause.[15]

It widened more when Curt Flood issued a salary ultimatum to the club in early-March 1969 that was printed in the *St. Louis Globe-Democrat*. After being offered a $5,000 raise from his 1968 salary of $72,500, he rejected the club's offer by telling them, "If you people want a .300 hitter who also happens to be the best center fielder in baseball, it will cost you $90,000, which is not $77,500 and it's not $89,999.99." Of course, Busch had a fit when he heard about it. Obviously, Flood no longer held that special place in Busch's heart.[16]

With labor discontent and Flood's outburst on his mind, Busch could no longer hold his anger about the perceived ingratitude of the players. So on March 22 he entered the Cardinals' clubhouse at Al Lang Field with a contingent of Anheuser-Busch and Cardinal officials as well as the St. Louis beat writers, to deliver a message to his players.

As a twenty-year-old in my first spring training, I had no idea what the speech was really about, as it definitely had an undercurrent meant for others in the room. I only wondered why it was being delivered in a public forum instead of just to the players.

In reading transcripts of it in 2011 and taking it at face value, it appeared that he wanted the focus back on the field and not on pension or contract matters, which he believed to be detrimental to the game. It was more a state-of-the-game message from management's point of view after a winter of baseball discontent that was meant for public consumption. Fair enough, but there was no mention of management's unwillingness to understand the players' point of view. Nor was there any mention of what management learned from negotiations with the players' union that would prevent a situation like this from ever happening again. What he said in this speech was one thing; his actions afterward told more about his true feelings.

An Unforgettable Spring

Even with all of the peripheral issues surrounding the team, there were some lasting spring-training memories. I remember when Bob Gibson delivered a knockdown pitch to the Mets' Tommy Agee on the first pitch in his first at bat as a member of the Mets; I remember my surprise when Steve Carlton yelled, "Welcome to the National League," as Agee was sprawled in the dirt; I remember the sad look on Orlando Cepeda's face when he came to the clubhouse to pack his bags after being traded to Atlanta; I remember Joe Torre, traded for Cepeda, when he put on his Cardinal uniform for the first time; I remember how Stan Musial and Red Schoendienst exchanged endless "Whadda-ya-say's" every time Stan came to the clubhouse; I remember the professionalism of the veteran Cardinal players working fundamental plays with rookies, knowing that the kid who stood beside him could be the one who would replace him; I remember the interviews with Jack Hermann and Bob Broeg, two writers from competing St. Louis papers that I read on a daily basis while growing up; I remember meals at a different restaurant every night that I bought with Major League meal money; I remember the hard work that players and coaches poured into every day; I remember watching the players who packed their bags, as some were reassigned to the Minors, had their contracts traded or sold, or were given their outright release; I remember when Red called me over and told me it would be my last day with the big club as he took the time to thank me for the hard work I did. I told him, "Thank you for inviting me and for the opportunity to spend the extra time around the Major Leaguers." After spending four or five weeks with the Cardinals, I developed a taste for the Major League lifestyle. I was willing to do whatever it took to be a part of it. All in all, it was one hell of a spring.

Tulsa, Oklahoma, Summer of 1969

Expansion opened a number of jobs around baseball, as the Tulsa club had just four pitchers return from the Pacific Coast League Championship club of 1968. This meant that many of us who would've stayed in AA ball another year had jumped a classification. I was one of them. In 1969 the American Association returned, as the expansion of Major League Baseball created a need for more Class AAA farm clubs. There were growing pains, as I was among the American Association league leaders in walks and hits allowed, but I was also among the leaders in complete games and led the league in innings pitched and games started. All of this happened when I was twenty years old in my first full season of pro ball.[17]

There was one day in early July when many of us received a registered letter from the Cardinals. It contained a check in the amount of fifteen hundred dollars, as all reached the ninety-day period in AAA ball that qualified us for part of our progressive bonus. There were some happy players but even happier wives when the checks were deposited in their respective bank accounts.

CHAPTER FOUR

Twenty-Four Hours from Tulsa

Anytime a Minor League player received mail from the parent club, it was opened immediately. Somehow, for better or worse, the letter inside the envelope changed your life. In this case, the letter was from the Cardinals' general manager, Bing Devine, dated August 25, 1969, and stated:

> Dear Jerry,
> Your contract has this date been recalled by the St. Louis National Baseball Club of the National League. You are to report to our club in time for a work out at 10:00 AM on Thursday, September 4.
> Best wishes,
> Bing Devine

That's how I learned I was called to the big leagues.

My First Day in the Major Leagues

When the AAA season ended on Monday, September 1, I was packed and ready for the six-hour drive home to St. Louis. I don't remember much about the actual drive except it was the first one as a future Major League ballplayer.

The workout on Thursday included seven other players from the Tulsa club. They were pitchers Santiago Guzman and Reggie Cleveland; infielders Chip Coulter, Jerry DaVanon, and Joe Hague;

catcher Ted Simmons; and outfielder Leron Lee. The workout gave the coaches and Red a chance to see what we looked like and an idea of how much we had improved since spring training.

On Friday morning I couldn't wait to drive to the ballpark. I jumped into the car and made the fifteen-minute drive to Busch Stadium around one o'clock. Because I had set up my locker after the workout on Thursday, there wasn't much to do. I do remember putting on the new uniform with my name on the back above the number 49. I walked across the locker room and stood in front of the bathroom mirror to admire the reflection. It was the same uniform I wore in spring training, but that was then. This was St. Louis on my first day in the big leagues. I remembered all the neighborhood games when we all dreamed of wearing our own Cardinals uniform. And there I stood, the first day of living that dream.

While sitting on the bench watching Nelson Briles shut out the Expos on Teen Night, that same promotion that once lured me to the ballpark, I looked a few sections above the visitors' dugout and spotted the section where I had bought seats for a previous Teen Night. I thought of how just two or three years earlier, I had sat there with a date, peering into the Cardinals' dugout, watching how the big leaguers handled themselves. There I was, staring back at those seats. On that day I was the luckiest twenty-year-old kid in St. Louis!

An Eye-Opening Experience

Long bus rides are normal for the Minor Leagues. When I played in Little Rock in 1968 and Tulsa in '69, we rode the bus for most trips, flying only on the longest ones. Things would be different with the Cardinals, with air travel being the rule, not the exception.

My first trip with St. Louis was to Philadelphia and Pittsburgh. Most teams in the late '60s flew commercial and chartered only as a last resort. From a private terminal at St. Louis's Lambert Field, the September call-ups boarded a United Airlines charter after everybody else and were told to find an empty seat. There was a protocol to be followed. Asking a veteran player for permission to sit next to him was a courteous and wise thing to do. No rookie wants to have his ass chewed out for taking a veteran player's personal space without asking. Besides, there were plenty of other opportunities to have your ass chewed out for some other real or imagined transgression.

To some of the older players, rookies were a pain in the ass. Realistically, a veteran knew one day one of the kids would take his job. We reminded him of that every time he laid eyes on us.

Playing a few years in the Minors taught me that certain seats in the front of the bus or plane were reserved for the manager, the coaches, front-office personnel, and veteran players. Once a player found a seat, it stayed his until a roster change opened another seat. If you wanted that open seat, you could make the switch. If two or more players wanted a seat change, then the one with the most time in the Majors had higher priority.

The same system was in place for seats on the bus to and from the ballpark and for a place in line for the postgame meal. Once the everyday players and veterans served themselves, then the rookies could sample some of what was remaining. It reminded me of a family breakfast when I was seven or eight. I was eating cereal like my brothers as Dad was served his favorite, soft-boiled eggs. I asked Mom while it was my turn to do the dishes why Dad had eggs and we ate cereal. Her answer was one of life's lessons. "When you earn the money that puts food on the table for the entire family," she responded, looking me straight in the eye, "then you can eat what you want." She continued, "And he'll have eggs every morning if he wants them. It's about respect and appreciation." The next morning I shocked the hell out my dad when I said, "Thanks for the cereal," as I was excused from the table and headed off to school. I was told Dad said, "Does anybody know what that was about?"

When Leo Ward, the traveling secretary, issued us our meal-money envelopes, we rookies were thrilled when we saw $75 in cash (the Major League meal allowance was $15 a day as opposed to $5 a day in Triple A). For most of us our monthly pay was around $1,000–$1,200 a month (my salary was $1,150 a month) during our Triple A season. After deductions, rent, food, and savings (we were paid only during the five-month season), not many of us walked around with money in our pockets. For our month in the Majors, we were all paid a prorated amount of the Major League minimum of $10,000, which was around $1,750. With the bump in salary and meal money, we were "living large."

Our first stop was Philadelphia and the well-aged Connie Mack Stadium. I couldn't wait to see the field, so I dressed and rushed down the runway to the dugout. Nobody mentioned the low overhang, and when I stepped up I banged my head. (I repeated this incident at Tiger Stadium in 1987.) I wonder how many players had that happen to them over the years.

The dugout was tiny, so before the game Red sent the three rookie pitchers to the bullpen. Once the game was under way, Tim McCarver, who wasn't in the starting lineup, brought over a half-dozen baseballs to sign. I signed them with no questions asked (signing balls during the game is another baseball taboo), as did everyone else in uniform. Tim gave the balls to a man waiting outside the bullpen, and I thought nothing of it. A few innings later the guy returned with a shopping bag, as the veteran players beelined to the grounds-crew garage in the back of the bullpen. With the help of McCarver and the unidentified man, those signed baseballs were magically turned into Philly cheese steaks. When Tim invited the rookies to the garage, there were still a few remaining. With one taste I was hooked. Only Dad's barbecued pork steaks topped this delicacy. I learned on that warm September evening, signed baseballs were instant currency, for cheese steaks or whatever could be negotiated.

We won the game, and as I was coming off the field Red grabbed me and asked, "How were those cheese steaks?" I was busted. "You knew?" was all I could say. "Hell yes, I knew," he laughed. "You still got cheese all over your face!"

The Miracle Mets

On September 1 the Chicago Cubs led the National League East by four games over the second-place New York Mets. The Mets won twenty-four of their next thirty-six games as the Cubs tanked, winning just ten of their last twenty-eight games. On September 24 the Mets clinched the first National League East Championship. I was there to witness it. Future Hall of Famer Steve Carlton lasted just a third of an inning, as five of the first six batters he faced came around to score. The Mets' starting pitcher, Gary Gentry, threw a complete-game shutout before a paid crowd of 54,928, as the Mets won 6–0.[1]

I was in the visitors' bullpen, watching the game through the panes of Plexiglas when Joe Torre grounded into a double play to end the game. Then all hell broke loose. New York's finest were in place around the playing field when the game ended, but they were no match for this crowd. Like ants after a fresh kill, they swarmed the field and in the process tore up everything they could. The Mets players barely got off the field, as the fans grabbed the bases and ripped up the grass from the infield. I stood there in a trance with Carlton, who got dressed just to see the celebration, when an off-duty policeman grabbed us and said, "You better get outta here!" We made our way to the runway as he lowered and locked the metal garage door behind us. Within seconds the crowd broke down the field entrance to the bullpen and ravaged the area we had left just seconds earlier. Through the Plexiglas window of the tunnel, I could see the crazed look on the faces of those people. I had never seen anything like it. I hope I never see it again.

My Major League Debut

My debut came just a few days after the Mets won the division against us. Red had every intention of putting the call-ups into the September games. Because the schedule had the Cards playing contending teams in the middle of September, it meant that my first outing would wait until we played one of the two teams below us in the standings, the Expos or the Phillies.

I got the call September 27, a cold, rainy Saturday afternoon, at Jarry Park in Montreal. I remember walking into the visitors' clubhouse, to my locker, and seeing my baseball jacket . . . moving. Mike Shannon, who called me "Rooster," brought a live chicken to the ballpark to commemorate my debut. Thanks, Mike!

All of the nonpitching call-ups from Tulsa were in the starting lineup with the exception of Ted Simmons, who had a U.S. Army Reserve meeting that weekend. My catcher was Tim McCarver, which was a blessing for me, maybe not for him. The start of the game was delayed by rain, which meant I had more time to think about my first Major League start. I was already nervous, so the delay just prolonged the tension. Of course, that tension was nothing like preparing to throw my first pitch in the bottom of the first inning. I swear my knees were knocking.

Gary Sutherland, the Expos' leadoff batter, grounded to short for the first out. Any pitcher will tell you that once you get the first out in an inning, you can relax a bit. Maybe I was too relaxed, as I walked Rusty Staub. After a flyout, a hit batsman, and a groundout, I completed my first Major League inning.

Rain fell steadily throughout the early part of the game, and the umpires called for the tarp in the top of the third. It just so happened I was the hitter with a 2–1 count. So it was back to the clubhouse to think about it. After nearly an hour it took just two pitches to finish the at bat, as I was called out on strikes.

The game was scoreless until the top of the sixth, when Byron

Browne homered. We then scored a second run in the top of the seventh, as Leron Lee and Steve Huntz singled. After a strikeout to Chip Coulter, I singled to right, scoring Lee with my first hit and RBI in the big leagues.

I allowed just the second hit off me with one out in the Expos' seventh. I retired the next two batters, as we led by a score of 2–0. Red approached me in the dugout and told me seven innings were enough. My line for my debut was no runs on two hits with three walks, three strikeouts, and two batters hit by pitches. Plus, I got my first hit and RBI. The RBI proved important. It was the difference in the score, as the Expos scored a run in the eighth. Montreal threatened in the ninth, as they had a runner on third with one out. But Tom Hilgendorf retired the next two batters, making me the winning pitcher in my first start.[2]

I don't remember celebrating that evening. I probably had dinner near our hotel, the Queen Elizabeth, as I spent the rest of the night knowing that I was in the books as I had just won my first Major League game.

When the season ended, the Cardinals invited me to the Instructional League in St. Petersburg. I was there for the duration. When I returned to St. Louis before Thanksgiving, I received a letter from the U.S. Army. It was time for basic training.

Greetings from Uncle Sam

I reported for basic training at Fort Lewis, Washington, outside Tacoma. True to the reputation of the Northwest, it rained nearly every one of those winter days. After eight weeks I was sent to the Military Personnel Records Center in Overland to complete my advanced training in military clerical services. Whatever needed to be done, I did. At least that was the description of my duties from the staff sergeant who trained me. Searching records (there were no computers), answering calls, cleaning offices, and making coffee (a few gallons a day for the entire office) were just part of my duties. I had no complaints, as my hours were from 7:00 a.m. to 4:00 p.m. After work I drove to Ritenour, as Coach Engert allowed me to work out with the high school team.

When my military duty was finished on April 6, I joined the Oilers in St. Petersburg for the final days of spring training. Fortunately for me, the American Association didn't begin their season until April 17. The late opening date allowed me some time to transition from a military lifestyle to a baseball schedule. Missing Major League spring training wasn't my choice. It was up to me to make the best of the situation.

From the Sleeper Bus to Sleeping in My Own Bed

A. Ray Smith, the owner of the Oilers, announced to the team that we would make all of our trips on a specially designed sleeper bus that he used on ski trips to Colorado during the previous winters. Instead of commercial flights to the Eastern Division of the American Association (Omaha, Des Moines, Indianapolis, and Evansville), the team would have the bonding experience of twelve- to fourteen-hour bus rides.

There were some advantages: No early-morning wake-up calls to catch a 6:00 AM flight. Hell, we were probably halfway through our trip by then! No need for the traditional sport coat to board a flight, as the rules were altered for the bus ride. Players boarded the bus wearing shorts and T-shirts, which were perfect for sleeping. If one of us couldn't sleep, the front of the bus still had traditional seating with reading lights. It was a trade-off of convenience. Leave after the game for the next destination, or try to sleep a few hours, wake up, and catch the first flight out the next morning. If one could sleep on the bus, the bus was an advantage.

Until I researched the games from 1970, I didn't remember much about my first start that year for Tulsa. I was surprised to discover that I pitched eleven innings for a no-decision on April 20. If a Minor League manager or pitching coach allowed a starting pitcher to go eleven innings today, especially a pitcher with less than two weeks of spring training behind him, they'd be fired immediately. It was just a different time and place.

I hit the ground running when I joined the Oilers. By mid-June I sported a 7–2 record in eleven starts with an ERA of 2.12. When Nelson Briles, one of the Cardinals' five starters, pulled a hamstring in mid-June, they needed someone to take his spot in the rotation, especially with doubleheaders in Chicago on June 21 and in Pittsburgh on June 22. Warren Spahn, now in his third year of managing the Oilers, gave me the news of my promotion to the Cardinals on June 15 after I defeated Wichita in Wichita. The rush from the good news kept me up most of the return trip to Tulsa. Who could sleep after hearing they were headed to the Major Leagues!

When we arrived at Oiler Park in Tulsa on Tuesday morning, I grabbed my equipment bag from the bus, emptied my Tulsa gear, and replaced it with whatever was in my locker. I drove to my apartment, packed my clothes and stereo components (I traveled with just the essentials), settled the rent, gassed my car, and headed east on Interstate 44 to St. Louis.

CHAPTER FIVE

Meet Me in St. Louis

June 16, 1970: Called Up to St. Louis from Tulsa

Because the Cardinals were completing a three-game series in San Diego on Wednesday, it didn't make any sense to fly there. Instead, I joined the Cardinals in Chicago on Thursday for the weekend series.

I started the first game of a doubleheader in Pittsburgh and defeated the Pirates 6-1, hurling my first complete game in the Majors. Plus, it was the only game that I ever pitched in Forbes Field.

Later in the year I had another first . . . my first fine. The Expos' Bill Stoneman had a reputation for buzzing opposing hitters. Once, he came too far inside on a pitch to José Cardenal, who then charged the mound. When he just missed Richie Allen's head with a pitch in a game against the Cardinals in St. Louis on August 9, Allen started to the mound to personally take care of business. Of course, both benches emptied, with the exception of one player, me. That was a serious breach of baseball protocol. Everyone went on the field when a hitter charged the mound. I figured if a fight started, I would be out there. If not, I would take care of Stoneman myself. When the players returned to the dugouts, Red looked my way and said, "I want someone to knock him [Stoneman] on his ass!" I figured that someone was me.

With two outs in the top of the fifth inning and no runners on base, Stoneman came to the plate. I drilled him with the first pitch. Ed Vargo, the home-plate umpire, issued a warning to both clubs, which meant I was fined either twenty-five or fifty dollars; I don't remember the amount.[1] What I do remember, however, was that Red pulled me aside a few weeks later and asked me, "Did you pay the fine?" I told him I did. Red, who had just received his meal money for an upcoming road trip, reached in the envelope, pulled out a few bills, and said, "This one's on me."

A Pleasure to Meet You, Mr. Mays

The Cardinals opened the 1971 season in Chicago with Gibson and Carlton starting those games. A quirk in the schedule gave us two off days before the Saturday-afternoon home opener against the Giants, followed by a Sunday doubleheader.

Red named me the starter for the Cardinals' home opener against the Giants on April 10, 1971. I was excited because this was an honor, especially when family and friends could attend. The game didn't go exactly as I hoped it would, although it had a memorable start. In the top of the first I struck out Willie Mays on three pitches. When I threw a letter-high fastball and he swung right through it, I thought, "There's some gas for ya, Willie!" When he took a called third strike to end the inning, I was feeling cocky.

When Mays batted the second time with a runner on and two out in the third inning, I got two quick strikes on him. I remembered that letter-high fastball he missed in the first. I fired another high fastball, and this time he didn't miss it. In fact, he hit it off the fence covering the Anheuser-Busch sign on the scoreboard! I watched him as he rounded second base and thought, "It's a pleasure to make your acquaintance, Mr. Mays!"

The Trades of Carlton and Reuss

Many years I've attended the Cardinals' Winter Warmup, which raises money for baseball fields around the St. Louis area. For me, it's a chance to give something to the community where I have roots. It also gives me a chance to visit with Cardinal fans, who are among the nicest and most passionate fans in all of baseball. During those visits it doesn't take long before someone brings up the trades of both Steve Carlton and myself and the alternate-universe theories about how many more games, pennants, and World Championships their hometown team would have won if those trades had never been made. I listen patiently, because the fans have put some thought into this and have some interesting conclusions.

This question has been discussed for years in newspaper columns, on radio talk shows, and even in some books. In his book *The Spirit of St. Louis*, Peter Golenbock says the trades of Carlton and myself cost the Cardinals at least four division championships, though he gives no details on how he arrived at that figure.[2] Rob Neyer believes the two trades cost the Cardinals division championships in 1973, 1974, and 1981 and goes into great depth when explaining why.[3] Bob Gibson in his 1994 book, *Stranger to the Game*, points out a ten-month period when Cards GM Bing Devine traded four pitchers (Fred Norman, Mike Torrez in June 1971, and Carlton and myself in the spring of 1972) who won a total of 714 games after leaving the Cardinals.[4]

In checking the numbers for the pitchers obtained in these deals and their legacies (players they were traded for), they won a total of 50 games for the Cardinals and a total of 171 from their time as a Cardinal to the end of their careers. There were some everyday players such as Reggie Smith and Ted Kubiak who were included in the labyrinth of deals, but I don't know of any metric that can convert the production of everyday players into wins and losses for pitchers. As I don't know why Norman and Torrez were traded, here's what I remember (with the help of the notated authors) on the trades of both Steve and me because both deals relate to the mind-set of Mr. Busch.[5]

"I Don't Care If He Throws Another Damn Ball for Us"

First, here's a look at the history between the Cardinals and Carlton. In 1970 negotiations between Steve and the club were so acrimonious that club owner August Busch Jr. stated publicly, "I don't care if he throws another damn ball for us." Carlton eventually signed a two-year deal. Carlton started negotiations in 1972 for $75,000, and the club countered with $57,500. According to Carlton, further talks left the parties slightly less than $10,000 apart.[6]

But the Cardinals had had enough of Carlton's holdouts. According to general manager Bing Devine, "Many times Mr. Busch gave me some leeway in the budget, but in the case of Carlton, Mr. Busch developed the feeling that Carlton was a 'smart-aleck' young guy, 'and I'm not used to having smart-alecks tell me what to do.'"

In August 1971 President Nixon had ordered wage and price controls for the country, and Busch informed Carlton it was his patriotic duty to honor the president's request for a salary ceiling. I often wondered how Mr. Busch would have responded had the president ordered profit controls.

Carlton held his ground and angered Busch so badly that as spring training approached, Busch finally ordered Bing Devine to trade him. Devine knew what a great pitcher Carlton promised to be, but was boxed in because Busch wouldn't bend on the question of giving Carlton the difference, and neither would Carlton.

"One morning the phone rang," Devine said. "It was Dick Meyer. This time he asked 'What have you done about Carlton?'" Devine said, "What do you mean?" Dick said, "Do you have a trade you can make for him?" Devine answered, "Yeah, I could probably make a deal with the Phillies. Why?" Meyer answered, "Because my ulcer is acting up. Mr. Busch comes in every morning and says, 'Have you gotten Carlton signed? If you don't have him signed, do you have him traded? If you don't have him traded, why not?'" Meyer continued, "I'm tired of putting up with that and having my ulcer act up, so my best suggestion to you is that you do me a favor and trade him today." Bing continued, "And that was it. I traded him to the Phillies for Rick Wise."[7]

Holding Out

After Carlton was traded the Cardinals still had four unsigned players to deal with as spring training approached: Joe Torre, the 1971 National League Most Valuable Player (MVP); reserve outfielder Bob Burda; catcher Ted Simmons; and myself.

About this same time the owners' contract with the Players Association that was signed in 1969 would expire on March 31, 1972. Marvin Miller asked for an increase in the owners' pension contribution that covered the past three years of inflation and an increase in health insurance benefits.

Marvin traveled through Florida and Arizona, explaining to players at every spring-training stop the current stalemate in negotiations, and gathered strike-authorization votes for a March 31 walkout. John Gaherin, the lead negotiator for the owners, was looking for a compromise. He told the owners, "We're just talking about money here."

For the owners, the issue went far beyond money. The issue was Marvin Miller. They weren't about to let him tell them how to run their business. After a mid-March meeting with the Players Relations Committee, Busch told reporters, "We voted unanimously to take a stand. We're not going to give them another goddamn cent. If they want to strike—let them."[8]

Negotiating My Contract

I learned in 1968 the Cardinals would split the difference on salary figures. We did it every year from 1968 to 1970. In 1970 on a Minor/Major League contract, I earned $1,750 a month in the Minors and the Major League prorated minimum of $12,000, which totaled a little more than $11,000 for the 1970 season. In 1971, after winning seven games for Tulsa and seven more for the Cardinals in 1970, I was paid $17,000, a raise of almost $6,000! This was the first time the club and I were in complete agreement on a salary figure that early in the winter.

After a 14–14 season with a bloated 4.78 ERA in my first full season in the Majors, I reasoned I was due a raise. The Cardinals agreed and offered me $20,000. It was a respectable first offer that came in late January. I was hoping to sign a 1972 contract for $23,000–$25,000, which was in line with the raise from 1970 to 1971.

With their offer, I thought we were back to negotiating contracts like the player-development people did. Why would I believe differently? I then asked for $32,000, knowing that it was just a starting point and we would ultimately meet somewhere in the middle.

While discussing our difference in my contract in his office at the ballpark before spring training, I asked Bing as an aside if there would be a possibility of my wife flying on the charter for one of our road trips. He was polite but told me firmly that there was no possibility of that happening. I thanked him for his consideration, and the matter was closed as far as I was concerned.

Bob Burns, a sportswriter and columnist for the *St. Louis Globe-Democrat*, reported in his March 4 column that I was "demanding fringes which the Cardinals refuse to grant. One would be for his wife to accompany him on Cardinal trips."

Who was the source that wrongfully tipped Burns that bit of information? It definitely wasn't me. I do know that I caught all kinds of hell from the media, fans, and even teammates, as this story was fodder used by newspapers and talk shows throughout the country.

There was no further movement from either Bing or myself as spring training opened. However, the dynamics to my situation were altered when the Cardinals dealt Carlton to the Phillies on February 25. I believed my negotiating position had improved, as I was the only left-handed starter on the club. So I decided to let Bing make the next move.

It's Just a Matter of Time

On March 7, the Cardinals renewed the contracts of Ted Simmons and me, which allowed the two of us to come to Florida and begin workouts with the club. To the Cardinals' credit, they renewed our respective contracts at their latest offer when they could have renewed them at a maximum 20 percent cut from our 1971 salaries.

The Cardinals also bought airline tickets for my wife and me. When I showed up in St. Pete, I sported a different look. With the braces on my teeth removed, I grew a mustache over the winter, liked it, and decided to keep it.

When I arrived at the ballpark I saw my locker, which had a piece of tape down the middle, separating the locker into "his" and "hers" compartments. I appreciated the handiwork and started laughing. What the hell else could I do? I was happy to be there and looked forward to starting my season.

I stayed in great shape with my off-season running program, and I threw when the weather allowed it. On the field in spring training I threw batting practice and pitched in a "B" game and a regular game before I shut out the Mets for six and two-thirds innings on March 29. That date was important because on the business side, Major League players, incensed enough to post the challenge of Mr. Busch in every Major League clubhouse, were ready to walk out on March 31. It was my last pitching appearance in spring training and, as it turned out, my last appearance in a Cardinal uniform.

Baseball's First Work Stoppage

On April 1 Major League Baseball players went on strike. Most players returned home from the spring-training sites. To stay in shape I met with a few other Cardinal players at Florissant Valley Junior College a few days a week. None of us had any idea how long the strike would last. Because many of us hadn't received a paycheck since the previous September, we were feeling the pressure.

Management also felt the pressure. The owners never imagined players would strike. Once the strike became a reality, their bottom lines came into play. Ultimately, the two sides came to an agreement on April 11.

It took two more days of wrangling, however, to determine whether a total of eighty-six games would be rescheduled (they weren't) and if players would be paid for their time out (they weren't). The strike ended April 13.[9]

The regular season for the Cardinals was scheduled to start on April 7 but was delayed until April 15. Only 7,808 fans were in attendance for opening day. There were just 7,148 on the sixteenth, as the St. Louis fans showed their displeasure with the business of baseball.[10] It was not a happy time for the Cardinal Nation. And my name was about to be added to a long list of unhappy St. Louisans.

Houston, We Have a Problem

It was around six on Saturday night, which happened to be opening day. I was talking to a contractor about some improvements to be made on a house I had bought less than twelve months earlier. The phone rang during our meeting. It was Bing Devine.

"Jerry, we made a deal that will send you to Houston," he said. My initial reaction was *OMG!* It quickly turned into *WTF!* "Bing, we haven't talked about the contract for a quite a while, and I'm sure we could have come to an agreement," I responded. "Jerry, I just didn't think we could have come to a deal to satisfy you. Here's the number of Spec Richardson, the Astros' GM. He's looking forward to hearing from you," Bing said in a manner that said, "What's done is done." "I'll be in early tomorrow to clean out my locker," I said in a state of shock. "There'll be some papers for you to sign before you leave," Bing stated in a businesslike manner. "They'll be in your locker" were his last words before he hung up the phone.

I took a deep breath and returned to the dining room, where the contractor had set up his plans. I told him, "I appreciate your time, but that was the Cardinals. I was traded to Houston." The gentleman, whose name I can't remember, might have initially thought that this was just a kiss-off from our deal. Once he saw the look in my eyes, he knew it was real. He packed his briefcase, shook my hand, and said, "Good luck!"

Bing and I never talked about my contract during spring training in 1972. When I was asked about contract status during spring training, I told the reporters that nothing had changed. The newspapers wrote that the Cardinals had reached their limit on that year's budget.

To this day I'm surprised that Bing never approached me. If we would have had a face-to-face meeting, I believe we would have reached an agreement. That is ... if he had been given some room to negotiate.

Out of the Bird's Nest

April 15, 1972: Traded to Houston
for Lance Clemons and Scipio Spinks

For years I believed I was traded because of the salary issue. Bing told the *St. Louis Post-Dispatch*, "In the background, is the fact that Reuss didn't appear happy with us, couldn't come to terms and we were still far apart."[11]

Bing said much the same thing to the *Globe-Democrat*. "The main basis of a relationship between employer and employee is a somewhat harmonious feeling," Devine stated. "We didn't feel he'd be satisfied enough or happy enough in his work, without being influenced by his feelings. And baseball is hard enough to play," added Devine, "without outside pressure. We saw no hope of getting together after two months in the spring."[12]

My first reaction was "Huh?" Those quotes were vague at best. The focus should have been on negotiating a contract and not my happiness. I never told anyone that I was unhappy. I wanted to sign a contract and get on with the business of playing baseball.

I didn't discover the other reason I was traded until 1998, when a trip to visit my parents in St. Louis also brought me face-to-face with Bing at Busch Stadium. He was in the press box, scouting for those same Houston Astros, so I stopped to say hello. Bing was cordial, so I took a chance and asked why the deal was made some twenty-six years earlier.

He told me it was because I grew a mustache. Mr. Busch didn't like it and demanded that Devine get rid of me. Thinking that this was another one of Busch's rants, Bing sat on it for a week. During that week Busch kept pounding Dick Meyer, the VP who developed an ulcer during the Carlton dealings, asking whether I'd been traded yet. Bing knew he had to make a deal.

With that great twenty-twenty hindsight of more than forty years, I believe I was traded for both reasons. The salary difference dictated a trade. That's common sense. The mustache "thing" was an emotional response on Mr. Busch's part. I also believe events that were put into motion with Flood's bold salary statement in 1969, the fallout from the negotiations regarding the Basic Agreement with the players in 1969 and 1972, Carlton's holdout in 1970 and 1972, as well as the four other players who were holdouts in 1972 were all part of Mr. Busch's state of mind when he demanded my trade.

"What We Have Here Is a Failure to Communicate"

This wasn't the last time I would deal with Bing. When I received my final Cardinals paycheck on April 15, I noticed a deduction for $77.87. I called Bing after joining Houston and asked about the deduction. "That was for your wife's return airfare from Florida," he told me. I responded, "Bing, I didn't agree to that. It was you that agreed to airfare for both of us if I would come to St. Petersburg, work out with the team, and continue contract talks." Bing replied, "Yes, that was before the strike." I answered, "What does the strike have to do with it?"

Reading from the arbitration decision from 1972, Bing asserts that "it was his intention of having my wife return to St. Louis on a chartered aircraft which, had the strike not occurred, would have carried the team and others to St. Louis from Tampa. Issuance of the round trip ticket to Mrs. Reuss resulted, Mr. Devine states, from a failure on the part of his secretary or himself to communicate clearly to each other."

Okay, that's much the same as he told me. I answered him, "Bing, you agreed to round-trip transportation and sent a round-trip ticket. There was no qualifier in that conversation." Bing, tired of the whole mess, said, "I don't have time to argue about this. If you don't like it, file a grievance." So I filed a grievance. The arbitrator heard the case (remember, we're talking about $77.87!) and sided with me.[13]

Who Really Knows?

To put another spin on the two deals, consider the potential economic impact. Let's assume the two of us (or four of us) won enough games to produce some division championships and maybe a World Series or two during the 1970s and '80s. What would have happened to the Cardinals, the city of St. Louis, and the fortunes of Anheuser-Busch? How many more tickets would have been sold? What about an increase in sales of ballpark concessions? How about the possible increase of fees for the radio and television rights? How many top-notch free agents would have wanted to play for a winning Cardinal team when the mid-1970s rolled around? What kind of economic impact would division-winning Cardinal teams have had on the St. Louis area? How much would the winning teams have affected Anheuser-Busch's bottom line?

The amateur economist in me guesses the number to be in the millions of dollars, but that's just speculation on my part. So the next time I'm asked about the deals and give my standard answer of "Who really knows?" understand that I have given the subject some thought.

Sorry, No Visitors Allowed in the Clubhouse!

I was up early that Sunday morning on April 16, as I had to make the trip to the ballpark to gather my gear. As I made the forty-minute drive from my home in Chesterfield, I thought about the reaction to my trade from the players, who were teammates Saturday and now former teammates on Sunday. Yes, I was apprehensive, being twenty-two years old and traded for the first time. How was I supposed to handle this? Should I let the trade roll off my back and come up with some witty quip? I wasn't in a witty mood. Should I make the occasion an opportunity to rip the club? Not a good idea, as my parents and other family members still lived in St. Louis. And my uncle worked for the brewery. How about if I just thanked everyone for their support and wished them the best? I chose option three.

My locker was next to the table that held the huge coffeepot just outside the training room and was two lockers away from Bob Gibson. Never at a loss for words, Gibby saw me quietly pass by, sit down on my chair, and pack my gear. "Hey, I told you to shave that mustache," he said with a laugh. He extended his hand and wished me the best. At the time I thought this was Gibson being Gibson and his way of dealing with an awkward situation. I didn't know at the time just how on the mark his comment was. Other Cardinal players soon followed Gibby's lead. I sensed that a lot of guys knew this feeling all too well, as their careers had them bouncing from club to club. Seeing me made them recall the uncertainty they painfully remembered.

After my bag was packed, I stepped into the coaches' room and thanked everyone for all they did. Then it was a trip to Red's office to say good-bye. Red criticized me for growing the mustache, but said it had no bearing on the trade. "There's no club rule against it," Red said.[14]

"Hey, this happened to me a few times. You'll be all right" were

Red's words to me. We shook hands, and I went back for my bag but was stopped.

Probably the most curious good-bye was by clubhouse manager Butch Yatkeman, who had been with the club in some capacity since 1924. "Could we square up the past few weeks before you go?" Butch asked me just inside his office door, which was on the other side of the coffeepot. "Butch, the players were on strike for twelve days. Yesterday was the first day back. Tell me what I owe you for yesterday," I said incredulously.

I wrote him a check, and I don't remember the amount. I know it was for more than a day. As I write this memory, I wish this had been the conversation with him: "Butch, thanks for reminding me. What's the tab? Suppose I put a home and away uniform and a jacket in my bag. Would 'x dollars' cover it?" Yeah, that's a conversation that never happened. Still, the money would have been spent wisely, as the gear would be family treasures today.

I sensed that I was overstaying my time in the clubhouse. Players are funny about that. After I packed my equipment bag, the players gave me a reasonable amount of time to say good-bye. Then, move on. After all, the Cardinals had a game to play, and now I was the opposition.

As I walked through the clubhouse double doors, I saw Scipio Spinks, one of the players from the Astros involved in the deal. I stopped, shook his hand, and wished him the best. He had his equipment bag in his other hand, so I asked him, "Did you save your orange-sleeved sweatshirts from the Astros?" "Yeah, I have them in my bag," he answered curiously. "Would you be interested in trading them for some red-sleeved shirts?" I asked with a smile. "How does one-for-one work for you?" he asked. "That works for me," I told him. We made the trade.

That was my first sign of acceptance of the deal. It was time to move on. Incidentally, I still have those orange sleeves.

CHAPTER SIX

Houston, I'm Comin' to See Ya

After saying my good-byes to the Cardinals, I arrived in Houston later in the day. Jimmy Lake, the home clubhouse manager, picked me up at the airport and told me about the Astros during the forty-five-minute ride to the Astrodome. I dropped my equipment bag in the clubhouse, but the general manager, Spec Richardson, wanted to see me before I got dressed.

I could smell his office before I arrived. Spec, with his ever-present cigar, invited me to sit with him. In his Texas drawl he said, "Bing told me where you were in your contract negotiations. If you had won fourteen games with me last year [the number I won for St. Louis in 1971], I'd give you the thirty-two thousand dollars you were asking for," he said with his tongue shifting the cigar in his mouth from side to side. "But you didn't," he said as he glared with narrowed eyes, drawing a long breath through the cigar.

The room was quiet until he exhaled. The cigar was perched between two fingers as he pointed in my direction and said, "Still, I wanna do right by you. I'll give you what you want prorated for the games lost to the strike if you sign the contract right now." He pulled out a contract from a folder and gave it to me. I looked at it, saw the salary figure of thirty-two thousand dollars, and then asked for a pen. "Mr. Richardson, thank you for the consideration," I said as I signed the contract. "Hell, boy, nobody calls me Mr. Richardson.

It's Spec. Got that?" he said with an outstretched hand and smile, cradling the cigar that was once again shifting in his mouth. We shook hands, and I was officially an Astro.

Maybe it was Spec's way of welcoming me to the club. Maybe a few more thousand saved him the hassles of dealing with an unsigned player during the season. Maybe it was good salary karma. I don't know. I was just happy to get it.

Important Cogs in the "Big Red Machine"

From 1962 through 1971 the Astros (and their predecessor Colt .45's) had finished every year below .500 with the exception of 1969, when they were 81–81. In 1971 the Astros were 79–83, the same as the Reds. Both teams knew they had to make some changes. On November 29, 1971, the Reds sent Lee May, Tommy Helms, and utility player Jimmy Stewart to Houston for Joe Morgan, infielder Denis Menke, pitcher Jack Billingham, and outfielders César Gerónimo and Ed Armbrister.

The deal led the Astros to a second-place finish in 1972 with an 84–69 record, the best in franchise history. It was an even better deal for the Reds, who won the Western Division and a trip to the 1972 World Series with a 95–59 record.[1] In fact, the deal was so good for Cincinnati that they went to the World Series in 1972, 1973, 1975, and 1976 (winning the latter two) and were dubbed the "Big Red Machine."

The 1972 Houston club was a run machine, as the Astros led the National League in runs scored with 708. The everyday lineup included four players with 20 or more home runs and five players with 80 or more RBI. Defensively, Doug Rader and César Cedeño were Gold Glove winners, and Roger Metzger played shortstop like a Gold Glover.[2]

The Next Willie Mays

The player who caught the baseball world's attention was twenty-one-year-old César Cedeño, who was touted by many to be the

'70s answer to Willie Mays. His numbers in 1972 included a .320 average, with 22 HR, 82 RBI, and 55 stolen bases. He also won his first of five consecutive Gold Glove awards in 1972.

When players perform the way Cedeño did, they make themselves immune to club rules. Like players around baseball, the Astros wore their stirrups higher and their pants lower. Spec didn't like it when the blue star on the orange stirrups disappeared under the pants leg. So he told Jimmy Lake to replace the stirrups in all the players' lockers with new stirrups that showed only a trace of the white sanitary socks. Any player altering these new stirrups would be fined, according to the line from upstairs.

Of course, the players bitched about it. Cedeño took one look at his leggings, threw them on the floor, and said, "I'm not wearing these." He reached deep in his locker and produced another pair of stirrups that fitted his style and wore them that night. We waited for a reaction from Spec, but nothing was said. The next day any player who wanted his old stirrups got them. Star players earn that right, says baseball protocol. This incident told all of us that Cedeño, with two-plus seasons in the big leagues, had arrived.

The Wit and Wisdom of Lefty Gomez

Like many starting pitchers, I took batting practice with my group on the day I started and then made my way to the clubhouse to change clothes and review my plan for the upcoming game. It was a routine I followed my entire career.

Once, while preparing for a start against the Giants at Candlestick Park in early 1972, I had the pleasure of a pregame visit by none other than Hall of Famer Lefty Gomez. At the time Lefty was a rep for Wilson Sporting Goods and served all of the professional players under contract to Wilson when they visited the Bay Area.

I was aware of his reputation as a great pitcher and had read some of his quotes that are timeless. He once stated, "I talked to the ball a lot of times in my career. I yelled, 'Go foul. Go foul.'"

Another time, he said, "One rule I had was make your best pitch and back up third base. That relay might get away and you've got another shot at him." I knew as soon as he entered the clubhouse I was about to hear my own Lefty quote.

I was sitting at one of the picnic tables in the clubhouse with that day's lineup card, reviewing the San Francisco hitters. When he walked into the clubhouse, we were the only two people there. Moving quite spritely for a sixty-four- or sixty-five-year-old man, he approached me. "Hey, left-hander. How's your change-up?" Normally, this was quiet time for me, but I always made an exception for baseball royalty. "It's my fourth-best pitch," I answered. He paused for a second, looked at me, and said, "You might want to work on that change and use it more often." When advice came from a four-time twenty-game winner, a five-time All-Star with a perfect 6–0 record in World Series play, I listened carefully to every word. When I asked why, he told me, "Because when you get to my age, that's all you'll have left."

A Near Miss

There weren't many highlights in my first Astros season that ended with a 9–13 record. I walked nearly four batters for every nine innings pitched and paid the price. The best game I pitched was on June 18, when I no-hit the Phillies for eight innings. Larry Bowa led off the top of the ninth with a line drive between a diving Doug Rader and the third base line. A flyout and two strikeouts retired the Phils in the ninth, as I settled for a one-hitter. Incredibly, Rader apologized for not catching Bowa's shot. Doug took a great deal of pride in his defensive acumen, as he collected five Gold Glove awards during his career. I told him, "There isn't a third baseman in the history of the game that makes that play. I appreciate the effort and acknowledgment, though."[3]

Harry the Hat

Harry Walker, the Astros' manager, was an excellent teacher in one respect. After I won a game early in the season, Harry shook my hand and told me to be at the park the next day at 10:00 a.m. I needed some work on my hitting. Harry and a coach were waiting when I arrived at 9:30.

I dressed, went to the field, and saw that a pitching machine was set up in front of the mound. Harry took one look at my thin-handled bats and told me, "Those won't work for you. Try this bat." It was a thick-handled Louisville Slugger, U1 model, used primarily by players of a bygone era.

"Matty Alou used this style of bat for me in Pittsburgh. He struggled one year, made the change, and won the batting title the next year," he said proudly. In 1965 Alou batted .231. After Harry presumably worked with him, he led the National League in hitting in 1966 with a .342 average. From 1967 to 1972 Alou hit under .300 just one season; in 1970 he hit .297.[4]

After suggesting that I change bats, Harry demonstrated the bunting stance he wanted me to use. Telling me to rotate my upper body while bending at the knees, he showed me how to fake a bunt and slap the ball on the ground while choking up eight to ten inches. This was a rare moment. Managers usually let the coaches handle these responsibilities. Harry, though, was hands-on. From his perch behind the cage, Harry would present a situation, and I'd respond with a bunt, a fake bunt/swing, a squeeze, a grounder to second, or a fly ball. Harry talked nonstop about when he would use these plays, as my respect and appreciation for him were growing.

Then somewhere along the way Harry started talking politics (hated Nixon), religion, the economy, the space program, or whatever else came to mind. I wondered if this time was to help me or serve as a forum for his opinion on everything Harry. Whatever respect I had in the early part of the session was lost by the time we returned to the locker room. Harry had me at "Be here at 10:00" and then lost me during his diatribe on the Cuban missile crisis.

My career hitting exploits will never be confused with the success of Matty Alou, but the lesson was learned. I used the U1 model my entire career and posted a .167 average, a respectable number for a pitcher.

Harry was fired on August 26, 1972, as the club was 67–54 and in third place, the best record the Astros recorded at this point in any season.

Why make the move? Astros great Jimmy Wynn believed it was because of Harry's racial attitudes as well as the front office refocusing attention from bad trades by hiring a new manager with marquee value.[5]

I was aware of Harry's attitudes on race when players exchanged stories in the clubhouse, on planes and buses, or in hotels. I never witnessed anything firsthand, as I came on the scene during his final year. But I probably would have heard all about it had I hit longer that morning.

Harry had a lot of baseball to offer, but he was his own worst enemy. Respect and trust from the manager were the missing ingredients for the talent-laden Astros of 1972, and Harry Walker couldn't and didn't provide either.

Many Astro players were thrilled when they heard Harry was fired. Their prayers were finally answered. These answered prayers should have come with a warning label like on the back of a cigarette package—"Be careful what you wish for!"—as his replacement was none other than Leo Durocher.

Leo the Lip

For all living things to exist they require certain essentials like air, food, and water. For Leo he needed constant attention, an enemy, and a mark. Though he stood maybe five foot six and weighed around 150 pounds, his persona was overpowering. When he entered a room his ego squeezed the air out of it. That booming voice bounced off the walls with his brashness and cocksure authority. His manner of impeccable dress wore well in his ever-present spotlight. When Leo moved in his calculated manner, he fully expected the earth to move with him so that he would always be the epicenter.

Such was the scene in the Astro clubhouse on August 28 when Leo was introduced to the club. Leo was very low-key and deliberate as he told us, "We have thirty-one games remaining, and we're eight and a half games behind Cincinnati. You got yourselves here, and I'm here to help you the rest of the way. I'm not here to change things, but I will observe." As we listened he looked around the room, sizing up each of us as if we were across the table in a poker game, hoping to spot our "tell." At twenty-three years old, this was the first time I witnessed a managerial change. So I sat there like a sponge, soaking up the moment.

Like my teammates, I had some questions. Why, at sixty-eight years old after a tumultuous stay in Chicago where he was at odds with the sportswriters, broadcasters, umpires, players, the commissioner, the league president, and whomever else, would he want to manage again?

It wasn't my place to ask the question then, but recalling it in 2013 I believe Leo looked at the situation like he would a card game. What was the upside? It was one more chance to grab the brass ring, as the club could catch fire, the Reds could falter, and he would have his name above the title as the man who finally led the Astros to the postseason. Just as important, making the playoffs would have helped erase his most visible failure with the 1969 Cubs, and he could have ridden off into the sunset as the credits rolled. His minimum bet was just thirty-four days of his time. At the end of the season, he could decide his plans for 1973. What was the downside? It was the same investment of time and the option to return in 1973.

Leo said he took the job after asking himself one question, "Can I win with this club next year? My answer was yes. They were a solid ballclub and they have the best young player in baseball, César Cedeño."[6]

He had a new game plan for 1973. "I decided I was going to do something I had never done before. I would be one of the boys, a pal, and a buddy. The times had changed, and you had to change with them. I was going to do it their way. I'd play cards with them for half an hour before we went out," Leo explained.[7]

What Leo failed to understand was that the Astros needed a manager the players could trust and respect. When you're a ballplayer in your midtwenties, do you really want a sixty-eight-year-old "pal" who takes your money in the daily card games?

With the best record in team history in the books for 1972, the Astros decided to fine-tune for the 1973 season. Rich Chiles was traded to the Mets for Tommie Agee, who batted .227 for the Mets in 1972. The reason for adding Agee was the planned move of Bob Watson from left field to catcher. Watson did his best making the adjustment but played only 3 games behind the plate and 142 in left field. Agee played in 83 games, spelling the regulars at all three outfield positions and pinch-hitting before being shipped to St. Louis in August.[8]

All I can remember about spring training was Leo dividing the team into three groups, the eight regulars, the bench players, and the pitchers. Because Leo was with the regular players every day, the only time I saw him was when we ran our team drills or when photographers showed up and followed him from field to field.

We were just 6–8 when Leo was hospitalized on April 19 with an inflammation of his lower intestine. Preston Gomez took over the club, and we went on a 14–3 streak. There was an entirely different atmosphere with Preston leading the club. The focus was solely on the game.

When Leo returned the club reverted to their early-season ways, winning just 9 of the next 20 games. We'll never know what could have happened had Preston led the club the rest of the way.

When Vin Scully Speaks, Los Angeles Listens

I learned during my first trip to Dodger Stadium in late-August 1970 that Dodger Stadium was someplace special. There were three reasons: the weather in Southern California was always cooler than the summers in the Midwest, the natural grass surface and the hard clay that composed the pitchers mound were the best in the league, and Dodger announcer Vin Scully.

When the Dodgers moved west after the 1958 season, the Southern California fans learned the Major League style of the game from Vin during his radio broadcasts. The phenomenon of transistor radios in the ballpark originated in the days of the Los Angeles Coliseum, where fans sat so far from the field that they brought radios to help them follow the action. When Dodger Stadium opened in 1962, the habit had become ingrained and continued.[9]

I pitched in six games at Dodger Stadium as a member of the Astros. If the crowd was around twenty thousand and was quiet, I could hear the radios from around the ballpark when standing on the mound. I couldn't clearly make out the words, but I could tell from Vin's cadence where he was in the broadcast. One night while staring at the catcher's signs, I noticed Vin was in midstory. As a courtesy to the best in the business, I stepped off the rubber, grabbed the rosin bag, gave it a shake, and threw it behind the mound. By this time Vin delivered his punch line, the crowd had its laugh, and I was back on the rubber, getting the sign from the catcher. Vin, ever the professional, never missed a beat. "Reuss winds and the pitch on the way …"

Regrets . . . Yes, I Have a Few

I've been asked over the years if I have any regrets for anything that I've done during my career. I always joked about the location of some pitches that I'd like to change, as I was always too embarrassed to discuss my more questionable behavior. But it's part of the narrative, and this is the time to tell it.

One such incident occurred on the night of July 6, 1973, at Jarry Park in Montreal. Leo talked about this game in his book but confused the facts.

Here's what happened. I started the first game of a twilight doubleheader and had a 7–1 lead entering the bottom of the fourth. A leadoff walk, an error, and two singles led to an Expo run. A sacrifice fly scored the second run of the inning, but we caught a break when the runner on second base tried to score and was thrown out at the plate. The next batter walked (my fifth of the game), and Leo replaced me with Jim Ray as Tim Foli came to bat.

In three and two-thirds innings, I allowed four hits, walked five, and left the game with two runners on base and a 7–3 lead. I was furious. This was the fifth time in the early part of the '73 season that I had at least a two-run lead and couldn't hold it. I figured he could have left me in there to face Foli and, hopefully, get on track.[10]

When I got in the clubhouse I picked up a folding chair and fired it into Leo's locker. I picked it up and was ready to throw it a second time when someone grabbed my arms from behind. It was the visiting clubhouse manager, Claude Lavoie, who told me in a very controlled voice, "You don't want to do this. Believe me, you really don't want to do this!" I put the chair down and continued my rant.

Eventually, word got to Leo on the bench about my tirade. He showed up in the clubhouse a short time later, and a spirited discussion ensued between the two of us. We took it to his office, as our "discussion" lasted through the second game of the doubleheader.

To Leo's credit he didn't raise his voice or lose his cool, as I'd seen him do with umpires. Nor did he blast me to the writers when asked why he wasn't on the bench for the second game. He just told them it was a private discussion between us and he had an upset stomach that kept him off the bench.

Now, looking back at this game, I have the perspective of time. I'll play manager. I would've taken me out of the game. With my then recent history of coughing up a lead and struggling again in this game, we had a chance to win, as we had a four-run lead. So I'd make the change. Win the first game however we can and then worry about the second game when we get there is sound baseball judgment.

With regards to my behavior, I'm certain some managers would have sent me to the Minors, traded me, or at the very least fined me. But nothing was done. Because the club was short on pitching, I, as the 2013 manager, would've recommended a large fine to send a message that this kind of behavior would not be tolerated.

Regarding the doubleheader, we lost both games using three relievers in the first game and four more in the second game. We lost on Saturday using one reliever, and when the club needed someone Sunday after using the only two pitchers available, I pitched two innings and, believe it or not, got the win.

Hank Chases the Babe

With all of the '73 pennant races decided, there was still some drama during the last weekend of the season. Henry Aaron was closing in on one of baseball's most hallowed records, as he approached Babe Ruth's career home run total of 714. Aaron had 712 notched into his belt when the Astros (with me pitching) faced the Braves on Saturday, September 29. I was very much aware of what was happening and would have been happy not to be a part of it. After all, Hank had touched me twice for homers before this game.[11]

Both times he connected on fastballs, so my game plan was to get him out on curve balls. Aaron singled in the first inning on a fastball and walked in the third inning. I recorded two quick outs in the fifth inning when Marty Perez doubled, Mike Lum singled, and Darrell Evans drove in Perez with a single. That brought Hank to the plate as I was on the ropes, trailing 3–0.

Hank was looking for a curve, got it, and hit number 713 over the left-field fence. The crowd of 17,836 went crazy, subsiding only when Hank made a curtain call.

Future Dodger teammate Dusty Baker followed with a solo HR to make the score 7–0. That made it five consecutive hits; the last two hits were home runs. I wanted to restore order. So when Davey Johnson, who hit 43 homers in 1973, stepped to the plate, I buzzed him with a fastball that caught him in the arm. I wanted to make sure there wouldn't be 3 home runs in a row. Home-plate umpire John Kibler issued a warning, which cost me fifty dollars. I eventually got out of the inning, but the damage was done. I lost the game, Hank Aaron stood at the precipice of baseball history, and I was fined again for the warning issued after I hit Johnson.

The stage was set for the season finale on September 30. With 40,517 present, Hank Aaron went three for four but didn't connect for the record-tying homer. That would wait until 1974.[12]

Being a part of this history was something I couldn't escape. I would have preferred to allow this honor to be bestowed upon another pitcher, but fate stepped in. When I first met Hank back in 1966 during that tryout at Busch Stadium 2, I would have never guessed our paths would meet again under these circumstances.

Some Guys Have Long Memories

Davey Johnson remembered this game for a number of years, not because of the home run chase but because he was hit by a pitch. Johnson was removed from the game after being hit but played the next day, going 0–4 against Dave Roberts and Don Wilson. Johnson's forty-three home runs were a record for a second baseman, but he trailed Willie Stargell for the league home run title by one. He blamed me for that missed opportunity.

On September 11, 1977, while playing for the Phillies, Johnson got two hits and a walk and drove in two runs against me while I was with Pittsburgh, as the Phils won the game by a score of 6–2. In his postgame interview he recalled the 1973 game. "Aaron and Baker just hit home runs," Johnson recalled. "I was the next batter and Reuss shook off two pitches and then hit me with a fastball." Davey continued, "I thought it was intentional. Ever since that day I've really been pressing to get Reuss. I really wanted to kill the ball."[13]

Fast-forward to 1999. While Johnson managed the Dodgers, I had the occasion to visit Dodger Stadium and meet the manager for the first time. "Hi, Dave. I'm Jerry Reuss," I said as I put my hand out to greet him in his office before a game. "I know who you are, you son of a bitch!" he said as he shook my hand. "You hit me with a pitch, and I lost the home run title as a result," he said with a forced smile. That took me by surprise. Whatever happened to "Hi, Jerry. It's a pleasure to meet you"?

Johnson continued as the members of the press frantically scribbled the notes of this story. Johnson recalled the events (incorrectly, I might add) about his home run chase. I said nothing. Finally, he asked me, "Did Leo tell you to hit me?" I started laughing as I answered, "If Leo had told me to drill you, I would have thrown the pitch down the middle in spite." I continued, "As I remember, I was getting hammered, and I wanted to put an end to it. It just happened that you were the hitter. It was nothing personal." Dave wouldn't accept that. He believed there was more to it. For me, I had forgotten about it until Johnson brought it up.

The Trade Winds Blow

The 1973 season ended as a disappointment to all associated with the club, especially after the 84–69 record of the 1972 team. We still had four players with 20 or more HR and three players with 80 or more RBI. But the number of runs scored dropped from 708 in '72 to 681 in '73 even though we played nine more games.[14]

On the pitching side Larry Dierker was injured most of the year and won just one game, while Don Wilson was five games under .500. Dave Roberts, with seventeen wins, and my sixteen wins picked up some of the slack. Overall, the '73 staff had an ERA of 3.75 against the 3.77 the previous year. However, we missed the veteran leadership that both Dierker and Wilson provided.[15]

With drop-offs in runs scored and players a year older, there were changes that needed to be made. The club still needed an everyday catcher and a new manager to replace the retiring Leo Durocher.

I'm Movin' On

Of course, I knew the club was looking for an everyday catcher. During the World Series between the A's and the Mets, the newspapers reported the rumors of a possible deal between the Astros and Pirates. The Pirates were willing to deal twenty-three-year-old catcher Milt May, who showed he could handle Major League pitching by batting .275 over four seasons in 212 games. The Astros, seeing his youth and left-handed bat fitting perfectly in a predominantly right-handed hitting lineup, knew he was the blue-chip catcher on the market.

According to news reports, Spec told Joe Brown, the Pirates' general manager, that he could have any starting pitcher he wanted from the organization except J. R. Richard or me. Joe insisted on me. After adding and subtracting different names in the deal, both clubs took a few weeks to see what else was available. Eventually, the deal was revisited and finalized, with Milt joining the Astros and me becoming Pittsburgh property.[16]

The deal made perfect sense. Trading a starting pitcher who gave you around 35 starts a season for an everyday catcher who played 125–30 games a year was a perfect trade for the Astros. And both clubs had replacements in mind for the players who were traded. The Pirates had Manny Sanguillén, who caught 89 games in 1973, return behind the plate as their starting catcher, with Dave Parker waiting in the wings as their everyday right-fielder. The Astros were working on another deal that involved Jimmy Wynn for Dodger lefty Claude Osteen, who would take the vacant spot in their starting rotation.[17]

Who's the Dummy?

On November 1, Jack Herman, a sportswriter for the *St. Louis Globe-Democrat*, called me at home in Houston. At twenty-four years old and still shocked by my personal reality (I just moved into a new home and was facing the prospect of living elsewhere for at least seven months for the second time in two years), I spoke with Jack about the deal. We spoke of the misfortune of Scipio Spinks, who was key to the deal that sent me to Houston, and how he performed for the Cardinals. Scipio, who tore up his knee in a home-plate collision against Johnny Bench of the Reds in 1972 and made his last Major League start in June 1973 before suffering from a shoulder strain in his pitching arm, ended his career prematurely with a 6–10 record for the Cards.

"With Spinks getting hurt, the Cardinals got the short end of that deal," Jack said. "Well, Jack, it was an unfortunate set of circumstances for Scipio," I answered. Jack, the professional that he was at sniffing out a possible story, asked me another loaded question. "You're already established as a starting pitcher over the last three years and were traded for a catcher that has yet to prove himself as an everyday player. Do you think the Astros got enough for you?" I took the bait. "When you look at the deal like that, yeah, the Astros could've gotten more for me," I responded. We talked a bit more about the future of the Astros and what transpired over the '73 season. By the time we talked about my 16–13 season, I mentioned that the "record would have been better if it hadn't been for that dummy of a manager that pulled me out of two games I had with a lead."

When we hung up I was uneasy about the interview, especially the part about Leo. There was no need to bury Leo as my arrogance got the better of me. Plus, he covered my ass in Montreal. So, how did the article turn out?

It began with these words: *Jerry Reuss hasn't changed. Still his own man, the St. Louis native is as outspoken as ever. "The Cardinals didn't get enough for me," said the tall lefthander, traded Wednesday by Houston to Pittsburgh, "and neither did the Astros."*[18] These quotes still appear in some form on the Internet today.

I don't blame Jack, as he was just doing his job. Still, after the article ran, I was apprehensive about talking to him anytime our paths crossed. I learned a valuable lesson: sportswriters have a job to do, and they're not always your friend.

Today, I see that interview as a missed opportunity. I had the chance to thank everyone for all the good fortune bestowed on me during my tenure with the Astros, and I threw it away.

Now for the quote about Leo being a dummy. It must have struck a nerve, as he mentioned it in his book. In 2013, with the play-by-play of every game I ever pitched posted for review, I discovered that, in 1973, I pitched in *eight* games with at least a two-run lead that I couldn't hold. After studying each of them and playing manager, I would have taken me out of each of those games. So who was the dummy? It wasn't Jack, Leo, or even Preston Gomez. I was the dummy!

One final thought on my time in Houston, and it has to do with Leo. In 1973 Leo Durocher was in his only full year of managing the Astros. It turned out to be a disaster for both Leo and the Astros, as the club went 82–80 and finished fourth in the division.

Off the field, I had some personal baggage, and, because of poor judgment and immaturity, it affected me at the park. It led Leo to refer to me in his book as the "asshole of all time."[19]

The asshole part had merit and I deserved that, but *of all time*? Didn't MLB commissioner Happy Chandler suspend Leo for a year for "association with known gamblers"? How about his alleged habit of passing bad checks during his Yankee days? This was a case of the pot calling the kettle black. Still, I think my behavior both on and off the field may have had something to do with my departure.

There's a postscript to my relationship with Leo. Years later, when I was with the Dodgers, Tom Lasorda called me into his office one day, telling me there was someone there who wanted to speak to me. When I walked in I spotted a frail older gentleman sitting on the sofa. "Jerry," Tommy said, "you remember Leo." Turns out that Leo was a hero of Tommy's and came in from his home in Palm Springs to pay his longtime friend a visit. "Leo, how are you?" I said as I smiled and held out my hand. Leo stood, took my hand, and said, "Tommy has a lot of nice things to say about you." Then he looked at Tommy and said, "Can we have your office for a few minutes?"

Tommy got up from behind his desk and said, "Take all the time you need," and walked out, closing the door behind him. Leo motioned for me to sit with him on the sofa. Then he looked me in the eye and started a conversation of fifteen minutes by stating, "You know, I said some things ..."

We cleared the air that day and finished the visit with a hug. Not often in life have I had a chance to right a wrong and apologize for my mistakes. I think the visit did the same for Leo, too. Many thanks to you, Tom, for making it happen. That was the last time I ever saw Leo. He passed in 1991.

CHAPTER SEVEN

Makin' My Way to the Steel City

My first trip to Pittsburgh after the trade during the off-season found me at Willie Stargell's bowling tournament. It was the perfect opportunity to meet some new teammates, including another lefty pitcher just acquired by the Bucs, Ken Brett. Brett, 13–8 in twenty-five starts for the Phillies, was traded for Dave Cash and, like me, was apprehensive about the deal because he was joining his fourth team in three years. "I took the phone off the hook because I didn't want to hear one general manager wishing me luck when he traded me and another telling me how happy he is that I'm with his club," said Brett.[1]

The Pirates' general manager, Joe Brown, told me in early 1974, "As an organization, we've been fortunate to draft, sign, and develop many players for our Major League club. Of course, we've been luckier with our everyday players than we have been with pitching. But we've been able to trade an everyday player to bolster our pitching and not miss a beat offensively."

Of the thirty-nine players listed on the Pirates' roster for 1974, twenty-seven were from the farm system. Under the guidance of Brown from 1970 through 1976, the Pirates won the Eastern Division five times and a world championship in 1971. The dynamic worked.

The Winning Ways of Danny Murtaugh

Danny Murtaugh was in his fourth tour as manager of the Pirates. In his first go-round, he managed the club from 1957 to 1964, including the world championship team of 1960, before retiring due to health problems. He then took a front-office job with the Pirates, evaluating players for Joe Brown. Murtaugh was pressed into service as an interim manager when Harry Walker was fired during the 1967 season. He then returned to his front-office role.

Murtaugh was well aware of the abundance of talent in the system and asked to reclaim the managing job after Larry Shepard was fired in the last week of the 1969 season. Once he received medical clearance, Murtaugh returned to managing. He led the Pirates to a National League East Division title in 1970 and 1971, winning the 1971 World Series. Murtaugh stepped down after the 1971 season, and his handpicked successor, Bill Virdon (his center fielder on the 1960 World Series champions), took over.

When Brown fired Virdon in September 1973, Murtaugh reluctantly came back to managing. Once again, with Murtaugh at the helm, the Pirates won the division championship in 1974 and 1975. He stayed through the 1976 season. He and Brown announced their retirements during the final week of the 1976 season.[2]

Like Red Schoendienst, Harry Walker, and Leo Durocher, the other Major League managers I had played for in my career to date, Danny Murtaugh had a history. Before I joined the club, there were already memorable stories circulating about him.

The Leprechauns at Work

When he was a second baseman with the Boston Braves in 1947, Murtaugh and his roommate left the team's roadside motel one night for a poker game. The game lasted into the next morning, and the boys went straight from playing cards to the ballpark. Unshaven and disheveled, Murtaugh and his roommate walked smack into Boston manager Billy Southworth. "Did you sleep well last night?" Southworth asked sweetly. "Like babies," the players said in unison. "That's good," said Southworth. "I was afraid you might have been disturbed by the truck that crashed through your room in the middle of the night."[3]

Danny told his players during one of his infrequent meetings that he had a curfew. He didn't like curfews, but the club needed one for their protection. "I'll probably check sometime during the year," Danny told the team. One night Danny gave the night-shift elevator operator (this is an old story!) two baseballs that he wanted signed, with the instructions to have them signed by the players who arrived after midnight, which was the curfew time. When Danny got on the elevator the next morning, he asked the operator for one of the balls. "You keep the other one," he told the happy gentleman. Once the team arrived at the ballpark, he called the players who signed the baseballs into his office one at a time. "Were you in your room by curfew last night?" The response, as expected, was an emphatic, "Yes, I was." Danny gave the unsuspecting player one more chance. "Are you sure about that?" Danny asked. "Absolutely, Danny." Murtaugh produced the signed baseball, catching the player by total surprise. Danny told the embarrassed player, "Your fine for missing curfew is doubled for not telling the truth." The story ends, as the rest of the players who signed the balls walked into the manager's office one by one and placed their fines on his desk without a word being spoken.

Danny always had a memorable quote for the media. This was one of his best. "Why certainly I'd like to have that fellow who hits a home run every time at bat, who strikes out every opposing batter when he's pitching, who throws strikes to any base or the plate when he's playing outfield and who's always thinking about two innings ahead just what he'll do to baffle the other team. Any manager would want a guy like that playing for him. The only trouble is to get him to put down his cup of beer and come down out of the stands and do those things."[4]

The first time I met Danny, he told me, "If you can give me six innings every start, you'll win a lot of games. We'll score a lot of runs, and we have some pitchers in the bullpen who can hold a game." He was referring to Dave Guisti and Ramon Hernandez, two pitchers coincidentally from other organizations that Brown shrewdly got in deals from St. Louis and the Mexico City Reds, respectively.

While Danny talked about the club, I could see something in his Irish eyes that I hadn't seen with other managers. Those eyes displayed an air of confidence and honesty, but behind them was a sense of humor that had leprechauns dancing in the background, waiting for a chance to conjure up their magic. I would see examples of their mischief in the weeks to come.

I didn't have many conversations with Danny during the three years we were together. In fact, few players did. Wisely, Danny let the players have the clubhouse and stayed out of their way. When he did speak, there was a good reason. Once, when some pitchers were complaining about the defense, he called us into his office and told us, "Gentlemen, you can't expect people to do things they aren't capable of doing. It's the philosophy of this organization to find the best players we can, and when they're ready for the big leagues, we plug them into a position. It's not always their best position, but we found the run production they generate more than makes up for any defensive shortcomings," he said sternly. After a pause, he smiled and said, "You'll thank me in the postseason."

Spring of 1974: Work Hard, Play Hard

Spring training of 1974 began at Pirate City, a four-field complex that included a barracks that the City of Bradenton, Florida, built for the club. With the four fields the players split into smaller groups to get their work done more efficiently. A day's work included all of the drills that every team practiced: covering first base, backing up bases on throws from the outfield, and reviewing the defense for bunt plays, to name a few.

One day Danny wanted to stress the importance of a sacrifice bunt to the pitchers. With the everyday infielders at their respective positions and Dock Ellis on the mound, the drill was run at game speed. Each pitcher had an outfielder or reserve infielder as his partner and was expected to lay down a bunt that would advance his partner to the next base. If the sacrifice-bunt play wasn't executed properly, both the pitcher and his partner were told to run down the first base line, touch the foul pole, and return for another round. Well, the first round looked like a parade to the foul pole, as nearly every pitcher failed to advance the runner against Ellis, who was told he would do the running if he let up during the drill. If a pitcher failed to bunt his partner over a second time, you can bet the pitcher's ass was being chewed out during that foul-pole run. Before the next round I learned the Pirates meant business when it came to scoring runs.

Not every drill was as intense as the sacrifice bunt. There were drills that had me puzzled. But I learned the Pirate way. Someone in the organization purchased a forced-air tube called Iron Mike that could shoot baseballs as high as one hundred feet in the air and as far as three hundred feet and was used by the outfielders, infielders, and catchers.

One spring day at Pirate City, Danny, who normally stayed in the background, ventured on the field while "Iron Mike" was still running and invited the pitchers, who were working on an adjacent field, to join him. "Gentlemen, I'm not one for changing what works. But the position players said they like what this machine can do. I'd like your opinion," he said as the leprechauns behind those Irish eyes were watching. "How about if we shoot some pop flies in the infield for you to catch so you can see firsthand what this machine's all about?" he said. So one at a time, we caught our first round.

"Well, you handled that pretty easily," he said with a smile. "Let's try another round, only we'll shoot them higher." Not every one of the sixteen pitchers in camp was able to handle the one-hundred-foot high fly ball. Still, Danny pushed on. "Let's try a squat position facing center field and see how we do," he said matter-of-factly. "Maybe that'll be more of a challenge for some of you."

Now, the pitchers were getting into the drill. As Mike shot a ball skyward, it created a loud pop, followed by the voices of pitchers shouting encouragement as the ball was in flight. If it was caught, we all cheered. If not, we laughed at our teammate's reaction when his effort fell short. Anyone who caught a pop-up that round was eligible for the next round. "Well," Danny said with a laugh, "we still have five of you remaining. How about laying on the grass in front of the mound, face-down, and counting to three before you get up to catch the ball?" I was thinking, "Where does he come up with this shit?" I'm sure I wasn't the only one. Eventually, the field was narrowed to two pitchers. I think it was Jim Rooker and Ken Brett. I don't remember who was the winner . . . Maybe it was even a tie, as we had been playing for more than an hour. Eventually, Danny took off his sunglasses, called us all together, and asked us our opinion of Iron Mike. We were in complete agreement that it was everything as advertised and a great training tool.

Finally, someone asked the obvious question: "What does this drill have to do with pitching? We never catch pop-ups in the game." Danny paused, then smiled and said, "Absolutely nothing!" The leprechauns were roaring with laughter as Murtaugh put on his sunglasses and walked away.

Rollin' Down Highway 41

The Pirates assigned me uniform number 27. There's nothing wrong with 27, but it just didn't feel right. I thought about it on the way to the park one day when the Allman Brothers song "Ramblin' Man" came on the radio and I heard the lyrics "... *rollin' down Highway*

41." I happened to look at a street sign that told me I was driving on Highway 41! I liked the way it looked, so when I got to the park I asked John Hallahan (Hoolie), the equipment manager, about the availability of uniform number 41. "I'll make the switch at the start of the season . . . provided you make the club," he told me with a smile as he took a long drag on his cigarette.

Dock Walked to the Beat of His Own Drum

During the last week of spring training, Dock Ellis injured his hand while packing a trunk, which caused him to miss his scheduled opening-day start. Instead, I was honored, as Danny named me opening-day pitcher against the Cardinals in St. Louis. It was my first opening-day assignment.

I had a no-decision against Bob Gibson, as we eventually lost the game. In fact, we were 0–6 to start the season. By the time the month of April was over, we were 6–12 and sitting in last place in the NL East. Nothing seemed to get us out of our funk. Dock decided to take matters into his own hands.[5]

On May 1, 1974, he tied a Major League record by hitting the first three batters of the game. In spring training that year, Ellis sensed the Pirates had lost the aggressiveness that drove them to three straight division titles from 1970 to 1972. Furthermore, the team now seemed intimidated by Cincinnati's Big Red Machine. "Cincinnati will bullshit with us, then kick our ass and laugh at us," Ellis said. "They're the only team that talks about us like a dog." Ellis single-handedly decided to break the Pirates out of their emotional slump, announcing, "I'm going to hit these *motherbleepers.*" True to his word, in the first inning of the first regular-season game he pitched against the Reds, Ellis hit leadoff batter Pete Rose in the ribs, then plunked Joe Morgan in the kidney, and loaded the bases by hitting Dan Driessen in the back. Tony Perez, batting cleanup, dodged a succession of Ellis's pitches to walk and force in a run. The next hitter was Johnny Bench. "I tried to deck him twice," Ellis recalled. "I threw at his jaw, and he moved. I threw at the back of his head, and he moved." At this point, Murtaugh came to the mound and told Dock, "I guess you don't have your good stuff tonight," and removed Ellis from the game.[6]

The Pirate Family

Dock once told me, Brett, and Rooker that we were orphans. "Orphans? What the hell are you talking about?" asked Rooker. "Most of us came up through the organization; we're family," he explained as his voice became louder and higher pitched. "You came from somewhere else, and we took you in," he said with a touch of arrogance. I guess Dock thought by coming through the organization and being a member of the family, he had trade immunity. When he was sent to the Yankees in 1975, I wondered how that family thing worked for him.

Dealing with Dock

I brought a boom box to the park so we could have some music in the clubhouse. Dock took exception and, then, a bat to it. I saw the pieces scattered around the clubhouse. I told him, "Wouldn't it have been easier to just turn it off?" I mentioned my displeasure about the radio to Tom Reich, who represented Dock. Tom put his head down, shook it, and told me, "I'll talk to him about it." When I joined the Dodgers in 1979, there was a big cardboard box waiting for me in my locker. When I opened it I was shocked to find a newer, bigger, and better boom box with a cassette deck. The note on the inside read, "Make sure you play it LOUD!" It was signed, "Dock Ellis."

The Corner of Boardwalk and Park Place

The first time I walked into the Pirates' home clubhouse, I noticed something different from the St. Louis and Houston clubhouses. Instead of being arranged numerically, the Buccos were divided by ethnic backgrounds. Along the back wall the Latin players dressed in *Spanish Harlem*. The wall on the left of the entrance was *The Ghetto*, home of the black players. Separated by the door to the shower room on the same wall was *Boardwalk*, while the adjoining wall was *Park Place*, where the white players dressed. Curiously, the only player out of place was Bruce Kison, who lockered on the corner of *Spanish Harlem* and *The Ghetto*. When I asked Bruce about it while writing the book, he said that he never thought about it until I had mentioned it. "Hell, I just went wherever I was told," he said with a laugh.

Equally surprising were the barbs tossed freely throughout the clubhouse. Al Oliver noted, "Nothing was off-limits, even racial slurs. Nobody was above the fray, not even the coaching staff. Nothing was said in a vicious manner, just a bunch of guys cracking on each other in ways that would never be accepted anywhere but in a locker room. In the Pirate organization we had so many black and Latin players that the white guys felt comfortable joking with us. A big factor in that was that we were winning. A losing team is more apt to point fingers. Much of what went on in the Pirate clubhouse wouldn't have been tolerated in a losing clubhouse."[7]

Always in the middle of anything was Dock Ellis. Whether he made sense or not, Dock's opinions were heard. There were times he would get so excited that his voice would reach a pitch that only dogs could hear.

Called for Traveling

The Pirates had a rule regarding wives joining their husbands on a road trip. The rule, as I remember it, was that your wife could join you on a trip just once and only after the player received the club's permission. I reasoned that if I paid her way, where and when she showed up was our personal business. I had family in St. Louis and a home in Houston that was for sale and wanted my wife (now ex-wife) in both cities. Not so fast, said the Pirates.

After a second trip I was fined a hundred dollars. I called Marvin Miller, executive director of the Players Association, and told him about the fine. Marvin, always cordial yet to the point, asked me a few questions. "Obviously, she didn't fly on a team charter. Did the Pirates pay for her commercial flight?" Marvin asked. "No" was my answer. "So, she flew independent of the club paying any of her expenses?" he asked. "That's correct," I responded. "Since she's a private citizen, she can go wherever she wants," Marvin told me.

Marvin filed a grievance against the club. By the time the grievance was heard, I was fined a total of five hundred dollars for breaking this rule a few other times. I never made this information public because the issue was between the Pirates and me.

Once news of the grievance being filed was made public, I told reporters that the issue wasn't open for discussion. Joe Brown also refused to talk about it. Ultimately, the money was returned to me. Joe Brown, when asked by the press if the rule was still in effect, said, "It means that Jerry Reuss has been refunded his money and nothing else."

What Was I Thinking?

Baseball superstition dictates that if you have vanity plates made for your car, jewelry with your number on it, or buy a house in the city where you play, chances are greater that you'll be traded. I was never superstitious, but I was traded twice after buying homes in the cities where I played. Thinking that there might be something to this, I moved to Santa Barbara, California, between the 1974 and '75 baseball seasons. I fell in love with the city. With the mountains, the ocean, and the warm winter, who wouldn't? Within a few months I bought a home there. One day I rode my bicycle on the campus at the University of California at Santa Barbara and found the baseball team practicing. After a short time I approached the baseball coach, Dave Gorrie, introduced myself, and eventually asked him about the possibility of working out with the team that winter. Dave needed a few days to think about it and clear it with the athletic department. True to his word, Dave called me and said that I could join his club for the workouts.

While on the field with the student athletes, I thought about the possibility of resuming my education. There was still money in my college scholarship fund set up by the Cardinals when I signed in 1967, and my high school and college transcripts allowed my credits to transfer.

There was only one problem. The winter term ended on March 8, which was three weeks into spring training. As I look back today, I had one of those *What was I thinking?* moments. I decided to enroll anyway and let the Pirates know about it after the first of the year. The proper and respectful way to handle the situation would have been to call Joe Brown and let him know what I was thinking. Then, I should have asked him if attending the winter term would have been feasible. Joe's answer probably would have been something like this: "Jerry, I'm all for you attending classes in the off-season. Your job requires you to be in Bradenton the third week in February. So, as much as you wish to continue your education, I can't permit you to show up after March 8."

Maybe I knew back then this would be Joe's response. So I did it my way. I sent Joe a letter (didn't even give him the courtesy of a phone call) around the first of February. Joe called me the morning after he read the letter and told me, "The Basic Agreement [between Major League Baseball and the Players Association] states that you must report to camp by March 1. If you're not in uniform by then, you'll be fined a substantial amount for every day you miss. Do you understand?" said the furious general manager. "I do," I responded meekly.

I took whatever final exams I could and flew to Florida. I saw Joe first thing the morning I reported to camp. "I'm glad you're here, but I'm in no mood to discuss this matter with you now. I'll come to you when I'm ready" was Joe's response. Joe and I eventually settled my indiscretion. But it took some time to rebuild the bond of trust.

Danny was more receptive. "I'm okay now that you're here. But you're gonna have to straighten this matter out with Joe. Also, be prepared for what you'll hear in the clubhouse," he said as the leprechauns behind his eyes turned their backs to me.

Entering the clubhouse, I was greeted with a sarcastic round of applause and was referred to as "the professor." I deserved this ration of shit, I thought. Finally, after a while, I told my teammates, "I apologize. I made a mistake in judgment, and it won't happen again." Most of them were good with that. Others reserved their opinion.

Fortunately, I was already in great baseball shape. Before I came to camp I threw five or six innings in a few college intersquad games. If there was a doubt as to what shape I was in, it was erased when I completed thirty-six innings that spring, tied with Dock for the most by a Pirate pitcher.

Hall of Fame Player, Hall of Fame Man

Willie Stargell (Pops), the team captain, was the heart and soul of the ball club. He was always there for a teammate. When Rick Langford, who was the pitching coordinator for the Toronto Blue Jays when I interviewed him, joined the club in Atlanta when he was first called up to the Majors in 1976, he got a phone call from Willie. Pops invited him to share a cab to the ballpark, and they talked about the differences between the Major Leagues and the Minors during the fifteen-minute ride. Once they got there Willie showed Langford the clubhouse and answered the questions that any rookie would have. "I didn't even know how much to pay the clubhouse attendant, how to get to the field, or where to sit on the plane," Rick told me in 2011. "Willie was there to make the transition easy. I was just one guy that didn't play a big part on the club, and he took that amount of time for me. I'll never forget that."

When Willie was offered a paid appearance, he would do it on the condition that he could bring along a young player and would split the fee with the kid.

Willie picked up the idea for his "Stargell Stars" from a friend who awarded rose-shaped stickers for good deeds to anyone who deserved one. Pops designed gold stars with adhesive on the back and gave them out to anyone as a show of appreciation for a job well done. It wasn't just for players but batboys, trainers, coaches, front-office personnel, and fans.

Willie not only talked the talk, but walked the walk. He preached a steady-as-she-goes philosophy, never too high when you win and never too low when you lose. He believed a player lost his effectiveness at either end of the spectrum. He lived those words daily, as he always replaced his helmet in his slot the same way, whether he homered or struck out. He never once lost his cool because of an umpire's call or because the game situation favored the opposition. "I'd rather turn that negative energy into a positive," Willie once remarked. For the same reason, he didn't share the eye-for-an-eye philosophy when players retaliated for breaking an unwritten baseball rule. Instead, he believed in a more global view. "What goes around comes around," he would say, understanding that karma transcended all things baseball. Probably, his most famous quote was, "The umpire says 'Play ball,' not 'Work ball.'" The quote said everything about Willie's perspective.

He also had a Hall of Fame sense of humor. Once when I struggling during a game, he walked over to the mound and told me, "Throw it down the middle and let them hit it. Let those 'brothers' [he actually used the dreaded N word] in the outfield run it down." He was also a Hall of Fame–caliber instigator.

The Three-Man Lift

Kurt Bevacqua, who joined the club in a trade with Kansas City over the winter, was another player who enjoyed the clubhouse stage.

Dirty Kurt (nicknamed *Dirty* for a multitude of reasons), always in a hyper state, was prime meat for the clubhouse pranksters. Once Bevacqua was offended when trainer Tony Bartirome refused to give him a rubdown. "I only give rubs to guys who actually play in a game," Tony told him. Of course, always willing to stir the pot, Stargell pulled the agitated Bevacqua aside and told Kurt not to mess with Tony. "*Bleep* him!" was Kurt's response. "Look," Willie calmly explained to the reserve infielder, "he may look small [Tony was maybe five foot nine, weighing around 165], but he's one of the strongest men around this team." "My ass," Kurt said in disbelief. Willie continued, "Watch him rip up these phone books." "Hey, Tony," Willie said as he and Kurt entered the training room. "Kurt doesn't think you're strong enough to rip a phone book in half." "I don't have to prove shit to backup infielders that come into my training room begging for courtesy rubs," replied the trainer as he was working on another player.

Now, Bevacqua was getting annoyed at the put-downs and challenged Tony. "Okay, you skinny shit, let's see what you got." Tony finished with the player he was taping and told Kurt, "I got work to do around here. If it'll shut you up, I'll do it." Willie handed him a phone book. Tony grabbed it and with a flick of his wrists ripped the four-inch phone book in half. "Now do you believe me?" Willie pleaded to Bevacqua. "That doesn't mean shit," said the surprised but unimpressed newcomer. Willie kept at it. "What if I told you he could lift three guys?" "What do you mean, 'lift three guys'?" was Kurt's reply.

Suddenly, the interest of the clubhouse was centered on Stargell and his mark. Guys were gravitating to the training room. I looked at Ken Brett, whose locker was the first address on *Boardwalk*, right next to mine, and asked him, "Any idea what this is about?" "Not a clue," was Brett's reply. "But something's gonna happen."

Bevacqua was louder than ever, as Willie explained Tony's exploits that he personally witnessed. "There's no way he can lift three grown men off the ground high enough to roll a baseball under," protested Kurt. "Hey, I got a hundred bucks that says he can" came a voice outside the training room. On cue another voice responded, "I'll take that bet." Suddenly, the clubhouse was alive with bets taken on the three-man lift. Kurt could still be heard above the rest of us. "I want some of this!" shouted Kurt. Both Willie and Dave Parker volunteered to be lifted, as the activity shifted to the center of the locker room.

Tony set Willie and Parker on their backs, laying parallel to one another on the floor with an opening in the middle for the third player. Looking around the faces that had closed ranks around the two players on the floor, he spotted Bevacqua and said, "Hey, part-time, how much do you weigh?" "One-eighty!" shouted Kurt. "Get your ass on the floor!" barked the agitated trainer.

Tony placed Bevacqua in the middle and had him put an arm around the head of Stargell and the other arm around Parker and told Willie and Dave to hold that in place. He then had Kurt overlap each of his legs between the legs of the guys on the outside, who then placed their outer legs over Kurt's. "When I count to three, I want you to strain every muscle in your body, especially you, loudmouth," Tony quietly told Kurt and the other two players. The crowd of standing players was unusually quiet, with smirks on their faces and hands behind their backs. I didn't understand why their hands had cans of shaving cream, aftershave, cartons of milk, and juice until I heard Tony shout, "Three!" Bevacqua's pants were pulled down with his shorts and jock as the bounty of products sprayed, splashed, and poured on his exposed person. It seemed like five, maybe ten, minutes passed before the laughter stopped. Tony told him, "Next time you want a rub, go to one of those places on Liberty Avenue [once the center of red-light activity]. You'll get a 'happy ending' there!"

"I'll Get His Ass!"

It just wasn't in Bevacqua's nature to let the joke pass, as he became obsessed with one-upping Willie. If Kurt walked past me and I said, "Hey, Kurt, how's it going?" He would respond, "I'll get his ass!" and walk away.

Kurt waited and his patience paid off. Willie wasn't in the lineup one night, and while sitting on the bench he crossed his hands over the knob of his bat whose barrel stood upright on the dugout turf. Once Willie pulled his hat over his eyes and rested his chin over his hands, he nodded off while appearing to be studying the hitter. Remember, Three Rivers Stadium was a multipurpose facility, and when in the baseball configuration the dugout was half pebbles and half turf.

Kurt found a bottle of rubbing alcohol and a lighter and belly-crawled through dirt, pebbles, turf, and who knows what else past the manager, coaches, and players to Stargell's location. He emptied the bottle on the turf and lit it. Poof! The flame shot up within a foot of Pops's chin. To my surprise, Willie didn't move a muscle until he slowly opened his eyes.

To me and the other players who watched this spectacle, we held our breath until we saw that Pops was okay. Willie took a deep breath, looked at me, and asked, "Bevacqua?" I nodded, and Willie went back to sleep.

On the Road with Dirty Kurt

When we returned from our next road trip, Kurt had an envelope addressed to him from a mall in upstate Pennsylvania. The enclosed letter read, "Dear Kurt, We are celebrating the Grand Opening of our new mall in Erie and we would like for you to be a part of the celebration. The ribbon cutting is scheduled for 9:00 AM Saturday morning and we would love to have you join us. For your time, we will pay you $1,000." Now, a thousand dollars was big money for an appearance in 1974, and Kurt let everybody in the clubhouse know he was getting it. Kurt had the traveling secretary, John Fitzpatrick, call and confirm for him. Night games on Fridays began at 8:05 p.m. at Three Rivers, and we played a long game the night before his scheduled appearance. But Kurt was up before 5:00 a.m. and on his way north.

Bevacqua found the mall using the directions provided but didn't see any grand-opening signs. So he parked in the empty lot and banged on the double glass doors at the mall's entrance. Finally, the security guard answered, as the high-energy Bevacqua was screaming about the appearance and the planned festivities. No matter how much Kurt inquired, the guard had no answers. "Can you call this lady who sent me the letter at home?" he pleaded. The guard looked at the name and said, "There's nobody here by that name."

Meanwhile, back in Pittsburgh, Willie woke with a smile on his face of scorched whiskers, sipping that first cup of coffee, wondering how Kurt was enjoying his appearance. A cup of payback always tastes best hot, with cream and sugar.

Within minutes of walking into the clubhouse that afternoon, everybody knew about Kurt's appearance. When Bevacqua arrived all conversations stopped as he walked straight to Willie's locker. Kurt put out his hand and said, "Truce? I won't mess with you anymore." Willie shook his hand and told him, "If you don't start no shit, there won't be no shit. It's the Bucco way!"

The Cobra Uncoiled

Dave Parker (nicknamed "Cobra" by Pirates announcer Bob Prince) probably benefited most from Willie's approach. When Dave first came to the Pirates in 1973, he was platooned in the outfield, much like Willie and Al Oliver (Scoop) were early in their careers, as both Bill Virdon and Murtaugh sat him on the bench when tough veteran pitchers were facing the Bucs. Dave, like Pops and Scoop, didn't like the platoon method but wisely listened to Willie and studied the game when he wasn't in the lineup.

He became the everyday right fielder in 1975. By 1978 he was the league's Most Valuable Player. In the years we played together with the Pirates (we were also teammates with the Reds), I never saw Dave lose his temper. After a strikeout Dave, much like Willie, would walk back to the dugout, place his helmet in the rack, drop his bat in its slot, light a cigarette, and take a seat on the bench. The demeanor of both Willie and Dave set the tone for the rest of the club. It wasn't always copied, but it was there to be noticed.

Parker Meets Muhammad Ali

Parker was probably the most physically imposing player in the game during my years with the Bucs. At six foot five and weighing around 225 pounds, he had a perfectly sculpted body. In fact, he had muscles where most of us don't even have places!

With his physique and a boisterous personality, Dave never had a problem getting the attention that he sought. He also had no problem handling the numerous interview requests. He could be humorous, thoughtful, intelligent, and arrogant within the same interview . . . much like Muhammad Ali.

During my Pirates tenure, we stayed at the Executive House in Chicago when playing a series against the Cubs. Dave and I were on the elevator when we stopped at a floor and Muhammad Ali joined us for the ride to the lobby. Ali looked at both of us, nodded, and turned to face the door. I looked at Dave, who stood there with his mouth wide open in shock and, for the only time in my memory, had nothing to say. So I thought I'd break the ice. "Well, Dave," I said matter-of-factly, "go ahead and tell him how you could whoop his ass like you told us in the locker room!" That got Ali's wide-eyed attention as he turned to face Parker.

"Jeez, Jerry, what the hell . . ." Dave stuttered. He recovered quickly, however, and put out his hand to greet the champ. "Hi, I'm

Dave Parker!" Ali replied, "Yes, I know who you are." Ali looked at me as I put out my hand. I had my biggest smile when I said, "Hi, champ, I'm . . ." I was interrupted. "You're an instigator, that's who you are," Ali said as his eyes narrowed. Dave and Ali exchanged pleasantries for the remaining ten or twelve floors. For me, it was the longest elevator ride in my life.

Baseball's Best Player

While playing for Houston in 1972–73 and watching César Cedeño play center field every day, I believed he would be the best ball-player that I would ever have for a teammate. He batted .320 with a total of 47 HR, 152 RBI, and 111 stolen bases during those two years. A Gold Glove winner from 1972 to 1976, he was a five-tool player (he could hit for power, hit for average, and field, run, and throw above average) who did something every day that made everybody take notice.

But when you compare Cedeño's production in 1972–73 with Parker's in 1977–78, César takes a backseat to big Dave. Parker, a right fielder and also a five-tool player, led the National League in batting both years with .338 and .334 averages, respectively, just two of the five consecutive years he batted more than .300. He also hit 51 homers and drove in 205 runs while winning Gold Glove honors from 1977 to 1979.

What separated Dave from César (and the rest of the league) was his intensity. Cedeño could turn his play up a notch when he wanted, while Dave was always at full speed. It seemed Dave was always in the right place, whether he was backing up the center fielder, backing up a play at first base, or running the bases. There's no telling how many shortstops or second basemen heard his foot-steps when covering second base on a possible play, as they knew instinctively that he would come into the base hard.

He played with such intensity that after breaking his cheekbone in a home-plate collision with Mets catcher John Stearns on June

30, 1978, he was back in the lineup on July 16. Dave's reaction to the injury was simple. "If I can see, I can play," he announced to the world. In order to protect his cheekbone, he wore two different face masks, one while batting and switching to the other when running the bases. When players throughout the league thought about their nagging injuries, they were reminded about Parker's courage and were inspired to play with pain.

In the late seventies I didn't know much about the players in the American League. So, based on the five years I played with Dave in Pittsburgh, there was no doubt he was the best ballplayer I saw during my twenty-two years in uniform.[8]

A Locker-Room Presence

In 1974–75 it was Dock who made the Pirates' locker room his stage. When Dock was traded to the Yankees in the winter of 1975, Dave Parker jumped into the locker-room spotlight. Unlike Dock, who would go off on a tangent to prove a point, Dave cut right to the heart. It didn't matter where you were born, your ethnic heritage, religious background, marital status . . . Nothing was sacred. Nor was it personal. But it was a daily comedy routine.

Dave was an equal opportunity offender. Players, coaches, and the front office were his favorite topics. "Pay me my money!" he would shout in the locker room, referring to his impending free agency in 1978. Pirate ownership heard him loud and clear, as Dave signed a five-million-dollar, five-year deal before the 1979 season, making him baseball's highest-paid player at a million dollars a year.

Unfortunately, many people in Pittsburgh who had lost their blue-collar jobs in the steel industry resented someone earning the kind of money Dave did. As a result the fans took out their frustrations on Parker, showering him with nuts, bolts, and radio batteries as he positioned himself in right field. On Bat Day, when replica-size bats were distributed to many of the forty-three thousand fans in attendance at Three Rivers Stadium, one fan decided to throw a bat on the field near the spot where Dave was standing.

Dave's reaction was to verbally attack the fans of Pittsburgh, which in turn infuriated them even more. There were numerous times his car was vandalized in the parking lot. He received death threats. These fan-resentment incidents became daily news wherever Dave and the club went. When the club struggled in 1980, the fans blamed him. With slumps and injuries from 1981 to 1983, the remainder of his contract, Dave chose his hometown of Cincinnati when he became a free agent.[9]

To those individuals who ventured into our locker-room world, Dave could be perceived as arrogant. When Dave was asked why he wore the Star of David around his neck, he told the reporter, "My name's David and I'm a star!"

He could also be cocky. Once, before an afternoon game in Chicago, he stood on the top step of the dugout stairs, sniffed the air, and told no one in particular, "I smell about twelve hits for us today. I'll get my four, and the rest of you sons of bitches can split the rest!"

One of Dave's favorite quotes was, "When the leaves turn brown, I'll win the batting crown." That's exactly what he did in 1977 and 1978.

He also had a great sense of what it took for him to be the best. "I come into the clubhouse and rave and scream to prepare me for the game. . . . [S]ome [players] meditate, I verbalize. I'm the type of individual who says what's on his mind. I've been that way all of my life."[10] With that approach, Parker never wrote a check with his mouth that his game couldn't cash.

Kicking the Bucket

Once the weather turned hot, the players dipped a towel in a metal bucket containing ammonia, water, and ice that was located down the ramp from the dugout. It took the edge off the heat.

No amount of that mixture could cool me off one night after I coughed up a lead and was taken out of the game. Baseball decorum dictates that a pitcher who is removed from the game must wait on the bench until the inning is over before he can retreat to the clubhouse. It was also a club rule on every team I played for.

I was still steaming from my performance when the inning ended. So, in my typical immature fashion, I took my disappointment out on the ice bucket. I kicked the metal bucket and shattered it, as water drenched the walls and runway.

When I got to the park the next day, I noticed a letter typed on Pirate stationery sitting on the stool in front of my locker. I picked it up and read it.

Dear Jerry,

Due to the fact that you destroyed our water bucket last night, we will deduct the cost of a new bucket from your next paycheck in the amount of $7.95.

Regards...

Of course, I lost it. "These no-good, cheap sons of bitches can kiss my ass!" I shouted. The attention in the clubhouse was on me. "Can you believe this shit?" I continued.

So Willie got up from his stool, walked over to my locker, and asked me what was the matter. "These assholes want to fine me $7.95 for breaking the ice bucket!" I told him. "No," Willie answers. "Oh, yeah," I said. "It's right here in this letter." Willie asks, "Can I see that?" I showed it to him. "Man, that's horseshit. A man can't even let off some steam every now and then around here," Willie said with mock indignation.

Other players walked over to my spot on *Boardwalk* and asked to see the letter. So they passed it around. "Man, that's a shame," one said. "That shows no respect," said another teammate, shaking his head. "You ought to go up to the front office right now and tell them what you told us," suggested another player.

By this time Hoolie came up to me and asked, "Is this letter bothering you?" "Your damn right it is!" I answered, still pissed off. "Here," Hoolie said in a quiet voice. "Let me take care of it for you." He grabbed the letter from my hand, tore it into pieces, and threw it into the trash. "There, that takes care of that," he said matter-of-factly, dusting his hands as he walked away.

I stood there dumbfounded. Suddenly, I looked at the faces of my teammates, as they could no longer hold back their laughter. Willie walked up to me with a half smile on his face and asked, "Hey, do you feel better now?" I paused, closed my eyes, and wanted to crawl into a hole. I had just been had! One by one my teammates walked up to me with big smiles on their faces, shook my hand, and said to me, "Glad your back with us" or "Don't worry, we got your back" and "Welcome to the Buccos!" Once again, I was reminded of being a Bucco!

Living Life on the Edge

In Jim Rooker's first five years in the Majors with Detroit (1968) and the expansion Kansas City Royals (1969–72), his record stood at 21–44 but with a respectable ERA of 3.93. His career turned around after he joined the Pirates in 1973, as he was 67–45 with an ERA of 3.00 through 1977. Maybe it was the change of scenery from last place in the American League to one of the top teams in the National League. Maybe he came into his own as a pitcher.

I asked Jim in the summer of 2011 what the difference was. "During a stay in winter ball in 1972–73, I switched my fastball to a two-seam grip," he explained. "When I changed my hand position slightly at the delivery point, I discovered a power sinker I could throw for strikes. Instead of pitching behind in the count, I was ahead of the hitters, as I could confidently throw my other pitches for strikes. Throwing my sinker for strikes changed my whole outlook on pitching and extended my career," Jim concluded.[11]

Whatever the difference was, Rooker, at times, was the best pitcher on the Bucs' staff. Without an overpowering fastball or a knee-buckling curve to add to his newfound sinker, he had what scouts would call average Major League stuff.

But he had the balls of a cat burglar. He walked the thin line that separated victory from defeat and came out a winner more times than not. When he wasn't in a game, his demeanor was much the same: live on the edge and don't give an inch. In July 1974 or 1975, Rook arrived at the park with a bag of assorted fireworks, which included some M-80s. A day or so later a group of us, which included Rook, myself, Bruce Kison, and Ken Brett, took his bag of goodies out on the field to see what we could do with them. Within minutes we placed a lit M-80 and a baseball into a ten-pound cast-iron posthole cover. Once lit the explosion propelled the baseball so high in the air that we had to hide in the bullpen bathroom, knowing the speed of what goes up like a rocket must come down even faster. The ball landed on the plastic outfield turf, and the first bounce went as high as the second deck . . . maybe sixty to eighty feet! Yep, we were living on the edge in Rooker's world.

Payback Is a Bitch!

When sitting on the bench during a game when you're not playing, guys like to get comfortable. The backs of the bench, which were small at Three Rivers Stadium, didn't afford that luxury. But we managed. Players who sat on the bench with one leg crossed over the other in an effort to sit comfortably found themselves at the mercy of Richie Hebner, who liked to spray the raised shoe of unsuspecting teammates with a spew of chewing-tobacco residue and then laugh in their faces. Most guys dealt with the defacement of their shoes in their own manner, such as cutting the laces on Hebner's spikes before the next game. Hebner, whose nickname was Hack, knew how the game was played. If the payback was fair, everybody had a laugh.

Rooker, however, didn't play fair. Hebner saw Rooker sitting with his legs crossed on the bench one night and sprayed Jim's shoe. It was precision aim, as he covered just the toes. Hebner was in full belly laugh when Rooker politely told him, "You might want to clean that shit off my shoe, Hack." Hebner was surprised at Rooker's reaction and responded, "*Bleep* you! I'm not cleaning anything. Maybe what you need is this," and spit on his shoe again.

Now it got interesting. We're trying to win a ball game, and both guys have drawn a line on the turf and won't back down. Rooker calmly watched his dripping shoe and very deliberately told a ready-to-fight Hebner, "I'll ask you one more time, Hack. Clean it off my shoe." "Or what, what are you gonna do about it?" challenged the now-crazed third baseman. Before the calm and collected Rooker could respond, the inning was over, as Hebner, still laughing, grabbed his glove, ran out of the dugout, and took his position at third base. Rooker's last comment about the incident was "I'll get his ass!"

Rooker's locker was located just two or three stalls away from Hebner's on the *Park Place* side of the clubhouse, a perfect vantage point for the relentless pitcher. For the next few days, Jim observed the unsuspecting infielder who had forgotten the verbal altercation, as he plotted his revenge. Hebner became a victim of his own daily habits. After infield practice he liked to strip down to his shorts, grab a newspaper, and head to the same stall in the clubhouse restroom to "pinch a loaf" before the game started.

Finally, Rooker struck. Jim skipped infield practice, cleared all clubhouse personnel from the restroom area, locked the door to the back entrance, and waited for Hebner to come off the field. Richie, in a bit of a hurry, grabbed a newspaper, and headed for his favorite stall, only this time he was still in his uniform. Rooker, once sure that Hebner was comfortably seated, pulled one of the M-80s out of his back pocket, lit it, threw it on the tiled floor by the stalls, closed the connecting door to the clubhouse, and just waited. Within seconds there was an explosion so loud that it brought the security officers who were stationed at the stadium entrance to the clubhouse.

Most of us players followed what Rooker was doing and howled with laughter when the bathroom door opened, pouring smoke into the clubhouse that silhouetted the dazed Hebner, pants and underwear at the top of his shoes, newspaper still in hand, with a shell-shocked look on his face as he tried to make sense of what had just happened. When Hebner saw the clubhouse in a fit of laughter, he shouted at Rooker, who was standing about ten feet away with his arms crossed and a look on his face that said, "I told you to clean my shoe, didn't I?"

Who's That Masked Man?

Fireworks weren't Jim's only props for pranks. One of the best in his collection was a rubber mask of an ogre that featured long, bushy white hair. He would put on the mask and catch unsuspecting teammates at a vulnerable moment. He caught most everybody at one time or another. The best reaction always came from first baseman and outfielder John Milner. "Hammer," as Milner liked to be called, would always jump and scream when Rook would surprise him, much to the delight of teammates who were glad it was Milner and not themselves.

It was custom in the '70s through the mid-'80s for most clubs to have beer available in the clubhouse after a game, as it encouraged the players to sit and discuss the game before heading home. During the years I was with the Bucs, the small clubhouse dining room featured Pittsburgh favorites Iron City on tap, Iron City Light in cans, and Rolling Rock in their trademark green bottles.

Hammer, who came over from the Mets as part of a huge four-team deal that also scored Bert Blyleven from the Rangers for Al Oliver, had his own way to relax after a ball game. First, he pulled off his uniform top, sweatshirt, and shoes and put on his robe/smoking jacket. Then he would pour a few ounces from a bottle of Martell Cordon Bleu in his locker into a brandy snifter, have a taste, and chase it with a Beck's beer, all while chain-smoking. I once asked him about this postgame scenario, and all he would say is "It's gotta be Cordon Bleu and Beck's. Otherwise, it's not right."

Parker, who lockered next to Milner, tried the combination, liked it, and joined Hammer, as the ritual now included their own chaise lounges, with a table, a lamp, and an ashtray full of butts between them. They kept it up for hours after a game as the cleanup crew vacuumed the carpet around them.

Hammer made it his responsibility to bring the Beck's beer to the park on a daily basis. For whatever reason, Beck's was sold only in a four-pack. Each day upon arriving at the park, Milner put each evening's postgame fare in the upright refrigerator before getting dressed. Because the beer was there for everyone to see, it was just a matter of time before the troops struck.

After one game Milner disrobed, put on his jacket, and headed for the fridge. He was shocked when he saw the empty bottles of Beck's sitting in the carton where he had left them. Hammer raised all kinds of hell about this. The next day, still pissed off about the transgression, he came into the clubhouse with another four-pack, placed them in his spot in the fridge, and walked in the clubhouse and told everyone within earshot, "There will be hell to pay if it happens again!"

Hammer seriously misjudged his teammates. Instead of heeding his warning, they accepted his words as a challenge. Sure enough, John found only empty bottles, as he prepared for his postgame sit-down with Dave. Milner was livid as he yelled in the middle of the clubhouse. Of course, the players had their heads turned away from the crazed first baseman while laughing.

Still determined, Hammer arrived at the park the next day, four-pack in hand, and headed to the dining room. He closed the door behind him and proceeded to clear a space in the top-loading cooler where the postgame spread was kept to hide his Beck's. Not saying a word, he went to his locker and prepared for the game. It didn't take but a few minutes before Rooker, who observed Milner's arrival and departure from the dining room, discovered the hidden Beck's under the trays of cold cuts. It was genius on Rooker's part to leave the beer alone and to keep other players from draining the contents. He had bigger plans.

After the game, much to Milner's surprise, the bottles of Beck's were intact. Milner, finding safety in his personal Fort Knox, repeated the process the next few days. Then Rooker struck.

Approximating the time the habitual Milner would arrive at the park, Rooker and a few other players emptied the cooler of its contents as Jim put on his ogre mask and crawled into the cooler. We carefully placed the original contents over Rooker, who was lying on his side, and covered everything with towels. We closed the sliding tops and took our seats at our lockers.

Like clockwork, Hammer entered the clubhouse a few minutes later, with Beck's in hand, and made a right turn into the dining room. Closing the door behind him, he opened the sliding doors as the masked Rooker grabbed Milner's arm. What we heard in the clubhouse was a blood-curdling scream, as Milner came running from behind the door into the clubhouse. All I could understand was "Dead white guy . . . grabbed me . . . he's dead! Ugly *motherbleeper* . . . dead . . . grabbed my arm." By this time the clubhouse was filled with uncontrollable laughter.

When Rooker entered the clubhouse still wearing the mask, Hammer let out another scream. There was an aftershock of belly laughs. For weeks Hammer stayed out of the dining room. He had one of the clubhouse attendants place the Beck's in one of the refrigerators. Surprisingly, nobody messed with it. Its presence always brought a smile to everyone's face, and who wanted to destroy the daily reminder of one of the great pranks of all time?

Scrap-Iron

Called Scrap-Iron for his gritty style of play, Phil Garner was the big prize for the Pirates when they traded six players to Oakland for a package of three in mid-March 1977. Garner's first day as a Pirate was on March 18. He arrived at McKechnie Field in time to get a uniform, get loose, and start the game at third base.

I was pitching that day against the Tigers. Tito Fuentes, who was in the American League for the first time after spending eleven seasons in the National League, came to the plate in the top of the first inning. Fuentes had this ritual he performed before every at bat. Batting right-handed against me, he held his right hand in the air, signaling for time to the umpire, and dug a hole in the batter's box with his right foot.

For pitchers of a previous generation, they would have drilled him in the ribs on the first pitch for that violation of baseball's unwritten rules. I was a bit more tolerant, up to a point. Then Tito adjusted his wristbands, his batting gloves, and something new he just added, his headband. I was ready to pitch before he came to the plate, and now I was annoyed, having to wait for this shit.

Fuentes finished his ritual series of tics by grabbing the barrel of his bat and tapping the knob on top of the plate so the bat flipped into his waiting hand. Now he was ready to hit.

I delivered my first pitch, a fastball down the middle. Fuentes swung from his ass, fouled the ball back to the screen, and fell to the ground in the process. I got a new ball from Satch Davidson, the veteran NL umpire who was working the plate, and in seconds I was ready to go.

Not so fast! Fuentes was still dusting his uniform before he repeated the whole ritual. The wristbands, batting gloves, the headband, and the bat tap were all adjusted and completed as he stepped into the box to hit . . . except he added something else. He signaled me with his left hand and told me to throw! I thought, "You piece of shit! You're gonna make me wait and then tell me when you want me to throw?" I shook off two curves and got the sign for a fastball, as the catcher, Duffy Dyer, knew what was going to happen.

I fired a fastball, elbow high (well, maybe closer to the chin), as Fuentes hit the ground, his helmet heading toward the dugout and his bat to the backstop.

I took a few steps toward the plate to get a new ball from Satch and stared at the prone infielder and told him, "Pull that shit again and I won't miss!"

Fuentes looked at me and then at Satch and barked, "He did that on purpose!" Satch walked from behind the plate, pulled his mask off, and told Fuentes, "Get your ass in there and hit, and no more of this bullshit." Apparently, Satch attended the same old school I did. I don't remember what happened the rest of that at bat, but Fuentes, who was understandably pissed off, just stepped to the plate without any more adjustments.

When the inning was over Garner, whom I didn't have the chance to meet before the game, came up to me in the dugout with a smile on his face and said, "Is that the way you guys play in this league? Damn, I'm gonna love it here!"

Garner was a breath of fresh air. He brought an aura of leadership with him from his days in Oakland. A quick study, he had the respect of manager Chuck Tanner, as Gar would position both the infielders and the outfielders as the game progressed, much like the manager that he would be after his playing career ended.

Because Chuck liked the running game, the Pirates, who were billed as the Lumber Company during the last year of Brown-Murtaugh leadership, changed their tag line to Lumber and Lightning the first year of the Harding Peterson—Chuck Tanner combination.

Garner fit the profile perfectly. There was a huge difference in the offensive numbers across the board when comparing the 1976 numbers of Hebner to the 1977 numbers of Garner.[12]

Defensively, Garner, primarily a second baseman for Oakland, was a huge upgrade for the Pirates at third. Suddenly, grounders between the shortstop and third baseman that went for hits in

1976 were turned into outs in 1977. Because Gar could cover so much ground in the hole, it allowed the shortstop to play a step or so closer to second base, which cut off a number of potential base hits through the middle.

As good as he was in the field, he was equally adept in the clubhouse, performing as the perfect counterpoint to the daily rants of Parker. On a typical day, one of them would say something loud enough for the other to hear, and off they would go, eventually meeting in the center of the clubhouse, the five-foot-eight, 170-pound Garner on his toes, pointing his finger in the face of the six-foot-five, 225-pound Parker, as both were shouting in each other's face some of the funniest lines ever heard. It was the greatest show on earth! One indelible image on my mind is Garner, once standing on a stool, going at it face-to-face with Parker.

Ever Hear the One about the Best-Laid Plans?

Free agency was in full swing by 1977. It seemed that every time a player signed a new contract, it would leapfrog a signing from the day before. Nobody had a grasp on what their dollar value was to a club. But you could bet the very next contract signed was for more money, more years, with every penny guaranteed.

I settled on a three-year deal with the Pirates starting in 1977. Harding (Pete) Peterson, who was in his first year as VP of player personnel after spending twenty-five years with the club, was part of the team that negotiated the deal for the Pirates. Pete told me during the first day of negotiations that he hoped we could reach a deal, because he wanted me to have a long and successful career and finish it with the Pirates.

I was happy in Pittsburgh. The problems that plagued me in Houston disappeared (with the help of a divorce) after my first year with the Bucs. I was on a winner, I was contributing, and I wanted to stay. So instead of seeking the largest contract, I was willing to accept less than the open market offered, if the Pirates would give me a no-trade clause. That way I could have security, buy a house, and become a part of the community. In the off-season I had speaking engagements and personal appearances, all in an effort to promote the Pirates and bring people to the ballpark. I was happy to do it, and the Pirates were happy to have me out there.

Chuck Tanner took over the managerial reins from a retiring Danny Murtaugh. I had a long-term contract, bought a town home, and was ready to have a great season. Everything was pointing in the right direction.

But ever hear the one about the best-laid plans? I had my first losing season with the Pirates in 1977, ending 10–13 with an ERA of 4.11. Considering that I didn't win my first game until May 24 and was 4–10 at the All-Star break, it took a good second half just to get there.

In 1978 a young man by the name of Don Robinson came on the scene for the Bucs. After a great spring training he won a spot on the club and eventually in the starting rotation with Bert Blyleven, Jim Bibby, John Candelaria, and Jim Rooker. Robinson ended a fabulous rookie season with a 14–6 record and an excellent ERA of 3.47. However, the spot he earned was the one I couldn't keep.

I began 1978 in the starting rotation. After my first three starts of the season, I was sporting a bloated ERA of 6.57. I was given a chance to redeem myself with two starts in mid-May, but the struggles continued. By the time the June 15 trade deadline approached, I pitched in eleven games and had a 0–0 record with an ERA of 5.97. The club was sputtering with a 27–31 record in fourth place, six and a half games behind the division-leading Cubs. The front office was getting restless.

I didn't notice the flashing message light on my phone at the Pirates hotel in Atlanta until the morning of June 16. The message was from Pete, who asked me to call him in his office at 9:00 a.m. So I did. "Pete," I said, "this is Jerry. What's up?" Pete, who loved talking on his new speakerphone, put me on speaker and said, "Let me get to the point. I have a deal in place that would send you to the Cubs [I found out later it was for right-handers Ray Burris and Paul Reuschel]. I talked to Bob Kennedy [the Cubs' GM], and he wants to put you in their starting rotation right away. To make it happen, I need you to waive your no-trade clause."

Shocked, I answered him, "Pete, do you remember why I asked for the no-trade clause?" He answered, "You wanted it in lieu of more money." I told him, "That's right. Plus, I didn't want to be forced into making a snap decision about my baseball future. You just put me in that place. I'll need some time to sort this out with my agent, Jack Sands."

Showing very little patience, Pete said, "The commissioner's office has given us three hours to complete the deal because it's after the deadline. Don't drag this out."

Apparently, Pete and I had different ideas about what the no-trade clause was designed to do. Pete thought of it as nothing more than a formality; he would still make whatever deals he wanted and then ask questions later.

For me, in addition to the security and sense of community, the no-trade was also an investment. If and when the Pirates attempted to move the contract, I could and would ask for a cash buyout to waive the clause.

There were other factors to consider. I asked Jack about the Deferred Compensation Trust, the part of the contract that took up the bulk of time during our negotiations. Because the papers were drawn in Pennsylvania, I wanted to know the tax ramifications with a move to Chicago. The same question was asked with regards to my salary. What about renting a place in Chicago? What out-of-pocket costs would result? Three hours just wasn't enough time to get the answers.

Jack and I just wanted to see how interested Pete was in making the trade. So we asked Pete if he would buy me out of the no-trade clause. "No way!" barked Peterson, sounding indignant. Jack, letting

Peterson's attitude roll off his back, told me, "Let's see just how interested the Cubs are." Bob Kennedy gave us a flat no on a buyout. He had payroll troubles of his own and didn't want to complicate them further.

So there was no deal. All that remained were some hard feelings on all sides. I was aware at the time I signed the contract that all general managers try to improve their clubs every waking minute and that trades can materialize in minutes. I was also aware that a no-trade contract didn't mean a club couldn't trade a player; they just needed the player to approve the deal.

Pete's back-door approach had an effect on me. I saw it as a lack of respect. It took a while to develop a new perspective. After all, the game of baseball is just a business, and anyone can be replaced at any time.

I didn't win my first game of the season until August 20, a complete-game effort against the Astros in the second game of a doubleheader. This win was one of ten in a row, as the Pirates were making a move on the division-leading Phillies.

I finished the season with the Pirates with a 3-2 record and a 4.88 ERA. I won two games in September. Both were complete games, as one was a shutout against the Mets. The Pirates finished a game and a half behind the Phillies in second place. But where did I stand with the club after another poor season and, more important, after rejecting a trade?

I considered Chuck Tanner an excellent manager and a straight shooter. In spite of all that had happened, I was comfortable asking him about my future with the club. So after our last game of the season, I asked him where I stood. Would I be given a chance to win a job in spring training of 1979? Would I be considered for a job in the starting rotation?

Chuck, one of the most positive people on the planet, told me, "Absolutely. With the job you did down the stretch run, you're definitely in my plans," he said with a smile. Chuck was always so positive that, if he came home and found a pile of horseshit in his living room, he would smile that smile, thinking somebody had just given him a horse.

I wanted to get my career back on track, so I moved to San Diego that winter and worked out with Padres trainer Dick Dent. I liked his program and believed it would rejuvenate my career.

I came to spring training in 1979 ready to go. I was in outstanding shape. When the games started I was paired with Blyleven. In our first game he was scheduled to pitch three innings, and I had two. Not a problem with Bert, but if I was being considered as a candidate for the rotation, as Chuck told me last September, why not three? So I asked Chuck. "Don't worry about it," he answered. "Next time out, you'll get additional innings." A few days later I was written in for two more. What gives? It was time for another meeting with the manager. Only this time I didn't see that smile. Instinct told me that whatever was said last year meant nothing now. And I was becoming a big pain in everybody's ass.

Change was in the air. It was time to move on . . . again. I had a meeting with Peterson and said if an opportunity came up somewhere else, we should consider it. Only this time we should work together.

CHAPTER EIGHT

California, Here I Come!

Within a week I was called into Tanner's office and told there was a possible deal with the Dodgers. Pete's demeanor was all business. It was not at all like it had been a few years ago when we agreed to the contract. "First of all, the Pirates will pay you nothing for your no-trade clause to accept the deal. Second, the Dodgers want you to sign a new contract. You have three days to make a deal with Los Angeles. Here's Al Campanis's number," Pete said as he dropped the number on Chuck's desk and walked out of the office.

It was hard to believe the relationship I had with the Pirates just two short years earlier had evolved into a "Don't let the door hit you in the ass on your way out" ending. Or maybe this was that baseball karma that Stargell had referred to when I showed Joe Brown disrespect by arriving at spring training late because of school in 1975.

I called Jack and explained the situation, and he gave Al a call. When Jack, who negotiated the long-term deal with the Pirates, called me back, he had a tone in his voice that I had never heard. "The Dodgers want to sign you to a deal for five years guaranteed at a 50 percent raise over your present salary," Jack said slowly. I thought for a second and responded, "Jack, I'm 13–15 over the past two years with an ERA over 4.00 [actually 4.33], and they want to guarantee a raise for five years?" "That's right," Jack said with a smile in his voice. "Jack, that works for me," I said. "I thought you'd like it," he responded. Jack called Al, and within a few hours I was a Dodger.

From the Golden Triangle to the Golden State

April 7, 1979: Traded by Pittsburgh to Los Angeles for Rick Rhoden
MapQuest says that Three Rivers Stadium in Pittsburgh was more than twenty-four hundred miles from Dodger Stadium. But the way the two clubs went about their business, the distance was much greater than miles. Walk into the Pirates' clubhouse in the mid- to late 1970s, and you would've believed you were at a frat party a half hour after the keg was tapped. A stroll into the Dodgers' locker room during those same years was much the same as attending a board meeting at a Fortune 500 company. It was two different ways of being successful.

Tom Lasorda

I can't even estimate the number of people I've met in more than forty years in the game. Many fade in and out, and it takes a while to remember a face, place, or time when someone asks about a certain player or coach. Others leave a lasting impression and become lifelong friends. Some had such a profound impact on me that they deserve their own chapters. Such is the case with Tom Lasorda.

I first saw Tom when he coached third base for the Dodgers in the mid-1970s. Using all that energy and enthusiasm, his personality was totally opposite that of Dodgers manager Walt Alston. But he was the right man for the third base coaching job, as he managed most of the Dodgers' roster while they were in the Minors. He was also the right man for the job when Walt retired in 1976 and Lasorda was named the Dodgers' manager.

Tom had a great relationship with fans. He would sign autographs tirelessly and talk with them one on one. One hot and humid July afternoon in St. Louis after a ballgame, he signed autographs from the time he walked through the glass doors at Busch Stadium 2 until he got on the hotel elevator. My wife and I observed him from our window at the team hotel just across the street from the ballpark. He made sure everyone in the crowd got his signature. He had to be out there in the heat for more than an hour on a day he ran a fever and should have been in bed.

Aside from Steve Garvey, Lasorda got the most fan mail. The intern who handled the mail put it in a box and delivered it directly to his office. To his credit, he opened and read every letter. If it was an autograph request for some enclosed baseball cards, he signed one or two and put it in the return envelope. If the letter was critical of him or the way he managed, he called the person directly and straightened it out. There's no way to count how many times Lasorda did this. But you can bet by the time that call was finished, the Dodgers and Lasorda had a fan forever.

Talking to him during a game could be an entirely different experience. On more than one occasion, Tom went to the mound to bring in a reliever, changed his mind, and left the pitcher in the game as Lasorda and the Dodgers came out on top.

But these decisions by the seat of his pants didn't always have a happy ending. One particular time after leaving the pitcher in the game, the Dodger hurler got hammered. So he had to make the trip a second time. A fan yelled at Lasorda as he made his way back to the dugout, "You should've taken him out the first time ya went out there!" Without missing a beat, Lasorda answered, "Did ya know they were gonna score all those runs? I didn't either. If I did, I would've taken him out earlier! You get the second guess. I get the first one."

Welcome to the Club

I joined the Dodgers on April 9, 1979, in Houston. Once I put my equipment bag in my locker, Lasorda invited me into his office for a brief meeting. "Welcome to the Dodgers!" he said proudly, putting his hand out to shake mine. "You spent ten years in the big leagues, and now you're in the Major Leagues!" I was about to hear excerpts from one of his speeches. "I looooooove the Dodgers!" he bellowed. He continued with a story about working for the Dodgers when he was dead.[1]

I never heard this kind of enthusiasm from anyone in the game. Maybe the Dodgers were the right place for me. Once I could get a word in, I saw another side of Lasorda. "Tom, I'll pitch any way you need me," I said, "but I prefer to start." Suddenly, he was all business. "I already have five starters. Besides, if you were that good, why did Pittsburgh choose five others guys over you and trade you here?" I responded, "Fair enough. Let me put it this way. If one of our starters can't pitch, keep me in mind." Lasorda paused and said, "All right, I'll keep that in mind. How are you for tonight?" I stood up and told him, "I'm ready to go."

I pitched four scoreless innings in relief of Bob Welch, recording my first save for my new club. But the day was more memorable because of what happened after I left the manager's office.

"Fined? For What?"

Joining the Dodgers in 1979 meant an adjustment on my part. It didn't take long for me to accumulate fines at a record pace for my indiscretions. Some were valid (missing the national anthem was legit for $25), while something like leaving the toilet seat up (a major, major no-no at home, but in the clubhouse . . . c'mon!) cost me $10.

The visitors' clubhouse in the Astrodome was huge, as it housed both baseball and football teams. That space included four to six picnic tables for the players to use.

Pete Prieto, the Cuban-born visiting-clubhouse manager, was known around the league for a couple of things. One was a clean clubhouse. It had to be, as the Astrodome was home to rats as large as house cats. Pete, who sipped his Cuban-blend coffee in a china cup, also had a state-of-the-art popcorn maker that rivaled those in theaters.

Players ate his popcorn so fast that he didn't have time to bag it. He just served it on beer trays piled in a mound on each of the picnic tables. Players scooped what they wanted on a paper plate from the trays.

After batting practice the first day as a Dodger, I removed my sweaty clothes, wrapped a towel around me, washed my hands, and then grabbed a handful of popcorn on my way back to my locker.

Davey Lopes took exception to this and yelled, "That's a fine!" I looked at him, knowing the unwritten clubhouse rule of grabbing food without covering yourself and said, "Look, I got a towel around me." Davey said, "That may work in Pittsburgh, but here you gotta be dressed."

Lasorda was passing by, heard Davey's loud voice, and came over to see what was happening. So Davey told him. "That's $10!" Tom said. "I was wearing a towel," I pleaded. "If you wanna fight it and you lose, the fine doubles. Now, if wearing a towel is all you got, the fine is now $20," Lasorda sputtered, sounding like a Philly lawyer.

I looked at both of them and quietly said, "Okay." I dropped the towel, stood on the seating area of the table, and lowered my bare ass in the center of the beer tray stacked with popcorn. "How much is this?" I asked.

Davey's eyes got big, and his jaw dropped. He grabbed his hat, shook his head, and as he walked away he muttered something like, "Where do they find these guys?" Lasorda stood there wide-eyed and started laughing while telling me, "You're crazy!" I guess I showed them. No more $10 or $20 fines for me. No, sir! From that point on, I graduated to the $25–$250 range!

There's a Pig in the Manager's Office

Tom Lasorda has a unique ability to reach people, which is part of what made him a Hall of Fame manager. Whether it's a speech before heads of state or a conversation with members of a player's family, I've watched all of them captivated by every word.

Once, while on a road trip to Atlanta, Joe Beckwith, a pitcher for the Dodgers in the 1980s who lived in nearby Auburn, Alabama, stopped Tom in the hotel lobby and introduced him to members of his extended family. Two hours later Lasorda was still telling stories. And they were laughing just as hard as when he started.

One of Beckwith's relatives was a pig farmer and was so impressed with Lasorda that he sent him a live pig when we returned from our trip as a way of saying thanks. Of course, there were some reporters, TV personalities, broadcasters, players, and so on who stopped by his office on a daily basis and seemed surprised that there was a real pig there! There were others who wondered what was going to happen next. They didn't have to wait long to find out.

The pig got the royal treatment, which included a solo ride on the elevator to the top of Dodger Stadium during the sixth inning. The look on Lasorda's face was priceless when stadium security called him while on the bench during the game and informed him of what had happened. He hung up the phone, beelined to me in a fit of rage, and suddenly stopped, shook his head, and said, "No. No. I'm not gonna ask you because I already know the answer. Just put it back in its cage."

Everybody on the bench wondered what that was about. When Lasorda told them about the call from security, the bench broke into howls of laughter. Truth be told, I had nothing to do with the pig being put on the elevator. Now, I may have mentioned the idea in passing to a couple of teammates . . .

Dodger Swag

There was always one element of the Dodger uniform that impressed me as a visiting player. Under the lights of a night game at Dodger Stadium, they seemed whiter than white—almost like a glow. Plus, the players didn't have just one team jacket, but had three different styles: a windbreaker, a medium-weight zipper jacket, and a heavy button jacket for the colder temperatures. I mentioned to the clubhouse manager, Nobe Kowano, that I'd like to purchase each of the jackets the club didn't supply. On the other three clubs I played for, the club issued one jacket, and I paid for anything beyond that. It was the same procedure for long-sleeve sweatshirts. Nobe looked at me with a puzzled look on his face and asked, "You mean you want to buy three more?" I corrected him, "No, I want to buy the jackets the Dodgers don't normally supply." Now, he corrected me. "We give you all three jackets. Have you looked in your locker? I gave you all three jackets with your name on the back and three sweatshirts. The club supplies you with anything you need. Let me know if you need more." Well, well, well! Maybe there was something behind Lasorda's welcoming speech.

You Wanna Do What?

I was traded to the club on April 7. Ken Brett joined the Dodgers on June 11. When we were teammates in Pittsburgh in 1974–75, we had adjoining lockers, so I knew what a free spirit he was. One day he asked me, "Is there anything you'd like to do in your career that you haven't done?" The question surprised me, as we never discussed a subject this serious. I thought about it and said, "Well, yeah, I'd like to win twenty games one year, play in another All-Star Game, and pitch in a World Series." I paused and asked him, "How about you?" He floored me with his response. "I wanna dress with the grounds crew and drag the infield in the fifth inning!" Of all the things he could have said, he hit me with this. Now I started laughing as he continued, "I'd like to do it tonight. You wanna do it with me?"

My mind flashed on all the reasons we shouldn't do it—like getting fined. Ken and I got fined twenty dollars for laying by the pool in San Diego. I was nicked for twenty bucks for the Houston popcorn incident. What the hell! At least this way I knew I was gonna get hit. The only question was the amount.

"I'm in!" I told him. "Great. Let's meet in the grounds-crew locker room around the third inning so we can get dressed," he answered. Of course, when we told the groundskeepers what we wanted to do, they looked at us like we were crazy. "You wanna do what?" they asked. "Dress in your clothes, drag the infield, and get back to the bench like nothing happened," we told them. Their minds flashed on all the reasons they shouldn't do this—like getting fired. Finally, one of them said, "See if these pants and shirts fit."

The hardest part of the plan was getting on the field undetected. After all, we had to walk down the runway between the clubhouse and field, hide in the storage room, and follow the two real grounds-keepers on the field as soon as the final out was recorded in the top of the fifth inning without being spotted by Lasorda.

Fortunately, Rick Monday (Mo) and Steve Yeager (Boomer), who were stationed at their spot in the far end of the dugout, saw us as we made our way down the runway. Holding their laughter, our partners in crime stood in front of the storage room and then walked in front of us as a screen from Lasorda as we made our way onto the field.

We grabbed our drag from the compartment just below the aux-iliary scoreboard a few feet from the dugout and made our way to the third base line as the players were laughing their asses off. Tom was in full four-letter voice as the last thing I heard him say was "Tell those sonsabitches, I'll get their ass for this."

The infielders and umpires loved it, as did the fans along the first base line who followed our tour from the start and gave us a standing ovation as we exited through the stands above the first base dugout.

Tom was still fuming as he met us at the top of the runway between the dugout and the locker room after we changed back into our uniforms. "Dammit, I can't have players pulling off stunts like this. If Peter [O'Malley] saw this, it could cost me my job. That'll cost you both a hundred dollars!" Ken and I thought it would be more than that. Maybe he gave us a break because of the great job we did.

Big Changes Help Revive My Career

Coming off the World Series years of 1977 and 1978, 1979 proved to be a real disappointment for the Dodgers, as the team finished under .500 for the first time since 1968. Yet for me the year was a confidence booster. I know a record of 7–14 with an ERA of 3.54 isn't impressive, but I proved to myself I could still start and win. Over a three-year span I was 20–30, not a record that secures one a place in the starting rotation, much less a spot on the roster. There were some adjustments that I still had to make. That winter I stumbled on some changes that turned around my career.

Dodger pitchers were a breed all their own. As far back as the days of Koufax and Drysdale, they were given free rein to train on their own, bypassing the traditional running programs used by other clubs. For starting pitchers the day after a start was an aerobic day, which meant a minimum thirty-minute jog. The second day was an anaerobic day with sprints after a ten- to fifteen-minute bullpen session. The third and fourth days between starts were a repeat of the first two days, with a reduced amount of running and no bullpen session.

When I joined the club Don Sutton pulled me aside and explained to me, "The Dodgers found that the pitchers work harder and have more success when they work on an individual program. As long as we do our work, we keep the program. If one pitcher doesn't do his work, all of us have run the traditional way the other teams do. I wanted to explain all of this to you to make sure you're not the guy who will screw up this privilege for the rest of us." I didn't embrace the idea of substituting jogging for sprints every other day, but I wanted to try it. From the center field fence inside Dodger Stadium, I jogged through the parking lot and past the Union 76 station and proceeded to a horseshoe-shaped path that returned me to the field. It was about a fifteen- or twenty-minute run. By the time the season was over, I was running the complete perimeter of the stadium parking lot, a forty-minute run, with ease.

After the 1979 season I visited Dr. Frank Jobe's clinic at Centinela Hospital for a complete physical. Dr. Jobe was the Dodgers' team doctor but also was the forerunner in sports medicine, as he was the first doctor to develop and perform the now famous "Tommy John" surgery. While testing for stability of my left shoulder, he noticed an area in the back of my shoulder where the muscles had atrophied. We discovered after some tests that my left shoulder, my pitching shoulder, had about one-third the strength of my right shoulder. I was prescribed a series of exercises to perform with light free weights to strengthen the area.

About this same time I was introduced to the Nautilus weight-training program. Dr. Jobe and the Dodger training staff endorsed the program because it increased muscle strength without adding bulk. After a few sessions on the newly purchased machines housed at the ballpark, I continued my winter workouts using Nautilus three days a week at a local gym with an aerobic run and alternated the free-weight program with racquetball for another three days a week. When the winter workouts began at Dodger Stadium in January 1980, I was ready to go. Throwing batting practice a few times a week at the ballpark allowed me to integrate the workout program with a baseball schedule before the start of spring training. This was my second year of a year-round workout program, and all was going well until the Dodgers dipped into the free-agent market.

The Odd Man Out . . . Again

On November 15, 1979, the Dodgers signed Minnesota's Dave Goltz to a six-year deal as a starting pitcher. That meant the Dodgers' starting rotation heading into the 1980 season was Burt Hooton, Rick Sutcliffe, Don Sutton, Goltz, and Bob Welch. Each of these five starters had a better year in 1979 than I did, earning their spots in the starting rotation.

Having faced this very situation the previous few years, I knew that no club had the same five starters from the start of the season to the end. It was a matter of time before I'd get the chance to prove myself as a starter. Rather than fight pitching in relief, I went with the flow.

Not needing four pitches in a relief role, I used just a fastball and a curve. I noticed that when I released my four-seam fastball on the inside of my middle finger, the pitch would run into the hands of a right-handed batter. In baseball language I developed a cutter, or cut fastball. Because I could throw this pitch consistently for strikes, I used it.

When the pitch was knee-high, it had late running action that made an adjustment difficult for opposing hitters. Much like Rooker did with the Pirates, I pitched ahead in the count and recorded early-count outs. When hitters looked for the pitch, I used my sinker on the opposite side of the plate and forced a routine fly ball or groundout.

If there were ever doubts as to the cutter's effectiveness, those were erased one day when Larry Bowa of the Phillies pulled me aside and accused me of cheating. "I know you're doing it. I just haven't figured out how. But I will." I told him, "I knew someone would catch me. I just didn't think it would be you." The only thing better than a successful new pitch was someone believing I was cheating and being hell-bent on discovering how!

I was like a kid with a new toy. My command of the cutter allowed me to throw my sinker and curve for strikes with complete confidence. For the first time in my ten-year baseball career, I was pitching to contact and enjoying positive results. In eight relief appearances my record was 3–0 with three saves. Then came the chance I anticipated.

Opportunity Knocked

Rick Sutcliffe, the National League's Rookie of the Year with the Dodgers in 1979, struggled in the early part of 1980 and was sent to the bullpen in early May after six starts, posting a 0–2 record with an 8.33 ERA. Lasorda wouldn't commit to Sutcliffe's spot in the rotation, as Dave Goltz came down with the flu and couldn't make his scheduled start on May 16. I started the game that night against the Pirates and won 8–6, pitching seven innings and allowing four runs on eight hits. Not a stellar performance but good enough to merit another start. I stayed in Goltz's spot, and Dave pitched a few days later, taking Sutcliffe's turn in the rotation.

Four days later I beat St. Louis, and five days after that I shut out Cincinnati. I was in the midst of the most consistent run of my career. Still, the best was yet to come.[2]

All I Can Remember about the No-Hitter

People have asked for more than thirty years about the no-hitter I pitched against the Giants on June 27, 1980. How did you feel before the game? At what point during the game did you know you had a no-hitter? Were you disappointed that you didn't have a perfect game? (That was the first question asked by a reporter after the game in the clubhouse!) Did anybody on the bench talk about it? Was this game your biggest thrill in baseball?

Here's everything I remember about the day, the game, the aftermath, and my thoughts about it today.

The Dodgers flew to San Francisco on Friday morning, the day of the game, so we could enjoy the off day, Thursday, at home. Traveling on the day of the game was normal for the Dodgers when flying to San Francisco or riding a bus to San Diego.

One could almost sense it was going to be a special night at Candlestick Park when the game started, if for no other reason than the weather. Vin Scully told the story best on the television pregame show. "First of all, let it be known and truly declared it is hot in San Francisco. I mean hot. It's been eighty degrees and higher all day, and it's still that warm in the ballpark tonight. It borders on the unbelievable." Only Vin Scully can turn a weather report into his own brand of baseball poetry. Still, with no wind and a higher than normal temperature, it made a Friday evening at Candlestick actually feel balmy. It was the only time in all the years of playing at the 'Stick that I remember weather like that.

I don't remember anything special about warming up. It probably was routine, as I worked both sides of the plate with the fastball, spun some curves, and maybe even threw a change-up or two.

We scored a run in the top of the first against Vida Blue, whom I had pitched against as far back as Triple A when he was with Des Moines and I was with Tulsa. The bottom of the first began with two quick outs and brought Jack Clark, who ultimately had a lifetime average of .371 and five home runs against me, to the plate. He hit an easy two-hopper to Russell at short, who fielded it cleanly and then threw it on a hop to Garvey at first. I can't count the number of times I saw Steve pull a ball out of the dirt for an out. This time he didn't. So Clark was on first as Rich Murray ended the inning, grounding into a force play.

We scored another run off Blue in the third and knocked him out of the game with five runs in the fifth. After working through the Giants' batting order the first three innings, I was aware that they were hitless. Still, the Giants' fans were their rowdy selves until we posted that five-spot in the fifth.

For my teammates and the rest of the people on the bench, it was a different story. Around the fifth or sixth inning, the bench got quiet, especially when we were batting. I kept the same seat on the bench, as I marked it with the jacket I wore between innings. It wasn't because of superstition; I just wanted to know where it was when I came from the field. No one touched it. In fact, the players kept the same seats, a baseball tradition celebrated daily to maintain a run of good tidings. In my hyperaware state, I knew they knew what the scoreboard told the world.

After the sixth inning many of the 20,285 fans in attendance acknowledged each out. Remember, this was San Francisco, where the Dodgers were the enemy from the South. The rivalry over the history of these two teams had always been intense. Both had roots in New York, where they had hated one another. I had no idea of the depth of feeling until years later when, at a Dodgers Fantasy Camp, Duke Snider revealed that he always hated Halloween because the colors were orange and black, the same colors worn by the Giants!

A smattering of fans cheered for me as I headed to the mound in the bottom of the seventh. When I went to the mound in the ninth, they stood and applauded. In between they cheered each out. I would have expected that at Dodger Stadium but not in San Francisco.

The Giants players, however, had other ideas. Nobody wants to be no-hit, especially at home. So when they came to the plate, each of them wanted to be the guy who broke up the no-hitter. Their breathing was different, their setup before each pitch was more intense, and they took just a bit more time between pitches. There was no guessing what pitch I was going to throw. I threw ninety-nine pitches in the game, with sixty-six of them being strikes. All but a few were fastballs, which I threw exclusively from the seventh inning to the end of the game.

As we had an 8-0 lead heading into the bottom of the seventh, I began "the finish," a quick review of what the hitter did against me earlier in the game and how I would pitch to him this at bat. This was where the possibility of the no-hitter factored into pitch selection. Each pitch and each out became a countdown. Just nine more outs . . . eight more . . . seven . . . were the words I heard. When I started the eighth, a voice in my mind reminded me, "Keep the

ball down, pitch for a groundout, and remember, six more outs . . .
five more . . . four!"

As I walked to the mound, oblivious to the cheering for the bottom of the ninth, the voice reminded me of the Houston game.
"You have another chance. Focus on location. Stay knee-high on
the corners." That's all that concerned me.

Catcher Mike Sadek led off for the Giants in the ninth. He fouled
back the first pitch for strike one. I missed inside for a ball. With the
count 1–1, I wanted another strike. So Yeager set up for a fastball
inside. Fouled back again. With two strikes, I had options: go for
the strikeout (Sadek struck out twice earlier) or just get the out.
I jammed him with a fastball, and he rolled an easy grounder to
Cey. One out.

Rennie Stennett, a former teammate in Pittsburgh, was the pinch-
hitter for the pitcher. The first pitch was way high and outside. "It's
not velocity, but location," the voice reminded me. Stennett swung
late and fouled the next pitch, a fastball belt-high and inside, down
the first base line. "Let's get in there again," I thought. Rennie
fouled off another pitch down the right side. The count went to 1–2
as Stennett stepped out of the box. "He doesn't strike out much.
But he can't catch up with your fastball inside. Stay in there and jam
him," I thought. Stennett jammed himself, rolling a two-hopper to
Russell, whose throw to Garvey was perfect.

Two outs and the voice said, "Take a short walk and reset. This is
the guy you waited for all night long." The batter was Bill North. He
had grounded out twice and flied out in his last at bat. While North
took his time getting in the box, I thought, "Let's go!" My first pitch
was a fastball that was high for ball one. "Make the adjustment," I
thought. I looked for the sign. Yeager called for a fastball inside, as
North tapped a routine two-hop roller to me in front of the mound.
"You have all the time in the world. Pick it up, turn, and throw to
Garvey's belt," I thought. Once I saw Steve catch it, I was airborne.

I don't remember the next thirty seconds or so as the emotions flowed. Gone was the struggle of the last two years in Pittsburgh. Being 7–14 in 1979 didn't matter anymore. I erased the memory of missing a no-hitter eight years prior and replaced it with a new reality.

Ron Cey was the first to the mound, followed by Yeager and then Garvey. In watching the replay of the game for the first time in years, I saw that Sandy Koufax, who joined us for the series, was there. I forgot about that until I saw him on the DVD I reviewed to write this book.

As the Dodgers exited the field down the right-field line, I was still accepting congratulations from teammates, coaches, and Tom Lasorda. Ross Porter, who worked the middle three innings on TV, asked me for a postgame interview.

If I could change just one thing that day, it would be the interview with Ross. Because of the adrenaline rush of the game, I was still in combat mode, and it showed in my answers to Ross during the postgame show. In what was one of the happiest days of my life, I appeared rude and a complete bore. Later, I apologized to Ross and he understood it wasn't personal, but it still pains me to watch it thirty years later.[3]

When I got to the locker room, it was time to answer questions from reporters. My reputation as an interview wasn't a good one. I was testy and impatient with reporters who didn't do their homework and challenged them to be better prepared. I also remembered how opening up too much had burned me. By this time the reality of the evening had sunk in as the adrenaline rush eased, and I was ready to talk about it.

"Are you disappointed that you didn't get the perfect game?" came the first question. I answered, "First of all, errors happen. Second, it was the same Russell who made an excellent play later in the game to keep the no-hitter alive." That night Billy fielded nine grounders and went three for five with an RBI. Knowing that some guys were on deadline, I answered all of the obvious questions before they asked them. "Besides, it was Russell, along with Cey and Dusty, who made some good plays later in the game that kept the Giants hitless. By the way, we scored eight runs on seventeen hits, which allowed for some breathing room."

For his part, Russell handled the questions about the error with his typical class. "At the time," Russell said of his error, "it was no big deal. I just took too much time, I guess, and threw it away."[4] Actually, Russell's error may have helped preserve the no-hitter. Jack Clark, who reached base on the play, strained his knee when running to second base on Murray's grounder to end the first inning. He eventually was replaced in the sixth inning. With Clark, who hit well against me, injured and then out of the game, the Giants had a weaker lineup.

"When did you know you had a no-hitter going?" I was asked. I told the reporter, "Right after the first out of the game." When I pitched I was hyperaware of everything that happened. I could spot a change in the batter's stance. I remembered a hitter's history against me. I knew how I wanted to pitch to him in this situation, and it could determine how I would pitch to him later in the game or even in the next game we faced each other. I knew each hitter's strike zone and, just as important, the home-plate umpire's strike zone. (Jim Quick, the home-plate umpire, had the same zone the entire game.) Because of this acute awareness, I have a hard time believing any pitcher doesn't know he has a no-hitter in progress.

"Okay. Let's try it this way," the same reporter asked. "When did you believe a no-hitter was a real possibility?" It was a fair question, so I elaborated. "It became more of a possibility after each out. Early in the game I wasn't thinking about a no-hitter. I was thinking about pitching to the Giants' lineup, one pitch, one batter, and one inning at a time. I had to maintain that focus," I responded.

What I didn't tell him was this: I stepped out of that mind-set, looked at the scoreboard, and realized that something special was happening. The score was just 2–0 until we scored five runs in the top of the fifth. Normally, I pitched with a margin of error with a seven-run lead. Being in the midst of a no-hitter, there was no such luxury. Each pitch meant something. One mistake could end it. Even a perfect pitch could be blooped for a hit. Making the pitches was my responsibility. I couldn't control luck.

"Were you aware of the fans applauding you when you left the dugout for the seventh inning and after every out you recorded?" was another question. "Absolutely," I answered. "I was aware of everything! My teammates were with me on every pitch. They treated each pitch like we were in the World Series. From the seventh inning until the last out in the ninth, I had three extraordinary plays behind me. Ron Cey made a diving stop on a hard-hit grounder in the eighth, Russell made an outstanding play on a grounder deep in the hole, and Dusty Baker made a nice play on a liner to left that he caught ankle high."

"Have you ever gotten this close to a no-hitter?" was the question from the back of the pack. I told them, "I pitched one in Little League and one in high school. Professionally, I was this close just once. It was on June 18, 1972, when I pitched for Houston. It took more than eight years to get this close again."

When Leonard Koppett, a highly respected journalist from the Bay Area, wrote about the game, he stated, "It was better than a perfect game in this respect. Reuss had to get 28 outs for the no-hitter instead of the 27 outs needed for a perfect game."[5]

Lasorda, when asked about the game, told reporters, "It couldn't have happened to a greater guy." He paused and added, "Well, yes, it could. I could have pitched it."[6]

The Next Day

On Saturday the game was scheduled for 1:05. Usually, the day after a start meant a forty-minute run before we took the field for batting practice. I'm not sure if I did the run that Saturday, as there were reporters who still needed some time for their Sunday column. There were also an extra couple of dozen balls to sign as well as appearing on the Giants' pregame radio show. I did my best to accommodate everybody and still get on the field on time. It's the job of the previous day's starting pitcher to collect the baseballs hit during batting practice in a bucket and fill the basket used by the batting-practice pitcher. There was a local TV crew that needed a few minutes after BP. I finished my work, handled the interviews, and signed the balls. I didn't know if I could make it to the dugout in time for the national anthem, which, if missed, was an automatic twenty-five-dollar fine.

In San Francisco the path to the dugout from the locker room meant walking through the Giants' bullpen in right field, which complicated things. I rushed like hell changing into dry clothes, putting on my jacket, and running through the hallway to the bull-pen door. I held my breath as I looked out the window to see if the players were lined up in front of the dugout.

I caught a break. Somehow, it just didn't seem right to throw a no-hitter one night and then get fined the next day for missing the anthem! So I took a deep breath, relaxed, and opened the door to make my way to the bench.

As I started my stroll to the dugout, I noticed applause. By the time I approached first base, the entire crowd of twenty-five thousand was applauding. I thought one of the "Willies," Mays or McCovey, was on the field. I looked around and saw just the starting pitchers, and then it hit me . . . this is for me! Imagine! A Dodger player getting an ovation in San Francisco . . . two straight days!

So I took off my cap and acknowledged them, and, to my surprise, they stood up. This lasted until I got to the dugout. It was the first time in my career that something like this happened, so naturally I milked it for all it was worth.

Lasorda came up to me and said, "That's fifty dollars!" "What for? I didn't miss the anthem," I protested. "That's fifty dollars for acknowledging San Francisco fans," he answered. I told him, "Do you see those fans wearing Dodger blue in the stands?" "Yeah, so what?" he asked. "I was tipping my cap to them and no one else," I said with total conviction. He looked at me, then at the fans in Dodger jackets, looked at me again, shook his head, and walked away muttering, "I'm the dummy for arguing with you."

The Aftermath

On Sunday afternoon there were no more interviews, no more balls to sign, and I was able to get my work done. So I was planning a leisurely grand entrance on the field. After all, it was a doubleheader with more than fifty thousand faithful attending the game. This should be some kind of entrance. It was show time.

I made my way on to the field, and there was . . . nothing. I paused, hoping by turning around that the fans would see my name on my jacket and the applause would start. Again, there was nothing . . . except for a guy in his forties with long hair, green teeth, and a scraggly beard wearing a Giants cap, standing over the Giants' bullpen roof. He looked at me and said, "What the hell you waitin' for? Get your ass in the dugout where you belong, you asshole!" Well, things were back to normal.

It was baseball tradition for a club to award a pitcher who threw a no-hitter with a new contract calling for a raise. The Dodgers signed me to a five-year deal in 1979 that took agents and lawyers a few months to settle. No way (and no need) for a new contract in those early days of free agency. But that didn't stop Dodger owner Peter O'Malley from showing his appreciation.

During the next home stand, the club gave me a beautiful giant-screen TV during a pregame ceremony. I thanked Peter, the Dodgers, and my teammates for making a dream come true. But now I had a problem. There was no room in the home I just bought for a TV this size. So when I stopped by Peter's office a few days later to thank him, he asked me how I was enjoying the new television. I told him that I couldn't thank him enough for his generosity, but there was no place to put it. He seemed a bit puzzled and then asked me, "What would fit?" "A table model would be perfect," I answered. A few days later a delivery truck arrived at the front door with a large table-model TV set along with the latest VCR. Peter found a place for the big screen. It was put in the manager's office for the entire club to enjoy.

Later that home stand Tom asked me to come into his office and sign a dozen balls. He instructed me to sign on the "sweet spot," usually reserved for the manager or Hall of Famer, as these balls were to be used in an auction where he would be appearing that evening. They were designated as baseballs used in the no-hitter. I looked at him as I was signing and said, "Tom, these balls are new. No one will believe they were used in any game." His response was classic Lasorda. "You know that and I know that. But the people who head the charity won't. Nor will the winning bidders. You'll look good and I'll look good. The charity gets the money, and they'll be happy. The fans in attendance will be thrilled, as will the people who buy the baseballs because they believe they're buying a piece of history. So, with one little white lie, we make all these people happy! How can you have a problem with that?"

With that, I signed the rest of the balls, closed the box, and said, "Have a safe trip!" I really doubt that he told everyone at the banquet that the signed balls were game-used from the no-hitter, but if there was anyone who could sell it . . .

Because videotape degrades after time, I wanted to transfer the game to DVD. So, I searched for the one-inch masters, only to hear that Channel 11 in Los Angeles threw them out some years ago. MLB Productions had a copy, but the audio was of the Giants' radio announcers. Fortunately, my good friend Mark Wolfson, who produced and directed the game for Channel 11, had the original masters for the first six innings in his garage. He found them in a box that was unpacked after his move to the Bay Area. The elements of a DVD were there. Mark sent his tapes to MLB. I sent my

VHS copies and my one-inch master from the final three innings to MLB for the audio featuring Vin Scully and Ross Porter. From these three sources and some excellent engineering, DVD copies were made. I now refer to the finished DVD made from bits, pieces, cuts, splices, and edits from the three sources as Frankenstein.

The Dodgers celebrated the twenty-fifth anniversary of the game on June 27, 2005, and invited me to throw out the first pitch at Dodger Stadium. It was also a special day for another reason. This was the first pitch I threw after my knee replacement. Both my new knee and old elbow survived and now live together in harmony to throw another first pitch when asked.

Introducing . . . Diamond Vision!

By the All-Star break of 1980, my record was 9–2 with an ERA of 1.96. I was one of six Dodger players selected for the All-Star Game to be played at Dodger Stadium. Ironically, the manager of the National League All-Stars was Chuck Tanner. I was curious as to how Chuck would greet me, as the last time we spoke was the day I was traded to Los Angeles. To Chuck's credit, he was his old bubbly self. "Congratulations," he told me. "It looks like you turned things around. I'm happy for you." In turn I congratulated him for winning the 1979 World Series.

Before the game I was asked by ABC, who televised the game, that if I started an inning to pause ten to fifteen seconds before throwing my first pitch so they could run some of the no-hitter footage. No problem, I told them. When I finished my warmup pitches and the ball was thrown by Mets catcher John Stearns to second base, I remembered the network's request. So I looked around the infield and saw Ray Knight at third and Dave Concepcion at short, both of whom played for the Reds; Phil Garner, my former teammate from the Pirates, at second; and Keith Hernandez of the Cardinals at first.

I called Garner in from second because he was the only one of the infielders I knew. "Gar, see that giant TV screen [making its debut in a Major League Baseball park that evening] above the left-field bleachers?" I asked. "Yeah, isn't that something!" he responded, having no idea where I was going. I told him, "There are over fifty-six thousand people in the ballpark tonight watching us on it right now." Gar glanced at the screen. "Yeah, I can see that." I continued, "There's probably another twelve to fifteen million listeners on radio and maybe more than fifty million watching on ABC!" Now he's laughing and asked, "What's your point?" I told him, "That's about seventy-five million wondering what the hell we're talking about!" He looked at me and shook his head. "They probably think we're talking about baseball, but we're talking TVs!" he said, laughing as he made his way back to his position.

It turned out to be a good meeting. I struck out the only three batters I faced, and when the National League took the lead in the bottom of the sixth, we held it, making me the winning pitcher.

"That Shit Can Cause Cancer!"

Most of the time when I wasn't pitching, I'd find a comfortable spot on the bench and watch the game. My favorite spot was a few seats from the water fountain toward the third base side of the bench. Like many players during my era, I'd pop open a fresh bag of chewing tobacco, grab a wad, pop it in, and enjoy a cheap buzz.

One night Reggie Smith, who could be as cantankerous as hell, sat down a few cushions from me. As we fell behind early in this ballgame, Reggie was observing the ritual of spitting on the dugout floor. Finally, he had enough. "That's disgusting. Don't you realize that people have to walk through that?" With the seed shells, paper cups, dirt, and everything else, the floor looked like a toxic waste dump! I spit again, looked at Reggie, and said, "Something on your mind?" "Goddamn right!" he replied.

Meanwhile, we got a runner on with Joe Ferguson coming to bat. "Don't you know that shit can cause cancer?" Well, now he had my attention. "It's worse than smoking. That wad sits right next to salivary glands, your throat, and everything else in your mouth." Well, Reggie succeeded in harshing my buzz. "I never thought about that," I answered. So I reached in my mouth and grabbed the chew, and, at that very moment, Fergie hit a two-run homer that put us in the lead.

Following baseball custom, everyone went to the home-plate side of the dugout to share high-fives with Joe . . . only I got the chew in my hand with no place to lose it . . . except for a coffee cup with maybe a half inch of coffee still in it. So I dropped it in the cup, wiped my hand, and gave Fergie his due. There's another baseball custom during a rally, and that is you return to the same seats. Which means, once again, I was sitting two seats away from Mr. Warmth.

No sooner did I sit than I heard, "Well, did you get rid of it?" What the hell, Reggie! He didn't let up. I was about to say, "Yeah, and thanks for letting me know," when I heard the noise of someone retching and throwing up at the other end of the dugout. It was Lasorda, with the trainer slapping him on the back, while Tom is spitting and yelling in the same breath, "Who the hell put chewing tobacco in my coffee? I'll kill the son of a bitch who did it."

That was a new baseball custom I hadn't heard about. If there's a half inch of coffee left in your cup, don't throw it out. There might be more runs in it. Tommy chugged the remainder of his cup and got more than he bargained for.

Once I realized what had happened, I lowered my head and tried to hide my laughter. Still, there was Reggie. I turned my head, looked at him, he looked at me, looked at Tom, who was still screaming, and said, "You didn't . . . You did!" Now, he had the giggles.

What a sight it was. A manager who just Heimliched my chew like a cat would a hairball, and two veterans, who never shared much more than a hello, laughing like ten-year-olds while fifty thousand Dodger faithful cheered their boys in blue.

Just How Many Games Did Sinatra and Rickles Win for Us?

The players who came through the Dodger farm system stayed much to themselves. They played great together, but off the field they went their own way. During 1979 my closest teammate was Ken Brett. When Brett was released late in spring training of 1980, I gravitated to Jay Johnstone and Don Stanhouse, who were signed as free agents over the winter of 1979–80. The reason was simple. We made each other laugh.

During batting practice at Dodger Stadium one day in 1980, Stanhouse and I took our normal position in right field while Jay took batting practice with his group. As Stanley (my nickname for him) and I stood there, he mentioned to me, "Things are just a little too slow for me today. We need to do something to liven things up." I asked him what he had in mind. "I don't know. Can you think of something?" he responded. "Okay," I said. "When Jay comes out here, just follow my lead."

Like clockwork, when Jay finished batting practice, he joined us in right field, throwing his glove aside while he hit the ground in front of us to do his daily sit-ups. I started my conversation with Stanley. "Personally, I think it's horseshit! He has their pictures all over his office while the guys that got him where he is are nonexistent." Stanhouse, not knowing where I was going with this conversation, came in on cue, "You're right. I agree. But what can you do about it?" By now Jay wanted to know what we were talking about. So I told him, "We're talking about the pictures of all the celebrities that hang on the walls of Lasorda's office. There are two walls of Sinatra, four or five pictures of Rickles up there, and who knows how many of everybody else!"

Jay got to his feet as Stanley was nodding his head. I looked at Jay and said, "But do you know whose pictures aren't on his wall?" Jay, of course, said, "Who?" I answered, "His players! The guys that helped him become Manager of the Year, the guys that took him to the World Series in 1977-78, and the same guys that are on this field with us today. Where the hell are their pictures?" Jay looked at me, as Stanley shook his head in mock disgust and muttered, "That just ain't right!" "I know it's not right!" I answered. "But what can we do about it?" Jay spoke up and said, "I can handle that." He grabbed his glove and jogged into the dugout and disappeared up the runway. "What do you think he's going to do?" Stanley asked. "No idea," I answered.

Jay never returned to the field, and about ten minutes before BP was finished one of the batboys came up to the two of us in right field. "Mr. Lasorda wants to see the two of you," he told us rather sheepishly. "Thanks, but can't it wait until batting practice is finished?" I asked the young man. "I think he means right now," the kid answered. "He told me if you don't come immediately, I'll be fired."

Stanley and I looked at each other and said, "I guess that means now." We jogged off the field, into the dugout, and up the runway and headed to the managers' office. I knocked on the door and said, "You want to see us?" A pissed-off voice growled, "Is Johnstone with you?" Jay suddenly appeared from behind us. "We're all here," I said. "Then get your asses in here and shut the door," Lasorda growled. I was shocked when we walked into his office and all of the pictures of the celebrities were gone! Even the signed picture of the pope!

Lasorda was standing at his desk, shuffling through some fan mail as he spoke. "I don't know how you guys pulled this shit off. I keep this office locked whenever I'm not here and give the clubhouse guys strict orders not to let anyone in." When he sat in his chair, I saw three eight-by-ten glossy publicity pictures, one of me on one wall, a picture of Stanhouse on another wall, and one of Jay on a third wall.

"How the hell did Jay do this?" I thought. I gathered my wits and went into denial mode. "You're not gonna fall for this setup, are you?" I started. "Would I be stupid enough to hang up one of my pictures . . . especially that one? That looks like hell! This is so obvious . . ."

He stopped me right there. "I don't give a shit!" he shouted. "Ever since you joined this club, shit like this has happened!" he sputtered, his arms waving. Then he pointed his crooked left forefinger at us and shouted, "I don't care who did it! I want those pictures back on the wall before you go home tonight!" With that he grabbed each of the three glossies on his naked walls, ripped them up, and threw them in his wastebasket. "Tonight, before you go home. Now get the hell outta here!"

As we closed the door to Lasorda's office, I had a whole new respect for Jay. All I could say was "Wow!" Stanhouse asked the logical question, "Where did you put them?" Jay just walked away from us chuckling. "Stanley," I said, "some things in this universe can never be explained. This may be one of them."

Stanhouse was in the bullpen during the game, and I was on the bench. I never gave a thought to returning the pictures to their place of honor. When the game was over I walked into Lasorda's office, where the postgame spread was set up, and all of the pictures were back in place. To this day, I don't know how Jay removed them, where he hid them, or how he remembered where each of them belonged. I guess it still remains one of the mysteries of our time.

Hangin' with the Garv

Unlike the previous clubs I played for, the Dodger players never went out for dinner together as a large group. There were groups of two or three players who ate at the same restaurant at the same time, but they would always occupy separate tables.

After Stanhouse was released prior to the 1981 season, Jay and I, for some unknown reason, partnered with Steve Garvey. It was an odd couple grouping, but it worked. Steve was and still is one of the nicest guys in baseball. Once, during spring training, Steve,

Jay, and I had dinner and met other teammates at a bar on the beach named Bobby's. A fan who was visiting Vero during the final days of the spring approached Steve in total awe. "My family back home won't ever believe that I met Steve Garvey," he gushed. Steve replied, "Let's get them on the phone right now." So the two of them went to a pay phone, and Steve spent a few minutes talking to this guy's family. When Garv returned and took his seat next to me, I asked him why he did that. "It took just a few minutes of my time to make some people happy," he answered in his matter-of-fact way.

It didn't take Jay and I long to know that Steve was recognized wherever we went. Not that it bothered us, because, more times than not, the manager or owner of restaurant would comp the meal. It was agreed by the three of us that this kindness meant a large tip for the server. On one trip the first meal was comped because of Steve. Jay worked his magic in Philadelphia. It was my turn when we arrived in Pittsburgh.

After dinner at a seafood restaurant, the check was brought to the table. I grabbed it, whipped out my credit card, and charged it. They had strange looks on their faces when I explained, "What? I don't have the same juice you have. Besides, you're still eating for free, aren't you?"

Eating for Free . . . the Lasorda Way

We thought we were good when it came to free meals. We were mere amateurs when compared to Lasorda. When Lasorda managed in the Minors and was on a long bus ride, he would stop the bus at a restaurant and instruct a player, trainer, or someone traveling with the club to tell the manager of the restaurant that Lasorda would bring his team of twenty-five to thirty paying customers if he and the person negotiating could eat for free. More than once this scheme worked. If the restaurant manager wouldn't do it, Tom said, "We'll keep driving until we find somebody who will!" This wasn't the only way he bartered his players for a free meal.

Getaway day for a road trip was always tough. At home it meant saying good-bye to family members for up to two weeks. Once on a road trip, it wasn't as bad. The hardest adjustment was from a night game to a day game on getaway day. If I packed the day before, left a wake-up call, and ordered room service for the morning, it made life on the road much easier. In the days before I used this method (it only took me twelve to fifteen years to figure it out!), I would get up early and eat in the hotel restaurant.

In San Francisco the Dodgers stayed at the Hilton near Union Square. On Sunday mornings they had the league's best buffet. So I got up early, held a table for four, and had a place for teammates to join me. One Sunday morning, while four of us occupied a table, Lasorda spotted us, grabbed a chair and place setting from another table, and ordered coffee. With his fork he speared food from all of our plates. "Hey, these sausages are great! When ya go up there again, bring the skipper back a few of those sausages," he said. "How are the eggs? Those potatoes look pretty good. Could ya get me some of those when ya go up there?" he continued. Within a few minutes he had everybody at the table running through the line for him. If you protested, his comeback was "With all the food I get you in the clubhouse, you're gonna treat me like that?" What could we say? Tom kept us running through the buffet line until he was finished. When the checks arrived he told the waiter he only had coffee, put the check on the table, and said, "You guys take care of that for me. I still gotta check out." And off he went. We sat there, looked at one another in total amazement, and then laughed because we knew we had just been "Lasorda-ed"!

Sign the Balls!

The Dodgers were the only team I played for that put out six dozen balls a day to be signed. Other clubs would have a player sign a dozen or so once a home stand. Why so many? It was because of the demand. And most of it would come from the manager.

Lasorda would send or personally deliver a dozen balls to a charity or religious institution for a fund-raiser. Maybe they were destined for a military outpost or a police or firemen's auction to help someone in need. Quite a few found their way to a children's hospital along with Dodger promotional items.

He could also take a dozen baseballs and turn them into free meals or merchandise. Many of the postgame meals in the clubhouse were the result of bartering the autographed baseballs. Many restaurant owners around the league delivered food to the clubhouse, rubbed elbows with Dodger players, and took home a dozen baseballs. Many of these restaurant owners have become good friends over the years. The players loved it, as they now had a place in town to take their family and friends with a good chance of the meal being comped, or, at the very least, they would enjoy preferred seating. So for Tom, the coaches, players, and trainers, it was a win-win situation. The lesson was a simple one: if you signed the balls, a lot of good things could come your way.

Because the food was in his office and he was responsible for procuring it, Lasorda treated the spread as his personal domain. Tom realized it was easier to get a player's attention by denying him postgame meals than by levying fines against him. I can't count the number of times I was barred from his office for various infractions.

Once I was given the heave-ho for commenting on Tom's penchant for double-dipping with his fork in a tray of barbecued beef, a gross breach of clubhouse etiquette. I stood next to him in a state of culinary shock and asked, "Rather than use the serving pan as your personal plate, why not get a dinner plate like the rest of us, take what you want, and eat at your desk?" He didn't bother to swallow before telling me, "Really? Why don't you get your ass out of my office if you don't like it?" Still sputtering, he added, "Make it three days!" Because there were other players who were banished at one time or another, we developed a system of hiding sandwiches under towels as we left the room to deliver to our shunned brethren.

Wait 'til Next Year

The 1980 season ended with three games at Dodger Stadium against Houston that were as exciting as any series I was a part of. Coming into the series, we had to win all three games to force a playoff to determine the division champion. Dodger fans had a different intensity, as they upped the excitement level a notch.

The Astros were leading 2–1 in the top of the ninth of the first game on Friday night against Valenzuela. Houston needed three outs to enter the postseason for the first time. With two men on and two outs, Cey singled to center to tie the game. The Astros went quietly in the top of the tenth. Leading off the home half of the tenth, Joe Ferguson hit a walk-off homer against Ken Forsch to give us the win.

I beat Nolan Ryan on Saturday night by a score of 2–1, as Garvey was the hitting star with three hits and driving in what proved to be the winning run. I retired ten consecutive batters from the sixth inning that took us to two outs in the ninth. The Astros wouldn't go quietly. Cedeño and Art Howe singled before Gary Woods grounded out to end the game.

On Sunday afternoon the Astros knocked Burt Hooton out early, as they led 3–0 after four innings. We scored a run in the fifth, another in the seventh, and two more in the eighth on Cey's two-run homer to take the lead. Like Saturday, the Astros threatened in the ninth. With two runners on base and two outs, Don Sutton, who started Friday's game, came in to retire Denny Walling on a grounder to force a Monday playoff.

The Astros scored two in the first against Dave Goltz, two more in the third, and three in the fifth. We managed only a run on six hits, as Joe Niekro threw a complete game for his twentieth win of the season. Art Howe drove in four runs with three hits, including a home run.

We went from the highest of highs to packing for home in the course of twenty-four hours. Losing the tough games with everything on the line made one appreciative of winning the big games. It was a lesson in perspective. Still, it was "Wait 'til next year."[7]

1981 and Fernandomania

As a result of my 18–6 record in 1980, I was voted the National League Comeback Player of the Year. Although many players scoff at the idea of the award ("Where did I 'come back' from? I was here the whole time!"), I accepted the honor quite seriously. I believe the Comeback Player of the Year Award is far more important than the Cy Young Award or even the MVP, because it takes at least three years to win it! Hell, anybody can have a great year and win the MVP. But just to be considered for the Comeback Player Award, a player must have at least one good year, then a lousy year, and then another good year.

After my comeback season of 1980, I was determined to maintain the momentum through the winter and hit the ground running in the spring of 1981. Instead of taking some time off to let my body recover from the 229 innings I threw (at thirty-one years old), the most since 1975 (at twenty-six years old) when I accumulated 237 innings in thirty-two games started, I kept my in-season pace, alternating my aerobic program with a few games of racquetball six days a week all winter long. Like many players, I had that Superman complex and believed I was immune to any injuries. That disregard for common sense would eventually cost me.

When the Dodgers opened the clubhouse in January 1981 for the annual winter workouts, I was there and ready to throw fifteen to twenty minutes of batting practice. Once we arrived in Vero Beach, I was ahead of everybody and threw four innings in my first spring game. As the innings accumulated and my workouts increased in time and intensity, I noticed my legs weren't recovering as quickly as they once did. Instead of backing off, I pushed

Fig. 1. I loved that uniform. I would have worn it to church if Dad had let me.
Courtesy of Jerry Reuss.

Fig. 2. Our Overland team was one of many from Missouri and Illinois that were invited to participate in of one of four games played simultaneously in the outfield grass at Busch Stadium 1 in July 1960. Courtesy of Jerry Reuss.

Fig. 3. Giving my all for the Ritenour Huskies during my senior year in high school. Courtesy of Jerry Reuss.

Fig. 4. (*above*) Ritenour won the Missouri State High School Baseball Championship in 1966 and 1967. We decided to "appropriate" the banner since we were the state champs! Courtesy of Jerry Reuss.

Fig. 5. (*right*) The Cardinals brought me to St. Petersburg during spring break of 1968. The rest of me eventually grew into those size 13 spikes. Courtesy of Jerry Reuss.

August 25, 1969

Mr. Jerry Reuss
% Tulsa Oilers Baseball Club, Inc.
P. O. Box 5382
Tulsa, Oklahoma 74104

Dear Jerry:

Your contract has this date been recalled by the St. Louis National
Baseball Club of the National League. You are to report to our club
in time for a work-out at 10:00 a.m. on Thursday, September 4.

Best wishes.

Sincerely yours,

Bing Devine
General Manager

BD:maq
cc: Commissioner's Office
    The National League
    Tulsa Oilers Baseball Club

AUGUST A. BUSCH, JR., PRESIDENT / BUSCH MEMORIAL STADIUM / ST. LOUIS, MISSOURI 63102

Fig. 6. Reading the contents of this letter always brings a smile to my face.
Courtesy of Jerry Reuss.

Fig. 7. If you look closely, you can see the mustache that led to my trade to Houston. Courtesy of Jerry Reuss.

Fig. 8. Danny Murtaugh and I share a lighter moment prior to opening of the 1974 League Championship Series at Three Rivers Stadium. Courtesy of the Pittsburgh Pirates.

Fig. 9. Jim Rooker, Bruce Kison, myself, and Ken Brett pose during a moment of relative sanity. One of us did something every day that made the others laugh. Courtesy of the Pittsburgh Pirates.

Fig. 10. Willie Stargell was a Hall of Fame man long before he was a Hall of Fame player. Courtesy of the Pittsburgh Pirates.

Fig. 11. Visiting with Sandy Koufax during spring-training stretching. When Sandy spoke, I stopped and listened. Courtesy of Los Angeles Dodgers LLC.

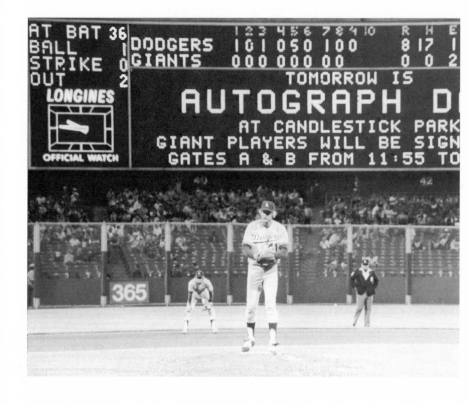

Fig. 12. The scoreboard tells the story as I deliver what turned out to be the final pitch of my no-hitter at Candlestick Park against the Giants. Courtesy of Los Angeles Dodgers LLC.

Fig. 13. Dodger owner Peter O'Malley gave me this beautiful big-screen TV for pitching the no-hitter. It was too large for the house, so it ended up in Lasorda's office for the team to enjoy. I'm shaking hands with Steve Yeager, who caught the game. Courtesy of Los Angeles Dodgers LLC.

Fig. 14. It was Old-Timers Day at Dodger Stadium in July 1980. What an honor it was to wear the same uniform as both Sandy and Don Drysdale. Courtesy of Los Angeles Dodgers LLC.

Fig. 15. Fans think that former teammate Phil Garner and I were reviewing the American League hitters before I faced them in the 1980 All-Star Game at Dodger Stadium. Actually, we were talking about the huge big-screen TV above the left-field bleachers that made its debut that night. Courtesy of Los Angeles Dodgers LLC.

Fig. 16. (*above*) Celebrating with Pete Guerrero and Derrel Thomas after the Dodgers beat the Houston Astros three straight games at Dodger Stadium to advance to the League Championship Series against Montreal. Steve Garvey and Davey Lopes exchange hugs to our right. Photo by Jayne Kamin-Oncea.

Fig. 17. (*right*) Defeating the Yankees in Game Five of the 1981 World Series was my greatest thrill as a player. At least it was until we beat the Yanks in New York to be crowned world champs three days later. Courtesy of Los Angeles Dodgers LLC.

Fig. 18. What happens when the bubbly and the beer run out during a World Series celebration? A food fight starts! I just gave Reggie Smith a face full of whatever was in my hand. Mike Scioscia, who started the mess, sneaks a peek behind me. Courtesy of Los Angeles Dodgers LLC.

Fig. 19. After a parade through the streets of downtown Los Angeles, I address a crowd of more than seventy-five thousand Dodgers fans (give or take a few) from the steps of city hall. It appears that Rick Monday and Steve Garvey were really into my speech! Courtesy of Los Angeles Dodgers LLC.

Fig. 20. Four days after winning the World Series, Steve Yeager, Rick Monday, Jay Johnstone, and I found ourselves inside the world-famous Capitol Records recording studio laying down some tasty tracks. Within a week the "Big Blue Wrecking Crew" sang "We Are the Champions" on *The Tonight Show* with Johnny Carson, *The Merv Griffin Show*, *The Mike Douglas Show*, and, for good measure, *Solid Gold*. Surprisingly, every once in a while, we were on key! Courtesy of Neal Preston.

Fig. 21. Seconds before we go on air, legendary Dodger broadcaster, Vin Scully awaits his cue as I rehearse some witty ad-libs! Courtesy of Los Angeles Dodgers LLC.

Fig. 22. Even when I wasn't pitching, I did whatever I could to help the Dodgers win. In this case I donned the ground-crew garb and dragged the infield. Courtesy of Los Angeles Dodgers LLC.

Fig. 23. When Steve Garvey returned to Dodger Stadium the first time after joining the Padres, he planted a big kiss on my cheek. I told him that's as far as we would go unless I got flowers, chocolates, and dinner. Photo by Jayne Kamin-Oncea.

Fig. 24. Jay Johnstone was the perfect partner in crime. Once while standing behind home plate before a game at Wrigley Field, a group of twenty or thirty kids lined up in front of us and started singing the national anthem. With nowhere to go we removed our hats and sang with them. Courtesy of Los Angeles Dodgers LLC.

Fig. 25. After a long spring-training workout, Tom Lasorda relaxed in the whirl-pool. While he was telling me how wonderful the water was, I decided to find out for myself. Courtesy of Los Angeles Dodgers LLC.

Fig. 26. Many times when Lasorda told the home-plate umpire to "bring in the right-hander," I wanted to fight him. This time we were just having fun. Steve Howe observes in amusement. Courtesy of Los Angeles Dodgers LLC.

Fig. 27. Orel Hershiser adds the finishing touches to this pie in my face. No idea who did it. No doubt it was well deserved. Courtesy of Los Angeles Dodgers LLC.

Fig. 28. I was a September call-up in 1969 and again in 1990. I'm ready to deliver a pitch in my final game. Courtesy of Jerry Reuss.

Fig. 29. Pirates manager Jim Leyland shakes my hand while catcher Don Slaught watches as I hear "Bring in the right-hander" for the final time. Courtesy of Jerry Reuss.

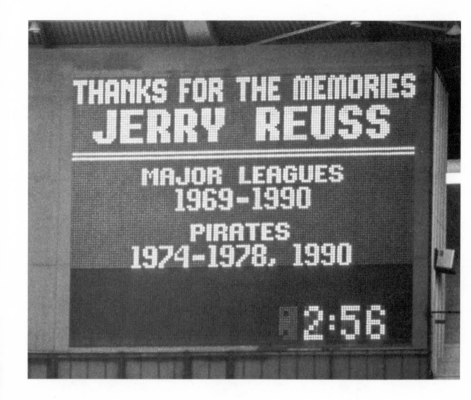

Fig. 30. This was the message posted on the scoreboard at Three Rivers Stadium as I stepped out of the dugout for a curtain call. My thanks to the Pirates for the classy acknowledgment. Courtesy of Jerry Reuss.

harder, knowing that I would be the starting pitcher at Dodger Stadium on opening day.

During the last week in Vero Beach and through the Freeway Series with the Angels, I had soreness in both calves. This time I did back off. But it was too little, too late. At the workout at Dodger Stadium the day before opening day, I felt a snap in my right calf while chasing a batting-practice fly ball. I knew treatment with a bag of ice wouldn't have me ready the next day.

Once Lasorda knew I would miss the start, he explored his options, as I wasn't the only starter experiencing health problems. Burt Hooton had an ingrown toenail, and Bob Welch's elbow was balking. Dave Goltz and Rick Sutcliffe had just pitched in the Freeway Series. Tom's last option was Fernando Valenzuela, a twenty-year-old rookie with all of ten games of Major League experience under his belt.

Fernando's opening-day start and ultimate five-hit shutout of the Houston Astros started a phenomenon that even after thirty years is hard to explain. Fernandomania was the legend that was created. It had an impact that went far beyond the baseball field.

Peter O'Malley said, "It was the most exciting period of time on my watch." Vin Scully described it as "beyond fan love of a player. It became . . . a religious experience." Jaime Jarrin, a Hall of Fame broadcaster in his own right who also served as Fernando's interpreter, stated that Fernando "created more baseball fans than any other player in history. Thousands of fans from Mexico and Central and Latin America, who didn't care for baseball, became fans overnight and still are to this day."[8]

Initially, the attention was more of a curiosity than anything else. None of us had ever seen the likes of what was happening. As the weeks passed we marveled at the spectacle. Every day there were more writers, columnists, and photographers waiting at the ballpark. On nights that Fernando pitched, we watched the stadiums fill. The Dodgers drew a total of 581,167 fans when Fernando pitched at Dodger Stadium during 1981 for an average of 48,431 a game.

The crowds kept the ballparks buzzing, and the team responded to the excitement.[9]

Lasorda, concerned that problems could arise from the focus Fernando was getting, called the other four starting pitchers into his office for a meeting. "With all the attention surrounding Fernando, I want you to know that you're just as an important part of this club," he stated. Searching for something to say, he added, "Each of you will have your own press conference after a game." I told him, "Tom, that's not going to happen." Burt Hooton added, "We don't have a problem with Fernando. It's allowed us to work without interruption." Burt's statement summed up the feelings of the players. It's a long season, and everyone will have the chance to contribute. We kept winning as the focus, did our jobs, and enjoyed the ride.

Everything about Fernandomania was positive. The attention given Fernando splashed onto the team, and we played well in the spotlight with the best record in baseball through the middle of June. The cultural significance was even greater, as Mexico and all of Latin America had a new hero. Wherever we played on the road, the stadium was filled when Fernando pitched. The only inconvenience was the crowded locker rooms.

Baseball clubhouses of that time were not equipped to handle that kind of media attention. Once the Dodgers used the auxiliary clubhouse at Dodger Stadium for press conferences and instituted a policy on road trips of one press conference held away from the ballpark per series, the problem was handled.

One question that everyone had on their mind was Fernando's age. No one could believe that a twenty-year-old could handle himself with poise beyond his years. After a while none of us cared. The fact that we were winning allowed us to enjoy the history being made right before our eyes. With Fernando leading the way, the Dodgers had a 14–5 April, were 33–15 at the end of May, and 3–7 in June when the players went on strike.[10]

The 1981 Strike

In a general sense the strike was about money and how it was to be distributed. Since 1976, when arbitrator Peter Seitz ruled in favor of players Dave McNally and Andy Messersmith, free agency was a spark that ignited controversy. Free agency caused salaries to rise (from an average of $51,500 in 1976 to $113,558 in 1979), meaning the owners were keeping fewer of baseball's dollars.

The issue in 1981, and this was the owners' demand, was Major League—caliber compensation for a free agent. At least that was the issue in the forefront. Behind the scenes the ownership negotiators wanted to dilute free agency to the point that it became much like a glorified trade.[11]

Marvin Miller recalled, "Ray Grebey [the owners' chief negotiator] maintained that the club that lost a free agent had to be able to receive direct compensation from the club that signed the free agent. And that compensation had to be a professional player on that club's major league roster. The Players Association proposed a variety of ways to compensate the club losing a free agent. But we focused on just that club, not on punishing the club that signed a free agent. If the punishment were severe, it would end free agency."[12]

Marvin made a proposal to Grebey that addressed the compensation issue. Each club could protect the twenty-five players on its active roster. All others on the Major League roster (up to a total of forty per club) were subject to being drafted as compensation. When a club lost a free agent, it could pick a player from a pool made up of unprotected players of all clubs combined.

Grebey rejected it. Marvin's proposal covered everything the owners wanted and needed. But it didn't restrict the movement of free agents and roll back salaries, which was what some owners wanted.

The owners had purchased an insurance policy months earlier that paid them around $100,000 for each canceled game from a $50 million policy that lasted until August 8. It took fifty days (coincidentally, the same number of days that owners received payments from this insurance policy) before the strike was settled. The agreement called for compensation for a free agent to come from a pool of unprotected players designated by each team, much the same plan Marvin had suggested before and during the strike. In addition, all players would receive credited service time for the fifty days missed with regards to pensions and other purposes involving service requirements.[13]

Before play resumed baseball implemented a split-season format with the respective first-place teams in each of the four divisions declared the first-half winners. If any of the first-half winners (Dodgers, Phillies, Yankees, and Athletics) won the second half as well, the team with the second-best record within that division during the second half would play the winners in a divisional series.

The hardest part for me during the strike was keeping in touch with my teammates. As the player rep, it was my job to keep everybody informed. I left messages with players with no response. If my call was answered, it was usually by someone employed by the players. Soon, I was on a first-name basis with their housekeepers. At a highly charged meeting with Marvin and the other twenty-three player reps during the strike, I mentioned, "I don't know where my players stand on the issues, but we have the support of their hired help!" Wherever players went and whatever they did, they returned to their respective cities on July 31 for a week of workouts before the season resumed on August 10.

Dragging the Infield, Part 2

Once the strike was settled, it was business as usual. When Jay Johnstone joined the club as a free agent in December 1979, he heard about Brett and me dragging the infield. During the 1980 season he pulled me aside one day and said eagerly, "I want to drag the infield. Let's do it, okay?" I answered matter-of-factly,

"Been there, done that. But we'll see." I was never one to dismiss an opportunity. So we kept it on the back burner.

On September 2, 1981, we moved the idea to the front burner. Because I was a veteran of antics like this, the planning was smoother than the first time. I told the grounds crew before the game about our plans, and they said, "No problem. We'll have your clothes ready." How I love working with professionals!

When I told Monday and Yeager, who, by now, found their own devious groove, Mo called a friend who worked on the Diamond Vision production crew to alert them of the event.

Still, we had to elude Lasorda. By the time Jay and I were dressed and making our way down the runway, we were quickly ushered into the storage room. It seems that Tom was taking a leak in the bathroom just across from us. We had to lay low and hope he made his way back to his spot at the other end of the dugout in time for us to make our entrance.

The final out was made, and now it was show time. Screened by Mo and Boomer, we made our way to the spot in front of the third base scoreboard where the drags were housed. As we make our way to our mark along the foul line, I heard Lasorda yelling at us. In one breath he managed to use the *F* bomb as a noun, verb, adverb, and adjective, hyphenating them in one breath.

Diamond Vision followed us from third to first, as we picked up the drags and put them away by the scoreboard just past first base. We made our way through the stands, high-fiving some of the thirty-two thousand fans who cheered our tour with a standing ovation. Anytime I got a standing ovation, I always acknowledged the crowd. So there I was, waving my hat to the fans and cameras as we made our way back to the locker room.

Knowing there would be hell to pay, we hustled back to the grounds-crew locker room, changed into our uniforms, and headed for the bench. The game was in the bottom of the sixth when Lasorda stopped us near the storage room and said, "I don't want to hear a word. That's a $250 fine for each of you. Jay, grab a bat. You're hitting for the pitcher." Even the coaches were trying to hold back their laughter as Jay stepped to the plate.

As fate would have it, Jay hit a pinch-hit home run, becoming the first player in baseball history to drag the infield in the fifth and hit a homer in the sixth. That's one for Cooperstown!

As Jay made his way around the bases, we could see a huge smile on his face. Lasorda stood there, his eyes looking to the "big Dodger in the sky," saying, "Why me? Why me?" When Jay got back to the dugout, he got the customary hug from Lasorda, who told him, "Your fine's cut in half." Then he looked at me and said, "Yours is still $250. Sit your ass down where I can see you and shut up!"

When I got to the park the next day, my focus switched to my next start just two days later. That wasn't the case with KABC radio's Bud Furillo, who had his daily two hours' worth of Dodger pregame show to fill with on-field interviews and live call-ins from fans.

During batting practice Bud, who witnessed the previous night's yard work, wanted the whole story. Bud was a good guy, and, besides, he always laughed at my antics. So I gave him the whole story, including the part concerning the $250 fine. I apologized to his audience, saying it wasn't very professional, but, I added, it sure was fun!

But my interview only whetted Bud's appetite. So he spoke to Jay, who told him his slant on the story, especially about his fine being cut in half during the greeting in the dugout. By this time Bud smelled a fun story, and being nobody's fool he knew it would cover his two-hour shift.

Now it was Lasorda's turn. Tom played the role of hard-ass. But to his surprise the call-in fans asked him to forget the fines and have some fun with our professional indiscretion. Lasorda, still in the cover-my-ass mode, held his own and said the fines would stick. With Bud stirring the pot and Tom playing the tough cop, the fans loved the tale that unfolded exclusively before them. By the time

Bud's slot was finished, fans called in and offered to pay our fines, in full and many times over.

So, after BP, Lasorda called Jay and me into his office and told us about the fans. "I don't approve of what you did, and I have to fine you. Most of all, I want this to go away. So let's do this: if the fans send you or me any money, we pool it and donate it to a charity. There'll be no fine as long as you both admit that it's been paid."

I never received any money to pay the fine, and the whole incident quietly went away, at least until Tom and Jay wrote their respective books.

Tom told a different story in his book. "When one of our announcers told the story on the radio, fans began sending in donations to cover the fine. Reuss and Johnstone ended up making a small profit. I then insisted I had been responsible for those profits and made them take me out to dinner."[14]

Jay had a different take on the story. He wrote, "We never did pay those $200 fines. In fact, people got such a kick out of the whole thing that they were sending donations to help pay the fines. We donated the money to a hospital in Orange County."[15]

The truth was in there somewhere. Whatever it was, any version of the story still brings a smile to my face!

The 1981 Season, Part 2

With the strike settlement giving us a guaranteed ticket to the 1981 postseason, we played okay in the second half (27–26) but not as well as Houston (33–20), Cincinnati (31–21), and San Francisco (29–23). Overall, the Reds had the best record in the Western Division, while the Cardinals had the best record in the East. The schedule worked against both teams, as the Reds played one less game than the Dodgers in the first half and the Cards played one less than the Expos. We didn't worry about that, as we had our jobs cut out for us heading into Houston for the first Divisional Series in modern baseball history.

There was a sense of urgency with the 1981 club. I mentioned to Dodger historian Mark Langill, who was writing another one of his fine books on Dodger history, that there were four sets of players on the ball club. The first set was the core group, the guys who came through the organization and played in the 1974, 1977, and 1978 World Series. That was the infield of Garvey, Lopes, Russell, Cey, and Yeager. Bob Welch played in the '78 series. Except for Welch, the first set of players, all over age thirty, had been with the Dodgers since at least 1972 and had yet to win a World Series. Since Branch Rickey, who developed baseball's farm system among other innovations, the Dodgers' policy was to move a player a year too early rather than a year too late. Time was working against the core group.

The second set was the guys who played in the '77 and '78 series but came from other clubs. That included Monday, Baker, Smith, Hooton, and Forster. Only Reggie played in a series with another club, and that was with Boston, which lost to the Cardinals in 1967. Only Terry Forster, at twenty-nine with a history of arm troubles, was under thirty.

The next set was the veteran players who joined the Dodgers from other clubs and enjoyed some degree of success. That group consisted of Thomas, Goltz, Landreaux, Johnstone, and myself. Only Jay played on a world championship club. Of the five of us, only Ken Landreaux was under thirty.

The final and largest group was the younger players that came through the organization since 1978. These players were the future of the Dodgers. Names such as Valenzuela, Sax, Scioscia, Marshall, Niedenfuer, Guerrero, Howe, Stewart, Pena, and Castillo dotted the roster. Their time had come.[16]

The World Series losses in the '70s haunted those veteran players, as did the more recent memory of losing the playoff game against Houston in 1980. The disappointment stayed with us all winter.

We were 8-4 against Houston overall but just 3-3 in the Astrodome in 1981. Nolan Ryan, who no-hit the Dodgers ten days earlier, was the starter against Fernando in the first game at Houston. We managed just a run on two hits (Garvey hit a seventh-inning home run) against Ryan, as Fernando allowed a run on six hits. The difference in the ballgame was the two-out two-run homer by Alan Ashby in the bottom of the ninth inning off Dave Stewart.[17]

We knew a win in the second game meant a split, a return to Dodger Stadium, and a big shift in momentum. It wasn't meant to be. The Astros' Joe Niekro battled his way through eight scoreless innings, as the Dodgers left ten men on base. I gave up five hits and a pair of walks in nine scoreless innings. Once again, the Astros won the game in their last at bat. Denny Walling singled to right with bases loaded and two outs in the eleventh inning to win the game and put the Astros in a position of needing to win just one game in Los Angeles to advance to the League Championship Series.[18]

The club scheduled a workout on the October 8 off day. Lasorda held a meeting before the workout and reminded us that we beat Houston three straight at Dodger Stadium in the final weekend of 1980, and there was no reason we couldn't do it again.

There always was electricity in the air during the postseason at Dodger Stadium. Maybe the fans sensed that our adrenaline was in high gear. Or maybe we rode the wave of excitement they brought to the park. Whatever it was, it was working. We put three runs on the board in the bottom of the first and coasted to a 6–1 win as Burt Hooton defeated Bob Knepper in Game Three.[19]

Because every game was a must win, Lasorda started Valenzuela on three days' rest. It was a gamble, as Fernando struggled during September, allowing four runs a game in three of his last six starts. Plus, Lasorda moved Welch, who started twenty-three games during the abbreviated season, to the bullpen. Fernando was at his best, as he pitched a complete game, allowing just four hits and a ninth-inning run against the Astros' Vern Ruhle, who gave up just two runs on four hits in a complete-game effort.[20]

With the series tied at two wins each, the season came down to one game, much like the playoff game at Dodger Stadium a year earlier. It was Nolan Ryan for the Astros, who won the first game of the Divisional Series and allowed just two hits and a run in his last eighteen innings against us, opposed by me, working on three days' rest after shutting down the Astros on five hits in nine innings in Game Two.

The adrenaline more than compensated for pitching on short notice. I was loose and ready to go after warming up ten minutes instead of the usual fifteen. Of course, there was the home crowd of nearly fifty-six thousand adding to the mental frenzy. Though my pitches had more action than normal, I worked out of the two jams in the first six innings. In the Houston second inning, a one-out single followed by an error put runners on first and second. Two ground outs ended that threat. In the sixth Tony Scott singled to lead off the inning but was thrown out attempting to steal. A single by Art Howe and a walk to Jose Cruz created another two-on, one-out situation. I worked out of the jam when Denny Walling popped out and Dickie Thon grounded into a force play.

Ryan allowed base runners in each of the first three innings and worked out of a two-on, one-out threat in the third. He appeared to reach his stride, as he retired eight in a row starting the bottom of the sixth.

I don't know if it was the home crowd ratcheting up the excitement level or the top of the order seeing Ryan for the third time, but suddenly we connected on pitches that Ryan had us missing the last twenty-three innings. After Landreaux flied to center, Baker drew a walk and Garvey drilled a pitch to center for a single. Monday hammered a pitch to right for a single, driving in Dusty for the game's first run. After Guerrero popped up, Scioscia lined a two-out single to center to drive in Garvey for the second run. An error by Walling at first allowed Monday to score the inning's third run.

With a 3–0 lead and the most excited crowd I ever played in front of, we moved in for the kill. Well, sort of. An error by Guerrero playing third put Ashby on first, leading off the Astros' eighth. It took a flyout, a groundout, and another flyout to retire Houston in the seventh.

A double by Landreaux off Dave Smith (it was literally off him, as he had to be removed from the game) and, one out later, a triple by Garvey produced our fourth and final run of the game in the home half of the seventh.

Each team left a runner on base in the eighth, as the Astros came to bat in the ninth. I remembered during my warmup pitches how I had approached the ninth inning of the no-hitter just a little more than a year ago. Get that first-pitch strike, and stay ahead in the count.

It was the bottom of the order for the Astros, with Dickie Thon grounding to short for the first out. Alan Ashby, the hero for Astros in the first game in Houston, flied to left for the second out. By this time the shadows were creeping up on home plate, making it hard to pick up the pitches. I threw the first two pitches to Dave Roberts, pinch-hitting for the pitcher, for strikes. The two-strike pitch was knee-high on the inside corner, but it eluded catcher Mike Scioscia and went all the way back to the screen. I never heard the strike call by home-plate umpire Lee Weyer, as the full house at Dodger Stadium was at full-decibel level. Apparently, neither did Roberts, as he stood at home plate. Scioscia heard Weyer, however. He flipped his mask and raced back to the screen. Roberts caught on and raced toward first. The final out of the fifth game would be decided by Mike's throw to first. There was nothing about this postseason that was going to be simple or straightforward. Why should the final out of this game be any different?

The one-hop throw to Garvey on his knees barely beat Roberts at first. Once I saw Steve with the ball, I was airborne. Within seconds the field was full of Dodgers ready to celebrate. It took three of the most exciting games I've ever been a part of, but we exorcised the ghosts of 1980 and advanced to the League Championship Series.[21]

Val-deri, Val-dera

At the workout on Monday at Dodger Stadium, it was easy to see just how drained everyone was. The series against Houston was a battle. There wasn't much time to catch our breath. The Expos, who defeated the Phillies to advance to their first League Championship Series, were headed our way.

The makeup of the Montreal Expos was much like the Dodgers. The Expos had six of the eight position players developed through their Minor League system. Add pitchers Steve Rogers and Bill Gullickson, also products of their farm teams, to the mix, and you could sense that the Expos were a team just coming into their own as they were entering their prime baseball years.

We beat the Expos in five of the seven games we faced them in 1981, including wins in all three games at Dodger Stadium. Plus, with Ron Cey returning to the lineup after having his left forearm broken on a pitch in early September, we were confident that we could beat Montreal at Dodger Stadium, win one more north of the border, and prepare for the World Series. The Expos had plans of their own.

Having Cey back in the lineup in the first game paid an immediate dividend. He drove in the first run with a double and scored the second run, as we took a 2–0 lead after two innings. The score remained that way, as Burt Hooton and Bill Gullickson matched zeroes on the scoreboard, until we batted in the bottom of the eighth. With two outs Cey singled and Guerrero homered. Scioscia connected for a solo home run, as we took a 5–0 lead. Bob Welch, who replaced Hooton with one out in the eighth, gave up a double to Gary Carter, leading off the ninth. A double by Larry Parrish scored Carter. Steve Howe restored order after a single put runners on first and third, with an infield pop-up and a game-ending double play.[22]

Game Two featured Fernando, who beat the Expos twice during the regular season, against Ray Burris, who lost in his only start against us. Montreal scored two in the second on three singles and a double. They added a solo run on two singles and an error in the sixth inning. Meanwhile, we couldn't mount any kind of an attack against Burris, who pitched well in his final two regular-season starts but was beaten by the Phillies in the Divisional Series. We had two runners on base in the sixth and ninth innings, but Burris and the Expos eased the threat with double plays and evened the series, winning by a score of 3-0 as both teams headed for Canada.[23]

With a split of the first two games in Los Angeles, the Expos had the advantage of momentum for the first game at Olympic Stadium. With the game-time temperature in the midforties, I was matched against Montreal's Steve Rogers. Steve and I had a history that went back to high school and American Legion ball. In 1966 I lost to Steve's Springfield team 1-0 in the American Legion State Finals in Springfield, Missouri. I returned the favor in the 1967 Missouri State High School semifinal, shutting out his Glendale High School team by a 3-0 score. Neither of us would have guessed at the time that we'd match up against each other fourteen years later in a game with a trip to the World Series at stake. Prior to the LCS, I held a 4-0 record against Steve. (Ultimately, I was 6-0 against him.) All of our matchups were close, as he was always an opponent to be respected.

This game would be no different. We drew first blood in the fourth, as Baker singled and advanced to third on Garvey's single. Dusty scored on a groundout by Cey. The score remained 1-0 until the bottom of the sixth. With two outs Dawson grounded a single past Russell. Carter walked. Larry Parrish ripped a single to left to tie the game. That brought Jerry White, an outfielder who batted .176 against me lifetime, to the plate. White lifted a fastball down the left-field line just barely fair but far enough for a three-run home run. That gave the Expos a 4–1 lead, and Rogers made it stand as Montreal led the series, two games to one.[24]

After the game many of the players didn't want to return to their rooms. After experiencing the highest of highs after the comeback against Houston, we were facing another unhappy ending. What better way to deal with reality than to head to the bar at the top of the team hotel with wives in tow and discuss the situation with teammates! Imagine if you will, highly talented athletes (with egos to match) and the adrenaline of a game still coursing through their veins mixing disappointment, frustration, and alcohol. Yeah, what could possibly go wrong? The alcohol lubricated the lips, as the pent-up frustration poured out. This was a veteran team with guys who spoke their minds, and the reality of this last chance to win as a team was evaporating. For the rest of us, who knew if there would be another chance to play in a World Series?

As the tension was building and the voices were getting louder, I had to visit the restroom. I made my way to the men's room, located up a long spiral staircase that had bright spotlights marking the way. What would possess someone to put restrooms at the top of a staircase in a bar anyway? Maybe it was a Canadian thing!

Even in my semi-inebriated state in this moment of relative calm, I observed the beautiful antique floor-to-ceiling mirrors in the men's room. Taking a moment to gaze at my reflection after I finished my business, I noticed my topcoat (I never bothered to remove it once in the bar) was a few inches short. I turned around and saw that it was just as short in the back. By now, the voices of my teammates were loud enough to pierce the doors of my fortress of solitude. I knew where the party downstairs was headed. Lasorda would make out lineups tomorrow based on who was out on bail.

Some players find solace in their religious faith. Other players hope to find it in the bottom of a glass. For me, in times of great stress, I find clarity and comfort in my humor. Besides, I had to deal with a more important problem at hand . . . a topcoat that was too short! But I needed another opinion or . . . maybe many opinions! That's when the solution occurred to me.

With all of those opinions flying around the bar downstairs, why not let my teammates, the ones at an emotional peak just below the stairs, help me solve this dilemma? So I removed the coat and, for good measure, my pants. I then put the topcoat back on and buttoned it. After neatly folding my pants over my arm, I was ready to make my entrance . . . after just one more look in the mirror, though.

Through the doors and standing at the top of the stairs, I noticed just how bright those lights were. I posed there with that faraway look in my eyes as the top models would . . . only with my pants hung over my arm! I made my way down the steps, pausing after each while changing the direction of my stone-faced gaze. After the first few steps the feverish, near-manic voices stopped in mid-sentence, mixed with the sound of quiet giggles from the wives who were present.

After the next few steps I spotted the faces of the men I called friends and teammates, with their eyes and mouths in suspended animation and total disbelief. Once I had arrived in front of the tables, I said in a quiet and controlled manner, "Since all of you have opinions to express, I beg for one more." I paused and did a 360. "Is this topcoat really too short for a man of my height?" The faces, red with anger just moments before, were sporting grins from ear to ear as laughter replaced the venom spewing from their lips. The clouds of doom disappeared, attitudes changed, and it was time to get some rest. Somebody said, "I'll take care of the tab, and we'll square it up tomorrow" (that's a teammate for life in my book!). My work in Montreal was done.

There were a few smiles on the bus regarding the night before. Once at the park the mood was all business, as the guys in the lineup put on their game faces with their uniforms. Pitching for us was Burt Hooton, who had two postseason wins, allowing just a run in fourteen and a third innings against Houston and the Expos.

We scored a run in the third, and the Expos answered with a run in the fourth. That was the score until the top of the eighth. With the home crowd of nearly 55,000 singing verses of "The Happy Wanderer," a German composition written shortly after World War II that featured the lyrics "Val-deri, Val-dera," Dusty singled with one out, and Garvey followed with a two-run homer to give us a 3–1 lead.[25]

The Expos threatened in the home half of the eighth with a lead-off single, a force out, and a single by Carter. Lasorda went to the bullpen to summon a well-rested Bob Welch. It was the right move, as Welch fanned Parrish and retired the previous night's hero, Jerry White, on a fly to center.

Welch's effort changed the momentum. Ten Dodgers batted in the top of the ninth to produce four runs and set the stage for Steve Howe's 1–2–3 bottom of the ninth and Dodger victory that evened the series.[26]

The fifth and deciding game was scheduled for 4:00 p.m. Thinking that the rain mixed with snow would stop, the powers that be waited until 7:30 to call the game. Looking at the positive side, the postponement gave Fernando, our scheduled starter, an extra day's rest. He pitched with just three days' rest in his last four starts, including all three of his postseason starts.

Just before game time on Monday, October 19, the home crowd was subdued, which is totally opposite of what someone would expect, as the winner of this game would travel to New York to face the American League champion Yankees in the World Series. They were more than subdued, because there were not as many of them. The announced attendance of 36,491 was nearly 20,000 fewer than Saturday.

The empty seats didn't affect the Expos, as they posted a run on a double, a sacrifice bunt, and a double-play grounder in the first. Expos starter Ray Burris, who had pitched a five-hit shutout against us in Los Angeles, picked up where he left off. He worked out of a jam after Russell tripled in the first and was left on base, as both Baker and Garvey were retired on ground outs.

The lead stood until we scored a run in the top of the fifth on singles by Monday and Guerrero, a line out by Scioscia, followed by a wild pitch that put runners on second and third. We scored our first run on a ground out to second off the bat of Valenzuela.

With one out in the Expos' eighth, manager Jim Fanning sent Tim Wallach to pinch-hit for Burris. Wallach, with home run power, could send the Expos to the World Series with one swing of the bat. Tim grounded to the pitcher, and Raines flied to center in a 1–2–3 inning.

Steve Rogers, who pitched extremely well in the postseason, allowing just two runs in twenty-six and two-thirds innings, came on to pitch for Montreal in the top of the ninth. He retired Garvey and Cey on flyouts. That brought Rick Monday to the plate. Life-time, Rick batted .176 against Rogers, with two home runs and twenty-six strikeouts in seventy-four plate appearances. But that wasn't during the postseason.[27]

With a 3–1 count, Mo lifted a fastball to right center that nobody on our bench could see. I watched Andre Dawson chase the arc to the track. Once he stopped running, he watched the ball clear the wall, and that told the story. The entire bench emptied to greet Monday when he crossed the plate.

"Rogers kept pitching me away, away, and he fell behind in the count, 3–1, forcing him to give me a pitch I could handle," said Monday. "He had to want the pitch more outside, but it got a lot of the plate and I crushed it to the right-center gap. As the ball cleared the fence, I just passed first base and was heading to second. I threw my left arm in the air and continued my jog around the bases, jumping a little when I got to home plate. My teammates beat the heck out of me, which I thought was a little premature, because the Expos had the heart of the order due up in the bottom of the ninth."[28]

Fernando, with a league-leading eleven complete games during the regular season, knew how to finish a game. A grounder to Garvey and a flyout to right brought two quick outs. None of us on the bench believed the Expos would go down without some kind of fight. Carter coaxed a two-out walk. Larry Parrish also walked. Now Lasorda had to make a decision: let a tiring Valenzuela face switch-hitting Jerry White or bring in a fresh Bob Welch. Tom chose Welch, and it turned out to be the right decision. White grounded out to second. The celebration began with Garvey on his knees and the final out in his hand. We cleared the field and the cold temperatures and proceeded to celebrate in the clubhouse.

Knowing that we had to face the Yankees the next day, we kept the festivities in check. Still, we sung a few bars of "Val-deri, Val-dera" between sips of bubbly to mark the occasion. The LCS was ours, as we came from behind, one game from elimination in our second consecutive series, to advance, this time to the 1981 World Series.[29]

New York, New York

Shifting gears from an emotional series is something every player should experience. From the high of victory and back to the business at hand with little time to make the transition is what the postseason is all about. Because of the Sunday rainout (or snowout!), we didn't have the luxury of an off day between the League Championship Series and the World Series. It was a quick transition from Monday in Montreal to Tuesday in New York. So, after a detailed meeting with the advance scouts about the Yankees, it was time for Game One of the 1981 World Series.

As a kid growing up in St. Louis, every October meant the World Series on radio and television. Because the games were played in the afternoon prior to 1971, the good sisters of All Souls School in Overland must have been baseball fans, as they allowed a radio in the classroom so we could get game updates. I'd either rush home after class to catch the rest of the game on TV or stand in front of the store window of Brockman's Television in downtown Overland to watch their color TV in the window. During the mid-1950s and early '60s, except for 1959, the Yankees represented the American League. Because of baseball's blackout policy, the World Series and All-Star Games were the only times I could see games other than the local Cardinals telecast. So that was my introduction to the World Series and Yankee Stadium.

Experiencing the House That Ruth Built in person had a profound effect on me. Everywhere you looked, walked, or sat was historical. That's fine . . . if you're a tourist. It's not so good if you're facing a well-rested Yankee team ready to beat your ass!

The Yankees started Ron Guidry, 11–5 on the season but 2–0 in World Series play, as he beat the Dodgers in both 1977 and 1978 with complete games. Guidry had a 1–2–3 first inning. My first World Series inning was memorable, but for the wrong reasons. With two outs and a runner on first, Lou Piniella (our respective career orbits crossed many times) doubled just inside the bag down the first base line. Bob Watson hit my first pitch to right-center for a three-run homer. One pitch, thrown belt-high over the middle of the plate, put the Yankees in the lead. I had a 1–2–3 second inning but in the third a single, a two-out stolen base, and a run-scoring double by Piniella, and my introduction to Yankee Stadium and the World Series was finished.

Guidry pitched seven innings, getting his third World Series win against the Dodgers, as the Yankees won Game One by a score of 5–3. That's not how I hoped my first World Series game would turn out. Hell, who would?[30]

Game Two featured two former teammates, Burt Hooton, who was selected the LCS MVP, and Tommy John, who had moved to the Yankees after six years with the Dodgers, including 1977 and 1978. T.J. had his sinker working, as he retired the first twelve batters he faced. Burt was nearly as effective, as he allowed a base runner in three of the first four innings but kept the Yankees scoreless. We had our biggest threat of the night in the fifth inning with two men and one out but couldn't score, as Landreaux struck out and Yeager grounded out. The Yankees scored their only run against Hooton on an error and a two-out RBI double by Larry Milbourne in the home half of the fifth. The Yanks scored two more in the eighth on three singles, an error, and a walk against Steve Howe to seal a 3–0 victory.[31]

Once again, we were in familiar territory, behind in another postseason series with our backs against the wall. Unlike the LCS in Montreal, there were no alcohol-induced reactions while returning to Los Angeles. I even kept my pants up the duration of the trip.

The Green, Green Grass of Home

The day off allowed everyone to breathe a bit easier, considering the ups and downs of the LCS and the first two games of the World Series. I bet everyone held his or her collective breath when an early-morning earthquake hit Southern California on Friday. As far as earthquakes go in the region, this one was memorable only when Yogi Berra, then a coach with the Yankees, said, "I didn't feel it. It must have bypassed me."[32]

Game Three featured rookie starting pitchers—Dave Righetti for the Yankees and Fernando for the Dodgers. This was just the third time in Major League history that rookies faced each other in a World Series start; the last time was in 1967, when the Cardinals started Dick Hughes and the Red Sox countered with Gary Waslewski.[33]

When Ron Cey homered in the bottom of the first with two on and two out, it gave us our first lead in the series. It was also the same way we started our three-game comeback against Houston just two weeks earlier. We hoped that giving Fernando a three-run lead would allow us to cruise to a win.

That didn't happen. The Yanks scored two in the second inning on a solo HR by Bob Watson, a double by Rick Cerone, and a run-scoring single by Larry Milbourne. They struck for two more runs in the third when Piniella singled and Cerone homered. With our team trailing by four runs, Lasorda went to the mound to talk to Fernando. "Everybody thought I was going to take him out," Lasorda said. "A lot of people wanted me to take him out. But I knew him. He loved to pitch out of jams. He used to pitch like he didn't know we had a bullpen. He didn't like to come out of games. A lot of guys, when they get in trouble, they're looking down there for help. But not him."

Lasorda eventually went back to the dugout, but not without giving Valenzuela a few last words of encouragement. "I said to him in Spanish, 'If you don't give up another run, we're going to win this ballgame,'" Lasorda said. "And then he says to me in perfect English, 'Are you sure?'"[34]

Righetti struggled through two-plus innings and was replaced by George Frazier in the third inning, as Garvey began the Dodgers' fifth inning with a single. Cey walked, Guerrero doubled in Garvey, and the score was tied at four. After an intentional walk to Monday, Rudy May was brought in to face Mike Scioscia, with the bases loaded and nobody out. Lasorda, recognizing the chance to break the game wide open, sent Reggie Smith to the on-deck circle to bat for Fernando in the event that Scioscia made out without producing the go-ahead run. Scioscia's run-scoring double-play grounder turned out to be pivotal, as it kept Fernando in the game.

"If Scioscia pops up, I'm gonna hit for Valenzuela," Lasorda admitted after the game. It was one of many times that Lasorda considered removing Fernando, especially when he was wild high early in the game with less than his best stuff. "I thought about it," Lasorda admitted, "but I said no. This is the Year of Fernando."[35]

Fernando held the Yankees in check in the sixth and seventh but ran into trouble in the eighth. Consecutive singles by Aurelio Rodriguez and Milbourne to lead off the inning brought Bobby Murcer, pinch-hitting for May, to the plate.

"At this point," admitted New York manager Bob Lemon, "I got greedy." Rather than have Murcer drop a sacrifice, Lemon told

Bobby to try for a bunt single on the first pitch. What Murcer produced was a foul pop-up that third baseman Cey picked off with a magnificent diving catch. Milbourne had departed from first with such enthusiasm that all Cey had to do was leap to his feet and throw to Lopes, covering first, for a double play. Next, Willie Randolph was in the process of legging out a chop to Cey, but the third sacker was spared making a futile throw because Rodriguez, advancing from second, obligingly ran into a third-out tag.[36]

The two base-running mistakes took the Yankees out of the inning. Fernando retired the Yankees 1-2-3 in the ninth, as we won the game 5-4. Valenzuela gave up nine hits, walked seven, and threw 145 pitches in a gutsy performance.

Lasorda's faith in Fernando paid off. Risking criticism if Fernando had faltered, Tom said, "He was like a poker player bluffing his way through some bad hands. And with that one-run lead . . . he closed out the game like the best of them."[37]

Game Four: Winning Ugly

Bob Welch got his first start in the postseason after giving up just a run in four relief appearances during the Division and League Championship Series. He lasted just sixteen pitches, allowing a triple to Randolph, a run-scoring double to Milbourne, a walk to Winfield, and a single to Reggie Jackson to load the bases without recording an out. Dave Goltz, who relieved Welch, pitched out of the jam, allowing a sacrifice fly to Bob Watson to limit the scoring to just two runs. The Yankees scored a run in the second on a solo HR by Willie Randolph and another run in the third on a single, a walk, and a run-producing single by Rick Cerone and led 4-0.

We scored two runs in the third on a pinch double by Landreaux and a single by Lopes, who stole second, advanced to third on a single by Garvey, and scored on an infield grounder by Cey.

Both teams had a chance for a big fourth inning, as the Yankees left the bases loaded and the Dodgers left two on base. Rudy May, who relieved starter Rick Reuschel, pitched out of a two-on, no-out situation. May, however, didn't stick around very long. He was relieved by Ron Davis after Garvey doubled and scored on Cey's single in the bottom of the fifth, to make the score 4–3.

In just five innings the game already saw seven pitchers, seven runs, sixteen hits, and fourteen men left on base. And it was about to get more interesting.

Tom Niedenfuer, who pitched a perfect fifth, ran into trouble in the sixth. Willie Randolph reached on an error by Russell. The next two Yankees batters flied out. Lasorda elected to walk Jackson intentionally to face Oscar Gamble. Sound strategy, but Gamble singled in Randolph. Bob Watson singled on a low liner to left that Dusty swore he caught but was ruled a trap, as Jackson scored the second run of the inning. The Yankees, who blew a four-run lead earlier, now led by three, going into the home half of the sixth.

Ron Davis, who manager Bob Lemon hoped would hold the three-run lead for an inning and give the Yankees a bridge to their closer, Rich Gossage, gave up a one-out walk to Scioscia. Jay Johnstone, batting for Niedenfuer, hit a 1–2 pitch for a pinch HR, only the thirteenth in World Series history, to make the score 6–5.

By this time the fall sunlight at Dodger Stadium took effect. Lopes hit a short fly to right that Jackson charged but lost in the sun, as the ball hit him in the chest and dropped for an error. Lopes, knowing how tough the shadows could be, ran hard out of the box and stopped at second. "I had a feeling it was going to drop so I busted tail to second," Lopes later relayed to reporters.[38]

Reggie had his own take on the play. "The ball was in the sun the whole way. I was hoping it would hit my glove but it didn't." The play may have unnerved Davis, as Lopes stole third uncontested on the second pitch to Russell. Russell made up for the error in the top of the sixth that led to a pair of unearned runs by singling to left on the next pitch and scoring Lopes with the tying run.[39]

In the home half of the seventh, Dusty, who was 0–11 in the

series up to this point, hit a high chopper to short for an infield single. Rick Monday hit a soft liner to center that was misjudged by center fielder Bobby Brown, making his only appearance in the series. Brown, playing in the bright sunlight as the ball came out of the shadows, took a roundabout route to the ball and never recovered. Monday was on second with a double, as Baker took third on the play. Guerrero was walked intentionally to load the bases with nobody out.

Tommy John, who pitched seven innings three days earlier in Game Two, was called on to relieve Frazier. With the managerial gerbils running full speed in their respective cages, Lasorda countered with Steve Yeager to pinch-hit for Scioscia. Steve drove in the seventh Dodger run with a sacrifice fly to right. Steve Howe, who came in the game for Niedenfuer in the top of the seventh, sacrificed Monday to third and Guerrero to second. Lopes then beat out a high chopper to third for an infield single, as Monday scored the inning's second run. Bob Lemon later noted, "They [Dodgers] know where the holes and rocks are. We have to go out at night and find those rocks." At the end of seven, the Dodgers held a two-run lead, 8–6.[40]

In the Yankees' eighth, Reggie proved that he gives and he takes. Jackson hammered a Steve Howe pitch to the right-field bleachers for an HR. On a day where he played a role in allowing a Dodger run on an error, he also reached base five times in the game, tying a World Series record held by six other players.[41]

It was up to Steve Howe, in his third inning of work, to hold the Yankees in check. Howe, who pitched as many as three innings twice during the regular season, was showing some signs of wear and tear. With two outs and a runner on first, Howe committed an error at first that put runners on first and second. Willie Randolph, with three hits in the game, sent a long fly to deep right-center that Derrel Thomas caught a step in front of the fence. The Dodgers had tied the series at two games each.[42]

The postgame reaction was equally varied and interesting among the participants. Rick Monday stated, "It wasn't your basic Picasso."[43] Lasorda said it was one of the most exciting games he had ever been involved in.[44] Bob Lemon said, "It was as exciting as hell when we were ahead, but I didn't find it very exciting after that."[45] George Steinbrenner, furious with his club for squandering first a four-run and later a three-run lead, refused to speak with an Associated Press (AP) reporter, adding he wouldn't be around after the game.

Probably the most predictable reaction of the day occurred after the game in the interview room. Jay Johnstone sprinted the length of the room, dived over a table, and tackled Steve Garvey, who was in the middle of his postgame discourse. Garvey collected himself, stood up, and, with every hair in place, told the shocked contingent, "Don't worry, folks! He'll be back in the home by 7 o'clock."[46]

Game Five: Two Pitches That Changed the Series

The first three days after Game One, I hoped I would get one more chance to pitch in the Series. Once I knew there would be a Game Five, I went into my game-face mode. I was on edge for five days. With this being the World Series, I was wound a little tighter than normal, which meant that I would walk right through you rather than say, "Get the hell outta my way."

The Dodgers hired some of the best scouts in the business. And it showed when their reports prior to the first game of the series were the best and most detailed I'd ever heard. The reports weren't responsible for the pitches I threw that were up in the zone that got hammered in Game One. I take responsibility for that and give credit to the Yankees for taking full advantage of it. On this day, October 25, 1981, I would pitch in the most important game of my career.

I retired the Yankees in order in the top of the first. My opponent, Ron Guidry, also recorded a 1–2–3 inning. Until Game One of the

Series, I never knew just how good Guidry was. He went about his business in Game One, pitching seven innings and allowing four hits and just one run, and was the winning pitcher. I sensed from the start that Game Five was going to be close.

In the second Reggie Jackson drove my first pitch between Cey and the third base bag for a leadoff double. Watson grounded to Lopes, who bobbled the ball for an error. Piniella drove in Reggie with a single, and the Yankees led 1-0. My next pitch set the tone for the first six innings of this game. Rick Cerrone, the Yankees' catcher, swung at my first pitch and grounded into a double play. Aurelio Rodriguez grounded out to end the threat. Walking off the mound, I knew if I could hold them, we'd find a way to score some runs.

The Yankees threatened in the third with a one-out walk to Randolph and a single by Milbourne. Dave Winfield, hitless in the Series, forced Milbourne. That brought Reggie to the plate with two outs. With all of his ticks and twitches, I struck him out to end the inning.

Again, I walked the tightrope in the top of the fourth by issuing a leadoff walk to Watson on four pitches. An error by Lopes allowed Piniella to reach base. Cerone grounded out short to first, as the runners advanced. Rodriguez was walked intentionally, bringing Guidry to the plate. He bunted back to me, and I flipped to Yeager for the force at home. With the bases still loaded, Randolph grounded to Garvey at first for the final out. I dodged a Yankee bullet, leaving three New York runners on base.

In the fifth Winfield singled with one out. It was his first hit in his first World Series. For me, it was a matter of history repeating itself. In his first Major League game on June 19, 1973, Dave got his first hit against me.[47] The Yankee bench asked for the ball, and I was more than happy to oblige. Even in a moment of complete game face, I respected the importance of the occasion. Back to the business at hand, Reggie grounded into a double play to end the inning.

In the meantime Guidry was coasting. Through the first six innings, he allowed just two hits and two walks and struck out eight Dodger batters. I sat on the bench in the bottom of the seventh, hoping we could put something together against a pitcher running on all cylinders. Guidry struck out Baker for the first out. Up to this point Guidry retired fifteen of the last sixteen Dodgers to face him, striking out eight in the process.

Then the game, and ultimately the 1981 World Series, changed over the course of two batters and five pitches. Pedro Guerrero slammed a 0–1 pitch for a home run to left. Suddenly, Dodger Stadium rocked more than it did when the earthquake hit about forty-eight hours earlier. Guidry later described the pitch. "It was a fairly decent slider. I got him out on it a couple of times. When you hit a slider like that you almost have to be guessing for it."[48]

Pete Guerrero agreed: "I hit a high slider. It was the same pitch he'd been throwing all day, except this time he got the ball up. As soon as I hit it, I knew it was gone." The score was tied at 1.[49]

Next up was Steve Yeager. Yeager, with a double in this game and a homer against Guidry in Game One, fell behind in the count 1–2. He drilled the next pitch into the left-field bleachers, giving us a 2–1 lead. Regarding the Yeager home run, Guidry said, "Maybe I put that in a little bit of the sweet spot. That's the only pitch I can second-guess myself on. Maybe I should have thrown him a slider."[50]

Yeager had his own thoughts: "I looked so bad on two sliders and I guessed he might try a fastball and he did."[51]

Within five pitches the Dodgers went from a 1–0 deficit to a 2–1 lead. The energy of the ballpark, which was already at all-time high, became a frenzied state. Derrel Thomas flied to center, and I lined to short to finish the seventh. When we took the field for the top of the eighth, we all sensed a shift in the momentum and the series. Now, this was our game.

The Yankees went down in order in the eighth, as Milbourne grounded out, Winfield struck out, and Jackson flied to left. This was especially important, because two of their power guys came to the plate with the bases empty.

When Lopes walked against Rich Gossage to lead off our half of the eighth, we were hoping to score some insurance runs. Russell popped up to first and Garvey flied to right, which brought Ron Cey to the plate. Gossage uncorked a ninety-four-mph fastball that hit Cey in the batting helmet. The entire stadium was suddenly quiet, as Cey lay motionless for a few seconds as the trainers attended him. "The ball disappeared as it approached the plate," Ron recalled. "I tilted my head down a bit and that's what saved me. I remember falling in slow motion. I remember trainer, Bill Buhler, coming out to the plate as I had my hands around my head. I asked Bill if there was anything sticking out of my head. After awhile, I got up and walked into the trainers room as we waited until after the game to have a CAT scan. Everything came out okay, but it was a scary moment."[52]

It was scary for all of us. Still, we had to shift gears and get back to the game. While Baker was batting, Lopes and Landreaux, running for Cey, executed a double steal. The eighth inning ended when Dusty grounded to third.

When we were ready for action in the top of the ninth, Dodger Stadium was rockin'. Watson, who batted .462 in his career against me (18 for 39), led off the ninth.[53] He hit one of the few curves I threw in this game on the ground to Russell for a routine out. Piniella singled to center. That brought Rick Cerone to the plate. Rick was having a tough day. He grounded into a double play in the second, which took the air out of a potential Yankee rally, and grounded to short with two on and nobody out in the fourth. This time he hit a shot to center at Landreaux for the second out.

All that stood between beating the Yankees three in a row was Aurelio Rodriguez. With fifty-six-thousand-plus standing, I got two quick strikes on Rodriguez. Then I did something that I never did before delivering the next pitch. I paused and scanned Dodger

Stadium from the upper deck in left field all the way around to right field and took in the moment. The inner voice, absent throughout the game, returned and said, "This is the time you waited for your entire life. Make it count."

From the stretch, with a quick look at the runner at first, I uncorked the best fastball I had in me. Rodriguez swung right through it for strike three, and we took a 3-2 lead in the Series! I was airborne as Yeager came out to the mound, grinning from ear to ear. We celebrated briefly on the field and gave the fans and TV and radio people their due, but we wanted to know how Cey was. The preliminary diagnosis was that he suffered a slight concussion. X-rays at Centinela Hospital were negative.

When the Yankees held a pregame meeting before the ballgame that was more of a pep talk from owner George Steinbrenner and manager Bob Lemon, Reggie Jackson spoke to *Los Angeles Times* reporter Ross Newhan and said it was a positive meeting. "They both stressed the things that got us here and reminded us that we had strayed from those things the first two games [of the Series]. George said it was time we got back to playing Yankee baseball."[54]

Steinbrenner's second trip to the clubhouse wasn't quite as positive. After the game George had a few things to say about his troops. "We lacked the killer instinct. We didn't get any production from Milbourne and Winfield. Winfield is 1-24 in the series. Cerone took us out of two innings when we had a chance to break the game open."

Steinbrenner also alluded that Guidry shouldn't have been out there for the seventh inning. "His ERA in the seventh, eighth and ninth innings is over 10," George growled. A reporter asked him if Guidry should have come out of the game. He told the reporter, "I'm not the manager."[55]

Bob Lemon defended himself. "That was the best I had seen Guidry pitch since mid-August," Lemon said. "I was definitely going to bring in Gossage to pitch the eighth and ninth. There was no way I was going to take Guidry out after just six, not the way he was throwing."[56]

In our clubhouse the mood was more upbeat but tempered because of the injury to Cey. Yeager, who batted .209 in eighty-six at bats during the regular season, while lefty-hitting Mike Scioscia got the bulk of the playing time as the Dodgers faced mostly right-handers, admitted that he had asked the Dodger management for a trade during the season. "I want to go where I can play. I have nothing against the Dodgers management. They've been good to me for 14 years. I'd love to stay here, if I could play," Steve said.[57]

When asked about Pete Guerrero's game-tying home run, Yeager admitted that he didn't even see it. He was swinging a weighted bat in the on-deck circle when the bat fell apart. "The commissioner [Bowie Kuhn] was watching the bat fall apart and I was watching him watching me," Yeager admitted to Mike Littwin. "I didn't see Pete until he was rounding second. I guess the commissioner missed it, too."[58]

Davey Lopes, who committed just two errors all year, made three in this game. Davey bobbled a routine double-play grounder for an error and then was charged with another error when he threw the ball into the Yankees' dugout. After getting out of the inning without a run scoring, Lopes dropped his glove on the dugout steps, ran up the ramp, and stopped at his locker. "I had to get myself together," he said. "Nobody else could do that for me."

Lopes, who misplayed a grounder in the second, admitted, "You can't hide out there. If you start thinking that way, that ball will find you." And it did in the fifth. Jackson hit a two-hopper with one on toward the middle of the diamond that Davey admitted he briefly lost in the sun. Lopes fielded it, stepped on second, and threw to first to complete the double play. "Somebody would have written that it was the first ground ball lost in the sun," Davey said. "I know if I didn't field that damn ball I would have run straight off the damn field and never come back."[59]

After the interviews we boarded the Dodger plane and headed back to New York in a much different mood after beating the Yankees in three games decided by one run.

The Monday workout and Game Six on Tuesday were canceled because of rain. Cey, who joined the club in New York on Monday, admitted he wouldn't have been able to play on Tuesday. He admitted he felt good on Tuesday morning, but "I didn't have a good afternoon. I had some light-headedness and dizziness."[60]

The extra day off worked to the advantage of both clubs. Cey was in the starting lineup, batting in the fifth spot, and Graig Nettles, who missed the series in Los Angeles with a thumb sprain, was back in the lineup for the Yankees.

The Yankees scored in the third on a two-out solo home run by Willie Randolph. They threatened for more, as Mumphrey singled and Winfield walked, but Jackson flied to left to end the inning.

The Dodgers tied the score in the top of the fourth with a one-out single by Baker, a two-out single by Monday, and a run-scoring single by Yeager, which was just out of the reach of a diving Nettles, for his fourth RBI of the series. This proved to be a good omen, as it was the same Graig Nettles who made so many great plays in the first two games of this series as well as the World Series between these two clubs in 1977 and 1978.

In the bottom of the fourth Lemon decided to pinch-hit for starting pitcher Tommy John with two men on base and two out. The strategy backfired, as Bobby Murcer flied to right. "I wanted to get some runs. I didn't think it was a gamble," Lemon said. "How did John look to you?" Lemon was asked. "I've seen him better and I've seen him worse. He'd given up six hits in four innings. I just thought I'd make a move and get some runs."[61]

George Frazier relieved John, and we got to him again. The fifth inning started with a single by Lopes who was sacrificed to second by Russell. After a flyout by Garvey, Cey singled in Lopes. Baker singled Cey to third, and Guerrero tripled both runners home. Frazier was on his way to losing his third game of the series.

Ron Davis relieved Frazier in the sixth and with one out walked both Hooton and Lopes. Russell singled in Hooton for a run. Rick Reuschel relieved Davis, and Lopes and Russell executed a double steal. Garvey was intentionally walked to load the bases. Derrel Thomas batted for Cey, who was feeling woozy, and drove in a run on a force play to third. Baker was safe on an error by Nettles that loaded the bases. Guerrero looped a single to left-center that drove in a pair, as the Dodgers led 8-1.

The Yankees threatened in the sixth, as Nettles singled with one out. Walks to both Cerrone and Milbourne loaded the bases, and Lasorda brought in Steve Howe. Piniella hit a run-scoring single, pinch-hitting for the pitcher, and it appeared the Yankees were on their way. But both Randolph and Mumphrey lined to right to end the threat.

Guerrero's solo home run in the eighth finished the scoring for the Dodgers, as Howe began the ninth entering his fourth inning of work. Howe, who worked three innings on Saturday, was again pitching in uncharted territory. After a leadoff walk to Randolph, Howe struck out Mumphrey and Winfield flied to right.

It seemed appropriate that Reggie Jackson stood in the box, as we were one out away from winning the world championship. It was Jackson, with three home runs in Game Six in 1978, who led the Yankees to the championship the last time these two clubs met. Jackson grounded to Lopes, who booted the ball for an error. So much for a storybook ending! Bob Watson lifted a routine fly to center that was caught by Landreaux, and that was the ballgame, and the World Series. While the Dodgers celebrated on the field, more than half the crowd in attendance was gone. We took the Yankees four in a row, just as they did to the Dodgers of 1978.

I never made it to the field, as I watched most of the game from the bullpen. After the game the guys from our bullpen walked with the Yankees relievers to our respective clubhouses. With class and dignity, they quietly congratulated us and continued on their way as we entered the door to our clubhouse, where all hell was about to break loose.

The crew from the bullpen was met with shouts and sprays of champagne. I grabbed a bottle, went to my locker that was covered with plastic sheeting, and slipped in my jacket, hat, and glove, cradling the bottle through a small opening at the bottom, and began to party. For the most part, players took a swig from the bottle and sprayed the rest on whoever was within distance.

World Champions!

In no time men who had fulfilled childhood dreams made their way from teammate, coach, manager, trainer, and everyone else associated with club to share this moment of pure joy with hugs, pats on the back, and tear-filled eyes. While cases of beer and champagne were poured and sprayed over unsuspecting heads, quotes were flowing just as freely as the alcohol.

"We're the champs!" shouted Lasorda. "Nobody in this room can take that away from us." "They can do anything they want with us now," stated Davey Lopes. "I've got the ring. They can't take that away from me." Ron Cey, who came out of the game because of dizziness, said, "If I pass out, there are lots of doctors nearby." Steve Yeager noted, "You can't put this feeling into words. I never thought this could happen to me this year. It's a great feeling. It feels great to be a part of what we've done." Steve Garvey mentioned, "We beat the Yankees mentally and physically. The best team won. The Yankees didn't give us anything."[62]

While some of the players were throwing out quotes, others continued the celebration. When there was no more liquid to spray (some players took a full bottle from the ice and hid it in their lockers, a veteran move, as they later shared it with wives and loved ones on the plane), a food fight broke out. Why not? Who thinks of eating after winning the World Series? Instead of eating the cold cuts (no clubhouse manager in his right mind would serve anything else on a day like this), we were wearing them! I only remember giving as much as I got. When I saw a picture of myself years later, I was covered with mustard and ketchup. If I'd been wearing a green T-shirt, I could have auditioned as a stoplight!

Eventually, the party wound down, and guys got dressed and met their families. It was time to board the buses and make our way back to Los Angeles. It was a subdued group on the players' bus and then the Dodger plane, as the excitement of the past few weeks caught up with us. After all, our lives had been pressure packed for the past three weeks.

Pause and Reflect

Like most everyone else on the late-night flight, I took some time to reflect beyond the current events, remembering all of the people over the years who played a part in this journey: my brothers, who played endless games with me in the backyard; my parents, who saw as many games as they could while making sure we had all the necessary equipment and, most important, family support; the friends I still have today, who were teammates and classmates who cheered from a distance; the coaches from Little League, high school, and the American Legion teams, who gave up time with their own families to teach me and other players the lessons that we used both on and off the field; and the professional coaches, managers, and players, who helped me make the transition from amateur play to the professional life.

I also thought about the years of never coming close and the years of near misses with St. Louis, Houston, and Pittsburgh. I also remembered the struggles during the past few years with Pittsburgh and wondered then where it would lead. I would have never guessed then that in a few short years I would go from that valley to the top of the mountain with the Dodgers.

I took a few minutes about an hour into the flight to walk the aisle of the plane and see the faces who shared the mountaintop. Most everyone was asleep at this time. To those still awake, I could still see the joy mixed with weariness on their faces. The dream of being a world champion that we all had as a kid was now a reality. That reality was the last thought on my mind as I returned to my seat and fell asleep.

For the first time in World Series history, three players shared the Most Valuable Player award. A panel of nine media members selected Pete Guerrero (7–21, 2 HR, and 7 RBI, including 5 in Game Six), Steve Yeager (4–14, 2 HR—including the game winner in Game Five—and 4 RBI), and Ron Cey (7–20, 1 HR, 6 RBI, and immeasurable courage for returning to the lineup) as co-MVPs.

Cey's comments put the whole season in perspective. "That's perfect for this team," said Cey. "It's most appropriate. We could have had 25 guys sharing this award. The most important thing was that this team won. It was a team victory."[63]

Looking at the 1981 postseason numbers for the Dodgers, there were other players who had a great postseason. Garvey hit .359 with two home runs among his twenty-three hits; Hooton was 4–1, allowing just three earned runs in thirty-three innings pitched; Howe had a win and a save in seven games with a 2.45 ERA; and Fernando was 3–1 in five games featuring a 2.21 ERA.

Other shining moments included Monday's dramatic blast in Montreal against Steve Rogers and Johnstone's pinch homer in Game Four of the World Series. I'll never forget my Game Five wins against Houston and the Yankees.[64]

Over a season of 110 games, everyone connected with the club played a part. There were key performances by players, behind-the-scenes help from the coaches, trainers, and scouts, as well as the confidence showed in us by Tom Lasorda. All of it made a difference.

Dodger Fans Share the Love

Everyone was groggy from the overnight flight but woke up in a hurry Thursday morning, as there were thousands waiting to greet the club at the airport. As we exited the plane and walked up the ramp, we could hear the faint roar of a cheering crowd. Once we arrived at the boarding area, it was a sea of fans, dressed in blue, cheering from the top of their lungs. Some of the players joined in the cheering, but most smiled, waved, and made it through the police lines to their waiting cars as quickly as possible. I was among the latter group.

The Los Angeles City Council wanted a downtown parade for us "win, lose, or draw." Initially, the Dodgers were cool to the idea, citing security reasons, according to a *Los Angeles Times* report. Some thought that the real reason was that the club wouldn't commit until they were certain of a world championship.

According to Fred Claire, the Dodgers' vice president of public relations and promotions, the club was on board with the idea of a parade whether we won or lost. With all that was happening around the World Series, there just wasn't the time to plan a parade or coordinate with those who could do the job from city hall.

Whatever the concerns, the Dodgers and the city put their heads together and agreed to the parade after our win on Wednesday night. It began at 11:30 Friday morning at Broadway and Seventh Street, with a ceremony on the steps of city hall at 12:30. What amazed me, more than anything, was how quickly plans for the parade could be set in motion. There were marching bands from all over Los Angeles and floats that were manufactured and pulled by classic cars that were organized by a police force that made the whole operation as smooth as glass. All of this was for a crowd of seventy-five thousand, with tens of thousands watching from the windows of the downtown buildings and millions more on local television.[65]

Once the three floats arrived at city hall, each player and coach was introduced to the crowd and made his way up the steps to a platform behind a podium . . . except for one player, the one that everybody wanted to see . . . Fernando!

As city officials made their speeches, there were a number of interruptions with chants of "We Want Fernando!" Lasorda attempted to placate the crowd, explaining, "Unfortunately Fernando was not feeling too well today and was unable to attend. But he wishes to extend his sincere thanks to all of you for what you've done this year."

Although the fans wished for Fernando, they heard a number of players speak from the heart. "I think we captured something the city of Los Angeles waited a long time to have and so richly deserved," said Burt Hooton. Rick Monday told the crowd, "Today is a celebration of bringing the championship to the city it really needed to be in—that is Los Angeles." "I've been waiting nine years to see this happen," Ron Cey told the multitudes. "I think our season closes this afternoon." "We can't stop here. We'll have to do it again next year," Derrel Thomas said excitedly. Those were highlights of some excellent speeches by my teammates. I mentioned that to the crowd during my turn at the podium and finished by saying, "If we had known it would be this much fun, we would have done it sooner!"[66]

After the parade, we boarded buses back to Dodger Stadium for a luncheon sponsored by the club. It was the perfect moment for members of the organization to celebrate the moment with one another. The World Series trophy, in glorious splendor, was front and center in the Stadium Club. I silently chuckled as I remembered the trophy in the visitors' clubhouse at Yankee Stadium . . . splattered with champagne, beer, and remnants of a full-scale food fight. I was seeing it for the first time as it truly appeared and knowing that, for all time, it would represent the efforts of everyone in the room.

Just because we were celebrating the moment didn't mean that business stopped. The Public Relations and Media Services Departments had their phones ringing off their respective hooks.

While hoisting yet another glass of something expensive, I was asked if I would like to appear on a late-night comedy show called *Fridays* over at the ABC studios. "Sure," I said, "When is it?" "Tonight," I was told. There was a limo on its way to pick us up. "Who is 'us'?" I asked. "You, Johnstone, Yeager, and Mo. They tape the show in a few hours" was the response from the Dodgers' public relations representative whose name I can't recall. This was the start of the craziest week and offseason of my life!

Living Like a Rock Star

When we arrived at ABC, we were taken to wardrobe and fitted in costumes from medieval times for a skit that opened the show. We each had a line to deliver after we were introduced in the skit as visitors from a far-off land bearing gifts and seeking an audience with the king, played by Michael Richards. After the show, while waiting in the parking lot of the ABC studios for our limo ride back to Dodger Stadium, Jay called the three of us to a pay phone, and the voice on the other end of the line had each of us singing a part of a song so that the voice could determine a key for his charts. It was time for our next stop in postseason 1981!

Bob Emmer, an executive at Warner Music and later Rhino Records, attended Game Five of the Series with his wife. While walking to their car after watching us take a three-games-to-two lead, he mentioned how much fun it would be to do a project with the Dodgers if the team went on to win the World Series. "I'll work on it," Bob said as they made their way home.

After watching us win on Wednesday night, he put a plan into motion on Thursday. Bob called Jay Johnstone, with whom he had some business dealings, and asked if he knew of three other players who would like to make a record. Jay recommended Rick, Steve, and me and asked us about it sometime Friday. "Why not?" we answered. We rode the crest of the postseason wave, not knowing where it would lead.

Bob enlisted the services of business partner Shep Gordon, president of Alive Enterprises, who managed Alice Cooper, Blondie, and Kenny Loggins among other prominent acts, to find musicians, a studio, and a producer who could put together a record on short notice.

A call to Christopher Bond, who produced and played guitar and keyboards for Hall & Oates's *Bigger than Both of Us* album[67] and was our mystery voice on the other end of the line on Friday night, yielded the producer, a studio, session players, and lead sheets. "Bob called me around 5:00 PM on Thursday and told me about the project. I knew it would be insanity, but it was going to be a lot of fun. I spent 18 hours on the phone on Friday getting players, lead sheets and a studio. We recorded the backing tracks on Saturday, the ballplayers on Sunday, and had the record on a plane to the pressing plant on Monday," explained Bond.[68]

On Sunday morning Mo and I shared a limo that took us to the iconic Capitol Records building in Hollywood. This was where Frank Sinatra and Nat King Cole recorded a number of great albums in the 1950s and 1960s. And now I would have the chance to walk the hallowed halls and sing in the same studios where artists with real talent had sung!

Chris Bond walked us through the process of laying down some tracks. He broke down the first four lines of "We Are the Champions," a song by Queen that reached number four on the *Billboard* chart in 1978, so that each of us had a minisolo. Eventually, Chris had a keeper, so it was on to the flip side, "New York, New York."

We sang for hours, loving every minute of it, until there were two usable takes that could be mixed to the outstanding instrumental tracks laid down by some of the world's best musicians, which included bassist Leland Sklar and Toto's drummer, Jeff Porcaro. Mo told the *Los Angeles Times*'s "Morning Briefing," "We'll need bodyguards to protect us from the musicians. We really messed up a good soundtrack."[69]

After the session and interviews for the networks and *Entertainment Tonight*, we headed to the rooftop of the Capitol Records building, where famed rock-and-roll photographer Neal Preston took full advantage of the golden hour of daylight for the record sleeve.

There still had to be a source of financing, even though the project wasn't going to turn a profit. "I knew from the start that the record wasn't going to make any real money," Bob said. "So, I asked the players for the name of their favorite charity and we drew the name of Children's Hospital of Orange County out of a hat. Any profits from record sales would be donated to CHOC."

Bob also had to ask for favors from different contacts in the record business to make the deal happen. "I approached the presidents of all the major record companies around Los Angeles. The best, and most interesting response, was from Steve Wax, the president of Elektra Records." Wax told him, "I'll give you the ten thousand dollars you want, if you can get these guys to make some appearances for me." "What kind of appearances?" Bob asked. "I have a sales meeting coming up, and I'd like them there. Also, there's a pressing plant in town, and I'd like to have them stop by" was Wax's response. Bob told him, "I'll work on it."

Meanwhile, Shep told Bob some good news. "I booked them on the Carson show for Monday night," Shep said proudly. "That's great news," Bob said, "except they don't have an act."

It was a call to Marty Krofft, who was the producer of Barbara Mandrell and the Mandrell Sisters TV show, that landed choreographer Joe Layton, an Emmy Award winner for his work on the 1965 TV special featuring Barbra Streisand, *My Name Is Barbra*. Krofft let Barbara Mandrell make the decision about letting Joe work for Bob. "They can have him for a day," she told Bob. "It didn't hurt that she was a baseball fan," Bob told us later.

All that remained was for Bob to work out a deal with Layton. "I'll do it for three large," Layton told Emmer. "I can't afford three thousand, Joe," Emmer replied. "Who said anything about three thousand! I want three large Dodger jackets," Joe answered. "I'll work on it," said Bob with a laugh. With that the Big Blue Wrecking Crew, our new name, had a record, a choreographer, and a date with *The Tonight Show Starring Johnny Carson*.

Mo and I were back in the limo Monday morning for another trip to Hollywood. This time, we were asked to bring our best suits, a dress shirt, and a tie. Once at the studio we handed over our dress clothes that had to be altered for the appearance with Johnny Carson that evening. We were in one of the rehearsal rooms as Joe Layton put us through the paces.

It was evident in just a few minutes that our baseball skills didn't transfer to the dance floor. If you ever heard the story about the monkey and the football, that punch line best describes our efforts. Working to the dub of the record we cut the day before, Joe walked each of us through our respective parts. Joe had an incredible routine, tremendous patience, and an unbelievable sense of humor. It was time to leave the comforts of the studio and head over to Burbank for our rehearsal with the *Tonight Show* band.

"Here's Johnny!"

We were taken to our dressing room that featured a huge spread from a nearby deli that surpassed anything we had at the ballpark. "Does Carson treat all of his guests like this?" I asked. "No, this is courtesy of Alive Enterprises. All of our acts have food backstage" was the answer from the Alive rep. "Is there anything else that you'd like?" he added. Mo asked, "Would it be possible to have a few cold Heineken?" "I'll have a case here in fifteen minutes" was the response as he left the room. "Yep, I could get used to the rock 'n roll lifestyle," I said with a smile. "Yeah, if we only had the talent to back it up!" Mo said with a laugh.

The door to the dressing room opened. "Get dressed, gentle-men," said the *Tonight Show* rep as he poked his head in the door. "Doc Severinson will be ready for rehearsal in ten minutes." We put on the suits we brought with us and noticed the alterations for our shirts and ties, as the buttons were resewn so the shirts would rip off and the ties were now the clip-on variety.

Once onstage and after accepting congratulations from many of the band members and Doc for the World Series win, it was time to get down to business . . . show business! Johnny would introduce us as the Big Blue Wrecking Crew singing "We Are the Champions," and then the curtain would rise as the four of us had our backs to the audience.

Because I was the first to turn and sing my solo, I took my cue from the band. Jay followed me with his part, and then it was Rick's and Steve's turns to sing their solos. Fortunately for us, Joe was still with us, out of camera range in front of the first row of the audience, taking us through the routine step by step.

The rehearsal with the band went pretty well, considering that when we finished the finale Doc had tears in his eyes from laughing so hard. Either that or he was crying from the fact that his career had sunk to a new show-business low.

Because the time for taping the show was just minutes away and we were the first guests, we stayed close to our marks while visiting with a number of people backstage. I don't know about the other three guys, but I was scared shitless. I could pitch in front of fifty-six thousand screaming Dodger fans and millions more listening on radio and watching on TV because I was in my world. But singing and dancing on *The Tonight Show* was out of my league.

Strangely enough, the excitement of performing before mil-lions meant the convergence of my real and fantasy worlds. What athlete hasn't dreamed of being a rock star? I was walking through the steps one more time when I heard a familiar voice. "Jerry, if you don't know the routine by now …" I looked up and there was Johnny, laughing.

From backstage we heard Ed McMahon's "Here's Johnny!" As Carson eased into his monologue, a stage manager told us that we needed to take our marks when the show broke for commercial. Joe, recognizing that all of us were a bit nervous, said, "I'll be out front between the cameras. If you need a cue, just look at me." The band went into their bumper music for the break as we took our marks.

As Johnny went into our introduction, I looked to my right as Mo caught my gaze. "Hey, what's your pucker factor?" he said, laughing. "You couldn't drive a greased needle up my ass with a sledgehammer," I answered.

Their laughter was the last thing I heard as Johnny said, "Would you welcome the Big Blue Wrecking Crew!" And the curtain and my adrenaline level rose as the band went into the first few bars. The audience noise was deafening, and I could barely hear the band, which was right next to us. I heard my cue and turned to sing my opening line, "I paid my dues," into the brightest lights I'd ever seen!

I scanned the room, looking for my lifeline, our choreographer, Joe Layton. I was lucky. I spotted him between the two cameras where he said he was going to be. He wasn't easy to see with the lights and audience members on their feet waving their arms. But I could follow his movement enough to maintain the pace. During the song, which included turns, moving the mic stand, and grabbing the mic, I had the mic in the wrong hand. I heard Joe yell, "Other hand!" Boy, he was good! But the mistakes I made through the number didn't matter to the audience, especially when we ended the number by removing our suit coats, ripping off our clip-on ties and Velcro-fastened shirts, and firing them to the floor, revealing our blue T-shirts with the Dodger logo encrusted in rhinestones.

After inviting us over to the couch and greeting us, Johnny's first words were, "I think people thought you were going to be bad," which had us howling. Johnny, being gracious and a true professional, took us through an interview that gave the world a chance to know us off the field.

This was my only *Tonight Show* appearance. When I think of all the talented artists over the years who never got the chance to show what they could do in the national spotlight, I appreciate those moments even more.

But Wait—There's More!

After we stopped in the dressing room for a quick bite and a taste or two of the chilled Heineken, Shep herded us into waiting limos for a trip to Carlos 'n Charlie's, a Hollywood restaurant that was owned in part by him and Bob.

Sometime during the evening, Shep and Bob told us that the Crew was booked on *The Merv Griffin Show*, *The Mike Douglas Show*, and *Solid Gold*. I don't remember the exact dates for *Merv* and *Mike*, but it was during the week of November 2–7. By the time we performed the routine on *Solid Gold* on Saturday morning, November 7, we had it down. Too bad, as we had taken the act just about as far as it would go.

We were booked for two holiday appearances with Norm Crosby at Knotts Berry Farm in Buena Park on December 29 and 30. Rick made the comment about just how far Norm's career was in the toilet since he was opening for us!

The final appearance for the Big Blue Wrecking Crew was on Super Bowl weekend of 1982 as we performed the skit one more time for the Hamilton/Amvet Corporation. It was as close to being a rock star as any of us would get. To this day, every time I see the Heineken logo, it reminds me of the best time of my baseball career.

CHAPTER NINE

Life after the World Series . . . Big Laughs, Great Times, and Transitions

Even with the schedule of the Big Blue Wrecking Crew and other promotional appearances in the winter of 1981–82, there was still time to prepare for the 1982 season. I stayed with the off-season conditioning program that worked the two preceeding seasons. Forty-minute jogs alternating with racquetball games and trips to the gym for Nautilus training and free weights became the norm in the winters from 1980 to 1984. When the Dodgers opened the doors to the clubhouse in late January, I was there to get my head start on spring training. When the Dodger plane departed Los Angeles for Vero Beach for spring training in 1982, I was ready and thinking of a World Series repeat.

All managers have a team meeting the first day of spring training. That's were the introductions are made of the new players, coaches, trainers, and other staff members. The next meeting occurred at the end of spring, once the rosters were trimmed. That's the way it was with every team I played for but one. Lasorda had a closed-door meeting every morning at 9:00 a.m. Attendance in full uniform was required. He believed that when everyone was in uniform, it was time to work. His first words in the spring of 1982 were about winning the consecutive world championship. "We have to work that much harder to repeat," he told all in the room. Personally, I couldn't have worked much harder. But I could certainly work smarter. No more five- to six-mile runs. Instead, I ran three to four miles at a faster pace. At this point in my career, I needed to take some of the stress off my legs.

Still, these morning meetings were more fun than business. Once the business and practice schedule for the day was covered, we never knew what would happen. Sometimes, he had a rookie stand up and tell the team all about himself. More than once the kid, as nervous as hell, had to sing his college fight song. Welcome to the club!

Even in spring training there were six-dozen balls to sign every day. Tom constantly had to remind guys to sign the baseballs, as the season's bartering was under way. One player who signed every ball every day was Ken Landreaux.

When Ken Landreaux Speaks, We All Listen

One day, after reminding us yet again to sign the balls, Tom thanked Landreaux in the meeting for being the only guy to sign them daily. "There it is every day, K. T. Landreaux," Tom remarked. He paused, then continued, "Landreaux, I was curious about your middle name. I looked it up in the press guide and it said your full name is Kenneth Antoine Landreaux." Now you can hear the laughs around the clubhouse. He then asked Landreaux if his middle name was Antoine. Kenny stood up and said, "Yeah, that's right." The laughs got louder. Puzzled, Lasorda looked at him, grabbed a ball, looked at it again, and asked, "But you sign them K.T. How in the hell do you get K.T. out of Kenneth Antoine?" The laughter was even louder. Landreaux paused and with a straight face said, "If two parallel lines mean equal and H2O can stand for water, then K.T. can stand for Kenneth Antoine Landreaux!" The clubhouse erupted in laughter. Meeting over!

Every year, Tom had to read aloud a letter from the commissioner. It's the standard letter regarding gambling and the penalties if you're caught. All he wanted to do was get through it. About a paragraph into it, somebody farted. He got the giggles and couldn't recover. We've all been there. So he stopped and said, "Look, let me get through this." He started from the top, read a paragraph, and somebody else farted . . . louder and longer! He laughed so hard tears filled his eyes. "Dammit, let me read this *bleepin'* thing!" he pleaded. So he started again, got back up to speed, and heard guys giggling like schoolkids. He paused, fought the urge to laugh, and battled on. Finally, when he finished, we all applauded. It was probably the only time a reading of a letter from the commissioner ever received a standing ovation!

Extra Work

Among the things I loved about Dodger spring training was the chance to get extra work when the schedule would permit. When the team was on the road and I wasn't pitching, it meant some extra BP in the cages or fielding some grounders back to the mound on one of the half fields. Because we shared the complex with the Minor League players, the Major Leaguers were invited to use the open cage at the far end of the row where the newly purchased curve-ball machine was installed. Because the baseballs used were either new or taken from the previous day's BP, we didn't fear a lopsided ball being spit through the rubber tires. This was the only kind of BP we saw during the spring. The other starting pitchers not in the game were great partners because we'd talk pitching and have competitive games involving bunting and situational hitting. The local kids hired to feed the balls loved us because we would tip them ten or twenty dollars for their time.

Getting grounders back to the mound was a bit more difficult because we needed a Minor League coach to hit them. My favorite coach for grounders was Terry Collins, currently the manager of the New York Mets, who was just beginning his managing career in the Dodgers' Minor League system. Terry carried a bit of an edge with him and always worked at game speed, except one particular day. After tapping easy one- or two-hoppers back to the mound on the half field closest to the batting cages where a crowd of Minor Leaguers gathered, he asked how I was doing. I answered, "Fine, but does your husband hit the grounders in the family?"

Collins stopped, his mouth opened in disbelief, and I could see the blood rush to his face from a pulsating vein on the side of his neck. In measured words he responded to my challenge of his manhood and said, "Oooh! I think I understand now. You want some game-speed grounders, don't you?" Boy, did I light his short fuse! The next grounder zipped past me like a bullet. Pausing to admire his work, Terry looked at me through squinty eyes and a full-beaded sweat and asked, "Is that better?" I nodded and said, "You're getting there." After that some I caught, some I knocked down, and others were too hot to handle. However, it was just a matter of time before I got nailed with a shot through the box. The killer shot caught me below my right kneecap, and down I went.

Terry told me years later when he managed the Angels and I was their road TV analyst that the first thing he thought of while running to the mound to see me was "I'm going to lose my job." He paused, laughed, and continued, "Then, I hope he's all right!" The voice of reason in my head said, "It doesn't matter—you're still gonna get fired!"

When he arrived he bent over and asked, "Are you okay?" I squinted, looked at him as he was silhouetted by the sun, and said, "Is that all you got?" He was ready to blow a fuse but stopped when he realized that I was working him.

His whole demeanor changed as he regained his composure. "Let's get a drink of water, and if you want more, I'll hit them," he said quietly with a smile. We got that drink, took our positions, and Terry, never one to miss a teaching opportunity, stopped to talk to the crowd of Minor Leaguers who witnessed the events and told them, "Gentlemen, this is what it takes to be a Major Leaguer, hard work and then more hard work!"

After that session Terry looked forward to meeting me on the half field. If I remember correctly, he invited a few Minor League pitchers to join me during our next workouts, allowing Minor League pitchers to work alongside a major leaguer. That was coaching genius on the part of Collins. For twenty to thirty minutes, four or five players got some concentrated work as opposed to standing around waiting for a chance to bunt in the batting cages. The players Collins chose were top-notch kids who came to play, so the drill became competitive and the experience was invaluable.

At the end of spring training, I put a fine bottle of chardonnay in his locker with a note that read, "Hope the time it takes to enjoy this vintage is as enjoyable as the time we spent on the half field!"

Traveling in Style

When I joined the Dodgers in 1979, a whole new world of player travel was set before my eyes. I had heard about the Dodger plane for years. To experience the reality was something else. First, the Kay-O II, named after Walter O'Malley's wife, was a Boeing 720B jet (the Dodgers were the first MLB team to own their own jet) configured for sixty-eight first-class seats in five compartments. Up front was a card table opposite the galley. Behind it was the section for the staff, front-office workers, and nonuniformed personnel. The players occupied the next two sections of seating, including the two card tables, which separated the players' section from the back of the plane. Members of the press who traveled with the club brought up the rear.

How important was the Dodger plane to the organization? For the traveling party, it meant that after a game on getaway day, there was never a wait for a commercial flight or a charter that was delayed. There was never a question about the safety of the plane, as it was painstakingly cared for. The meals served on board were as good as could be found on any plane.

While other clubs traveled exclusively on buses during spring training, the Dodgers flew to Tampa or St. Pete. It took twenty-two minutes from liftoff in Vero to landing in Tampa. The commute from Dodgertown to the beach where many players spent their spring usually took a half hour.

The Dodger plane transported entire families from LA to Vero Beach before spring training. When spring training was over, the Kay-O II returned everyone to Los Angeles if opening day was in Los Angeles. During the years the club opened on the road, families would return to Los Angeles a few days before camp broke, as the plane returned to Vero to take the team to their destination.

The plane also played a big part in the Dodger mystique. Seeing it up close and personal with the blue Dodger wordmark against the white background, it was a symbol that declared, "This is as good as it gets."

Of course, all good things come to an end. After the 1982 season the plane was retired, as the costs of using it just couldn't be justified. I remember Lasorda telling us that flying on a charter commercial airline like other clubs would be just as good. I knew better. And I know he did too.

Dodgertown—the O'Malley Way

Another great perk of playing for the Dodgers was spring training at Dodgertown in Vero Beach. When Dodger personnel and their families arrived in Vero Beach on the Dodger plane in late-February 1980, it marked the beginning of a new era of my baseball career. When the families exited the plane, fans from around Florida greeted us, as each player and his family were ushered to a member of this welcoming group and given the keys to a rented car and directions to the rented home or apartment for spring training. I never witnessed this kind of reception anywhere except in Vero Beach.

Although many of the players stayed off campus from Dodgertown, we were always invited to the events that marked the warm spring evenings. Once a week there was an ethnic food night in the cafeteria. Whether the theme was Spanish, German, French, Greek, or a barbecue . . . it didn't matter, as everyone in the organization was invited. I never attended the St. Patrick's Day celebration, but the stories over the years were legendary. When someone mentioned Christmas at Dodgertown, the O'Malley family put plans in motion for Santa to appear and hand out presents to the younger kids around the swimming pool that was decorated for the occasion with a Christmas tree and a pile of snow. There were lunches and activities planned for the families while the players worked, including a day of picking strawberries and a day trip to Bermuda for lunch and shopping for the wives on days when the Dodger plane needed to be flown.

For Dodger front-office personnel and members of the media, Dodgertown was the ultimate in convenience. Meals in the cafeteria were just a few steps from their temporary office, which was a short walk from their room. The media members used the pressroom, which was complete with phones and outlets for each at their personal work area. Many writers claimed that the room's best feature was that it bordered the bar!

For fans, Dodgertown was a dream come true. Though some areas were roped off, fans had easy access to players for autographs, pictures, or just a chance to say hello. Of course, if you're a player trying to get from the clubhouse to Holman Stadium where the games were played or even from one field to another, navigating the crowds could be a problem. Most of the time, the fans were well behaved, and players would take some time with them.

By far the best spring-training experience in my career was in Vero Beach. I've never heard of a player from another organization who experienced spring training the way the Dodgers had it.

That Once-in-a-Lifetime Thing That Happens Every So Often!

Every year I pitched there was a subtitle to the season. Something unique occurred that defined that year. In 1980 there was the no-hitter, and in 1981 we were the world champions. There were four games in 1982 that most pitchers experience maybe just once a career.

On April 21 at Dodger Stadium I pitched my second career one-hitter against the Astros. Then, just ten starts later, on June 11, I allowed a leadoff double to Eddie Milner of the Reds and then retired the next twenty-seven Reds batters in order. It was a perfect game after the first batter! That was my third and final one-hitter of my career.

On August 17 at Wrigley Field, the Dodgers were tied with the Cubs 1–1, as the game was suspended after seventeen innings because of darkness and rescheduled for completion the next day. Lasorda pulled out all the stops to win the game and as a result used every relief pitcher we had.

With no relievers available, his solution was to have me pick up the suspended game in the bottom of the eighteenth inning. The game, already strange because of the length and substitutions, took on a whole different dimension in the nineteenth inning.

Steve Sax walked to start the top of the nineteenth. John Vukovich, who was the acting manager for Lee Elia, the Cubs' manager who was ejected the day before in the eighth inning, was ejected for arguing the balls and strikes with home-plate umpire Eric Gregg. The umps were just getting started.

In the top of the twentieth inning, Ron Cey singled to right and was picked off first base before the next pitch. Cey was ejected for pushing first base umpire Dave Pallone, who also ejected Lasorda for arguing Cey's ejection. Are you still with me? The game became crazier because of the Dodgers' defensive moves.

In the home half of the twentieth inning, Pete Guerrero moved from right field to third base to replace Cey, and Fernando Valenzuela went to right field and batted in Cey's spot in the lineup. After I retired the first two Cubs batters, left-handed-hitting Bill Buckner came to the plate. Dusty Baker, who was playing left field, switched with Fernando for Buckner's at bat. Buckner singled, but left-handed-batting Leon Durham forced Buckner at second to end the inning.

I grounded out to start the twenty-first inning. Steve Sax doubled to right and advanced to third on a wild pitch. Ken Landreaux walked. With runners on first and third and one out, Dusty hit a fly ball to right field. Sax tagged and headed home and scored on the play, as Gregg had his arms in motion to call Sax out but switched to signal safe at home. Of course, the Cubs protested vigorously, but surprisingly no one was thrown out of the game. After Guerrero was walked intentionally, Fernando grounded out to end the inning.

As we took the field with a one-run lead, Fernando was replaced defensively in left field with another starting pitcher, Bob Welch. After Cubs pitcher Steve Ripley flied to center to start the inning, Dusty switched from right field to left field with Welch before right-handed-hitting Jody Davis grounded to short for the second out. Once more Baker and Welch switched positions for righty-hitting Steve Henderson. Henderson grounded to second to end the game.

When the dust settled the game of six hours and ten minutes saw the Dodgers use all twenty-five players, as the Cubs used twenty. Walking off the field with the win, we were informed the regularly scheduled game would begin in thirty minutes. Lasorda met me at the bottom of the stairs as I made my way to the clubhouse. "How do you feel?" he asked. I told him, "I'm fine." He responded, "Then you'll start the regular game and go as long as you can." I asked pitching coach Ron Perranoski, "I've never pitched in two games thirty minutes apart. Any idea on how I should warm up?" Perranoski looked at me, laughed, and said, "How should I know? I've never done it either!"

In the clubhouse I changed into a dry uniform, drank some water, walked down the stairs, and returned to the field. I was ready in five minutes on that warm August day. I lasted five innings, allowing two runs on four hits, as we led by a score of 6–2. Three Dodger relievers held the lead, and we won 7–4.

For me, it was the strangest day in my Major League career. I won two games in the space of four hours. Prior to August 18, 1982, I won a total of just two games at Wrigley, one in 1970 with St. Louis and the other in 1977 with Pittsburgh, over the course of twelve years! There's another note of interest: I never won again at Wrigley, as I appeared in four more games through 1990.[1]

Frank, May God Bless You!—Tom Lasorda

When the subject of umpires comes up in conversations with former players, many guys have favorites, while others have umps they can't stand. For me, they were all good. I preferred umpires like Lee Weyer, who would clean home plate with his brush and proceed to dust off a couple of inches beyond the black edge as if to say, "This is the zone today, gentlemen!"

When behind the plate some umps controlled the game as it came to them. Others took charge of the game before it began, especially if there was bad blood between the teams. Frank Pulli was the exception to both types of umpires. Frank challenged the game to come to him! If somebody had something to say, Frank pulled off his mask and took care of business on the spot. He'd let you have your say but not without a look in your direction that could melt steel.

As a pitcher I not only wanted all seventeen inches of the plate but a few inches of Lee Weyer's strike zone from every home-plate umpire. If a pitcher was consistently down in the zone and stayed on the corners, umpires would give him the benefit of the doubt on a close pitch. Frank worked the plate that way for the first two strikes. But for that called third strike, the pitcher had to get some of the plate. Granted, Frank would take a longer look at that borderline pitch, but would then take a deep breath, look at you, and shout, "No, that's a ball!"

There was a game when this happened to me a few times. Now, I had a habit of glaring at an umpire if a close call didn't go my way. Frank let it slide the first time I did it. The next time, he came out from behind the plate, pulled off his mask, and told me, "That's the last time you'll do that, Jerry!" he shouted. "Next time you're gone!" I guess I showed him. No more stares or glares from me.

Frank also kept the pace of the game moving. He'd let a player know if he took too much time at the plate or a pitcher taking too long between pitches. He'd also let a manager or coach have his say on a disputed play, but if he took too long, Frank ejected him.

Frank was behind the plate on a hot, humid Sunday afternoon at Dodger Stadium, and his edge that day was sharper than I had ever seen. His voice was louder, and his actions were more demonstrative. I figured he'd had a tough Saturday night. Being the sympathetic soul I was in those years, I thought I'd help him through the game.

First, I sent the batboy out to Frank with a cup of coffee. Frank, who had already sweated through his shirt, looked at the batboy like he just handed him a turd, took the cup, poured the contents onto the grass, and gave the kid the empty cup.

So I had to try a different approach to bring back the Frank we all knew and loved. I watched the game from the home-plate side of our third base dugout, standing behind the seated ball boy. I noticed every time a ball was fouled into the stands or had a mark on it from the clay-dirt combination that composed home plate and was thrown out of play, the ball boy would reach into the leather bag on his left, remove a new ball, and place it by his right foot. This way he knew how many balls to deliver to home plate when the ump signaled for them.

It occurred to me that an uplifting message on one of these new baseballs might inspire Frank. So I pulled a ball out of the bag and wrote on it:

Frank,
May God Bless You!
Tom Lasorda

(You really didn't expect me to sign my own name, did you?) I placed the ball near the kid's right foot with the writing facing the dirt so he wouldn't see it. Frank finally asked for new baseballs, and out went the ball boy to deliver them.

Time to take a seat on the bench as far away as I could from Frank . . . and Lasorda . . . and wait for something to happen. Only nothing happened! Frank never checked a ball going into the game. He just reached into his pouch and threw a new one to the pitcher.

Oh, well! I forgot about it and went on to something else when the inning ended and we came off the field for our turn at bat. Tom Niedenfuer, who was pitching for us, sat down next to me with a big smile on his face. "What's so funny?" I asked him. "You're not going to believe this. I got a new ball from Pulli that had some writing on it," he told me. *So Frank did put it into play!* "Well, don't they all have writing on them with the commissioner's signature and all?" I asked him. "No, this had handwriting," he told me. "What did it say?" I asked, not admitting to anything. "It said, 'Frank, May God Bless You! Tom Lasorda,'" he said, still laughing. "No shit! So what did you do with it?" I asked. "I threw it," he answered proudly. "I got two pitches with it before it was fouled into the stands in the family section," he said dejectedly. (The family section was directly behind home plate in the second deck.) "Damn, I was hoping to use that ball for the whole inning," he said. "Well, look at it this way," I told him. "You used it for two pitches, and you have a great story to tell." It was a great story for Niedenfuer. Still, I had no reaction from Frank . . . at least not yet.

After the game Lasorda called me into his office. "I just got a call from Jo [his wife]," he started. "How is she?" I asked. "She's fine.

She just told me a story, and somehow I think you're involved in it." He took a sip from a cup and continued, "She was sitting in the family section when a foul ball landed two rows behind her. The guy who caught the ball came up to her and said 'Mrs. Lasorda, I thought you would enjoy seeing the autograph on this ball.'" It was Niedenfuer's ball, I thought. Lasorda paused, took another drink, and continued, "Jo told him that mistakes happen, and sometimes an autographed ball can slip into a game. Well, the guy told her, 'Well, that may be so, but this ball is special for me. You see, Mrs. Lasorda, my name is Frank!'"

Lasorda took a long swig from the cup, burped, and continued, "Why is it that I think you had something to do with this?" I paused, looked away, and started to answer as he stopped me. "No, I know you're gonna come up with some kind of bullshit right now, and I don't want to hear it." "Tom . . . ," I blurted before he interrupted, "What did I just say? Go home and enjoy your evening."

As I walked out I passed Vin Scully walking into Lasorda's office. "Vinny, sit down. Have I got a story for you!" Lasorda said as I left the ballpark.

Apparently, the story that Lasorda told Vin was about the ball signed to Frank. Vin spun it into verbal gold and shared it with the Dodger faithful on the radio the next night. For the next few days, people asked me if I really put a signed baseball into play. Normally, I deny everything. But it was a good story. Besides, Vin Scully said it on the radio. It had to be true.

I had no idea how far the Dodger network reached. I found out the next time Frank Pulli came to town. There was a note on my chair that said, "See me *NOW*! Frank." I knew it wasn't Sinatra.

I made my way to the umpires' dressing room and knocked on the door. The attendant asked, "Who is it?" I told him it was me and that Frank wanted to see me. I heard Frank's voice in the background shouting to the kid, "Tell him to wait a *bleepin'* minute!" I guess Frank put his game face on early!

I knew I was in for a Major League ass chewing. As I entered the locker room, there was Frank, standing in his underwear, hands on his hips, head tilted, and that steel-melting look in his eyes.

"What the *bleep* were you thinking?" he started. "And how are you, Frank?" was what I thought. "You know I don't tolerate any bullshit, but no, you pulled this shit off," he said, just warming up. Then it was about the game's integrity and how he had to write about this in a report to the league office and then to the commissioner's office. When he finally stopped to take a breath, I said, "Frank, okay, it was wrong. I'm sorry, and it won't happen again. Honest to God, I thought you'd look at a ball before you put it in the game," I said, stating my case. Frank was on a roll, and he wasn't about to lose that head of steam. "So, it's my fault? My fault because I don't read the balls before putting them into the game, is that what you're saying? Now I gotta read the *bleepin'* balls before I throw them to the pitcher?" I wanted to respond but thought better of it.

As Frank paused, I heard muffled laughs from behind the wall in the bathroom. I looked at the wall and back at Frank. He had a sliver of a smile. Then the full force of pent-up laughter filled the room. The three other members of the crew were behind the wall, enjoying every minute of Frank's tirade. Frank got me and got me good. The other members of the crew came out, still laughing their asses off.

"Frank, if I . . . ," I started. "Uh-uh. Don't say a *bleepin'* word. I don't want to hear your bullshit story," he started. "Just shake my hand and promise me you won't do this again . . . then get your ass out of here," he finished. I shook his hand, looked at the crew, and said, "Gentlemen, see you tonight!"

All of this took place sometime in the early 1980s, though I can't pinpoint the exact date or even the year. After spending the last half of 1987 and all of 1988 and 1989 in the American League, I lost track of Frank.

Fast-forward to 1990. I returned to the National League with the Pirates in September and had just announced my retirement. Before the game in Pittsburgh on Monday, October 1, I stood in the bullpen as the umpires ran to their respective positions after the lineup cards were exchanged at home plate. I looked at the umpire making his way down the first base line, which was near my spot in the right-field bullpen. And there was Frank, with his back turned to me. He was a little grayer (who wasn't?), but still dared the game to come to him. I had to let him know I was there. And I knew just the way to do it.

I grabbed a new ball out of the bag, took out a pen, and signed it:

Frank,
May God Bless You!
Jerry Reuss

I instructed the ball boy located in front of the bullpen gate to give it to the umpire. I watched as Frank, who thought he was possibly getting another turd, read the ball.

Suddenly, his head dropped, and he turned to the bullpen with a smile as big as it was in the locker room back then and walked my way. I came out to meet him. Instead of shaking my hand, he gave me a hug. It surprised me in the same way a hug from an old friend from the past would.

"How you doing?" he said. "It's good to see you. I don't see many guys from your era still playing." "Frank, it's good to see you," I said. "Still enjoying the life?" I asked. "Yeah, but it's different now," he told me. "Everybody's gotten younger," he said with a sigh. "Look, the game's ready to start. I wish you the best!" he said as he turned. "Frank, good luck to you," I said. As I made my way back to the bullpen, he yelled at me. I turned around and he said, "Thanks for the ball. At least this time you owned up to it!"

The Breakfast of Champions

The path from my locker to the field at Dodger Stadium took me past everybody's locker. One Sunday morning as I headed for the field, I spotted Steve Yeager, who was in the early stages of getting dressed while sitting in his chair with a lit cigarette, stirring his coffee with cream and sugar, and eating a glazed donut. "You know, you're gonna be late and piss off Lasorda," I told him, knowing my inquiry would set him off.

"You worry about *you* being late, and I'll take care of *me*," he groused. "Besides, I need to eat something. I'm in there today," he said, taking a bite out of the donut. I looked at him and asked, "You're in there and that's what you're eating? That's hardly choosing from the four food groups," citing what I'd remembered from a report I wrote in high school. He swallowed and answered, "I'll be fine. Besides, I *am* eating from the four food groups." I wondered what four food groups he was thinking of. He gulped down his coffee and responded, "Yeah, sugar, fat, caffeine, and nicotine. Should be good for a few hits!" Who can argue with that?

1983: The Walk Year

After posting the three best years of my career from 1980 to 1982, I wanted to be absolutely sure I'd be in the best marketing position following 1983 as I reached the final year of my contract and free agency approached. Not fully learning the lesson from 1981 of what overwork did to my body, I rationalized that I would rather risk working too much as opposed to not enough. Besides, I would take some days off as a precaution. So I kept my off-season workouts at full speed from the end of the 1982 season through the winter.

I attended the January workouts at Dodger Stadium and hit the ground running once we arrived in spring training. But something was different. My baseball mojo was out of whack. And my left elbow showed some signs of strain.

On the field the year was split in three distinct sections. With a record of 5–1 on May 14, I was right where I wanted to be. Then the problems began. There were some tough-luck losses that followed, as I pitched ten innings against Houston on June 25, striking out eleven and walking none, when I experienced some elbow problems. I missed the next thirteen days and struggled in my next six starts before missing twelve days from July 30 to August 11. All told, in fourteen games started between May 20 and August 11, I went 1–9 but with an ERA during that period of sore elbow and bad mojo of 3.55. Once the elbow soreness disappeared, I was 6–1 in the ten games I started from August 16 through the stretch run, as we won the Western Division by three games over Atlanta.[2]

After losing to the Phillies in the playoffs, the time came to file for free agency. There was an exclusive negotiating period with the Dodgers, and I wanted to explore my options with them before looking at other possibilities. I wasn't interested in becoming the highest-paid player in the game. As long as the dollars slotted me among the other top pitchers in the game, staying with the Dodgers was my top priority. And why not? I had my best seasons in Los Angeles, and the Dodgers were willing to do whatever it took to win championships.

The Price Was Right

The Dodgers and I agreed to a four-year guaranteed contract with a fifth-year option in early November. There was an emotional toll that had to be paid for this contract. Even though I was able to compartmentalize the game on the field, the negotiations, and just life itself, there were moments when the stress from that moment of truth regarding the contract overwhelmed me. There were more than a few nights during the 1983 season that I tossed and turned. I hesitated taking or making phone calls to friends or family members because my contract status would inevitably come up. Mere mention of the contract from reporters, announcers, and other players started my heart racing. As the season progressed the stress intensified. The elephant in the room was making its presence known.

I don't know of any metric that quantifies the toll this stress had on me. I learned, however, that it found an outlet in 1984. But first . . .

A Standing Ovation from the LA Beat Writers

I had already played for three teams before landing with the Dodgers in 1979. And it takes a while to adjust to new surroundings: new teammates, a new city, a new organization, and a different group of writers who cover the club. The writers who covered the Dodgers during my tenure were a good group both professionally and personally. Instead of the every-man-for-himself attitude that I witnessed in other cities, these guys would share quotes and work as a team.

Of course, there was a break-in period for both the writers and a new player when he joined the club. The writers asked general questions after a game with hopes of landing a good quote. If they didn't get something they could use, they would ask a question to illicit a yes or no answer and then alter their question into a comment and attribute it to the player. Not exactly accurate, but their job is to report the game and make it an interesting read.

When I turned my career around in 1980, I still didn't trust any media types—meaning reporters, broadcasters, and even the Dodgers media department. For instance, when I was asked if this was my best season (it was), I was defensive and answered, "Up to this point, yes." The next question was "What was a better season?" "Probably 1975," I answered, still giving them virtually nothing. "Do you remember how that season went?" they pressed. "Not really. But isn't that info in the press guide? You can look it up," I responded. An interview with me was like pulling teeth.

Finally, after a few more press-guide references, they set me up. After a win on a shutout at Dodger Stadium, I was asked about the most shutouts that I had in a season. "Guys, it's all there in the guide," I answered as nicely as I could. At that point, all ten or so of them reached in their pocket, whipped out the press guide, and went directly to the sentence about my best season for shutouts.

Gordy Verrell, then with the *Long Beach Press-Telegram*, read aloud: "Had six shutouts in 1975 . . ." Another writer continued, "tying him for second in the National League." Gordy looked at me and said, "Thanks for all those references to this handy guide. We'd have never known if you hadn't pointed it out." There was a pause. "Okay, I understand. Your point is well taken," I told them. "I'll give you whatever you need." After that verbal attitude adjustment, we never had another problem with an interview.

Players and the media seldom met socially, as if it were an unwritten code. Players avoided talking to media other than in postgame sessions lest they be branded as a leak if something unfavorable appeared in a newspaper or on TV. Reporters and broadcasters stayed away from the players socially because they had to maintain the air of impartiality in their work. That code was put aside on a train ride from Philadelphia to New York on a warm summer evening in August 1983.

The Dodgers beat the Phillies 8–3 on August 28, 1983. It was a Sunday day game, and afterward the team boarded buses to make the trip to our next series in New York. I pitched a complete game that day and asked Lasorda if I could take the train to New York, as I had a business meeting with members of a public relations firm. Tom said it was okay, if I'd give him a call once I got there.

I had my meeting, boarded the train to New York, and took a seat in the back of the dining car. As I pulled a book from my briefcase and got comfortable, I noticed the LA writers were riding in the front of the same car, near the bar. I waved, sat down, and opened my book.

Terry Johnson (T.J. as he was known) of the *Pasadena Star-News* came back to my seat with an interesting proposition. I would be welcome to sit with the "dignitaries" (the name he chose for the writers; players were known as "oafs") if I wished. However, I would have to pay the same initiation fee as a new beat writer would. "Just what is the initiation fee?" I asked curiously. "You would have to purchase a round of drinks for the dignitaries," he said seriously. "T.J., I'm honored that you would ask. Sure, I'll pay the price," I said with a smile.

Because the trip to Philadelphia was the first leg of a three-city trip that included New York and Montreal, I had cash in my pocket. With T.J. and the *slant* of dignitaries,[3] I made my way to the front of the car to the makeshift bar. As the writers hovered, I pulled out a crisp, clean hundred-dollar bill, put it on the bar, and said to the bartender, "The first twenty is yours. The remainder will be for these fine gentlemen. Please, make sure their glasses are never empty. If you need more, just let me know." I turned, looked at the ten or twelve writers, as they stood wide-eyed with their mouths open in amazement, and told them, "Enjoy! The honor is mine."

As I made my way back to my seat, I heard the deafening applause. To my knowledge, it was the only time in baseball history that a player received a standing ovation from sportswriters.

"Bring in the Right-Hander!"

When I pitched I liked to work fast and control the pace of the game. I didn't like casual visits from infielders, pitching coaches, or managers. I tolerated catchers only because of their instant feedback. The pitching mound was my place of work. I had a job to do. And no one was welcome without an invitation.

Of course, there were some memorable meetings on the mound with Lasorda. Once, he came out to talk to me, and I immediately told him to get the hell off my mound. He looked at me and asked, "It's your mound, huh? Who the hell gave it to you? Me, that's who! I can give it to you, and I can take it away. Right now, I'm giving it to Castillo." He turned to the home-plate umpire and said, "Bring in the right-hander!" I guess he wasn't that impressed with my approach.

One night during a rain delay, Tom was telling the story about a shortstop who had a rough game while playing in a game he pitched. When the manager came to take Lasorda out of the game, Tom told him to take the shortstop out of the game. "Hell, I'm pitching a pretty good ball game. He's the one who's struggling. Take his ass out." What pitcher can't relate to that story?

While pitching in a game a few starts later, Dodger shortstop Bill Russell had an awful game in the field behind me. He booted a ball for an error and threw another one away for another error. I gave up a couple of hits, and the wheels fell off the wagon. So out of the dugout came Lasorda.

He made his way to the mound and waited before signaling for a reliever. I knew he was going to take me out, so I thought I'd give it my best shot to stay in the game. "Hey, you remember that story you told us on the last trip about the shortstop who had a bad game while you were pitching?" I asked. "Yeah. What about it?" he asked. "You gotta chance right now to correct that injustice!" I said. "What the hell are you talking about?" he asked. "Go over to Russell, talk to him, and then signal for Derrel Thomas to replace him. Hey, I'm only asking you to do the same thing you wanted your manager to do." He started laughing. "You are crazy. And you gotta a lot of me in you. I like that. What I don't like is the fact we're three runs down." He turned to the umpire and said, "Bring in the right-hander!"

For a while Steve Yeager caught me exclusively. Over time we developed a rhythm. And we were winning some games. All was right with the world. Only this night in Dodger Stadium, it wasn't happening. True, I was struggling, but I knew I had enough left in the tank to complete the inning. Also, I knew when Lasorda came out of the dugout that he wanted to make a pitching change. So I had to head him off at the pass.

"Okay, just hear me out!" I said when he got to the mound. "I can tell by the way you walked out here you want to take me out of the game. I want to stay in it. That's one vote for and a vote against the change. How about letting the democratic process determine this move and have Yeager cast the deciding vote?" I was shocked that he agreed to it. So when Yeager got to the mound, Tom told him, "He wants to stay in; I wanna take him out. You cast the deciding vote." I figured, "I'm so still in this game. Me and the Boomer are tight!" Yeager looked at me, then Lasorda, and said, "You should've taken him out two innings ago."

As my mouth dropped to my belt, I dejectedly gave Lasorda the ball, but as I started my trip to the dugout, Lasorda grabbed my arm and said, "Is this a great country or what? Even on the mound at Dodger Stadium, we see democracy in action! Now get your ass outta here!" He looked at the home-plate umpire and said, "Bring in the right-hander!"

Rub-a-Dubbin' in the Tub

After a spring-training workout was finished in early-March 1984, Lasorda chose some players for extra batting practice at Holman Stadium, as he wanted to throw that extra BP. Fans who stuck around were treated to a show of nonstop taunts, encouragement, and challenges issued by the man on the mound. Usually, he threw for twenty minutes, thirty minutes if he really felt good. This particular day he overdid it and threw for an hour!

By the time he made it across the fields to the training room, he was struggling mightily from the heat. With his clothes dripping and his skin turning white, he made it to the clubhouse, where team personnel attended to him. Trainer Bill Buhler filled the whirlpool with cool water, knowing this was the best way to bring Tom's temperature down. Getting him in there was a different story. "I've never been in the whirlpool . . . and I'm not starting now!" he proclaimed. Finally, Lasorda listened to Buhler and got in the tub. But he wouldn't stop talking.

While I worked my free-weight program (the training room was dual purpose, as it also served as a weight room), I heard Lasorda's story over and over whenever someone new entered the training room.

Finally, Tom stopped talking about his BP session. Instead, he talked about how great the whirlpool was. "Now I know why guys love this so much. This tub is outstanding!" he said at the top of his voice. I had heard enough. It was time to take one for the team.

So I walked over to the tub and said to him, "Hey, Skip, tell me about your day." He started about the BP again. "Sounds like you had quite a time," I said. "But I'm surprised to see you in the tub. How does it feel after your workout?" He answered, "This is the greatest thing going." I asked, "Is it that good?" He put his head back and said, "It's the best!" I peeled off my shorts, climbed in the pool, and lowered myself right between his feet. "Oh no you don't," he screamed as I took a seat on top of his feet. "You can't . . . Dammit . . . No. Get out!" he yelled. Once settled, I wiggled my toes, touching the skipper in a place where the sun never shines, and he got the giggles. "Hey," I said. "You're right! This does feel pretty good." He started yelling, but with one more wiggle I tamed the beast yet again, as he started laughing. "Now," I said quietly, "let's talk about my day."

1984: My First Trip to the Disabled List

After signing with the Dodgers in the winter of 1983, the elephant in the room disappeared. However, the notoriety of the new contract caused people to react differently to me. There was no more performing for the big payday in their eyes. Now, the expectations were to justify the investment. I didn't anticipate this reaction. But it wasn't going to be a problem. I was determined to perform at the same level I did for the previous four years.

I started my Nautilus program in December, much like I had since 1980. While working the overhead press in January, I heard a pop in my left elbow. After X-rays at Dr. Jobe's office, I was diagnosed with a loose bone chip that had to be removed immediately. Because the surgery, performed by Dr. Jobe on January 24, was arthroscopic, my down time was minimized. Still, my routine was altered. I didn't throw before spring training, and I couldn't perform any weight work that involved my left elbow.[4]

I had no problems with my elbow through spring training, but I was behind the other pitchers in camp so the Dodgers kept me in Vero for another week to work in some Minor League games.

My elbow surgery seemed to be a thing of the past after I beat the Cubs in my first start on April 9. Then I experienced inflammation on the inside part of my elbow after my next two starts. This put me out of commission for the next sixteen days.[5]

During spring training I noticed that pain in both heels had worsened. When I returned to Los Angeles, X-rays diagnosed the problem as bone spurs. Bill Buhler, the trainer, cut out some heel pads for my shoes, which helped some. Eventually, I needed cortisone shots to handle the inflammation. To make matters worse, I pulled my right hamstring running to first base in a game against Montreal. It cost me another two starts.[6]

With my heels and elbow hurting after a game against Houston, I was put on the disabled list for the first time in my career on June 7. To ease the elbow pain, Dr. Jobe gave me a series of cortisone shots around the inside of my elbow. Dr. William Wagner, a foot specialist located in Whittier, gave me a cortisone shot in each heel. It seemed I spent more time visiting doctors than I spent on the field.

The pain in the elbow gradually subsided, and I was activated on July 11. I pitched once in relief and started a game in Pittsburgh on July 18. I lasted all of eighteen pitches, the first seven of which were balls. After three runs, two walks, two singles, a double, and a ground out, my night was finished. It was the low point for my season and one of many low points during my career. I believed I was throwing okay, but Lasorda saw things differently. "He had nothing on the ball, absolutely nothing."[7]

I pitched out of the bullpen through August 26, a total of fourteen games. Gradually, my elbow came around. Although I had a few early bumps in the road, I allowed just two earned runs over my last eight innings, all pitched in relief. That was good enough to earn another start.

I pitched six innings against the Mets, giving up just a run on five hits. It was not a great game but good enough for me to turn the corner. I finished the season, winning three of my next four decisions. Over the course of those seven starts, I pitched fifty-one innings, allowing just thirteen earned runs. I was back on course, and my confidence was restored.[8]

The elbow inflammation was gone. The pulled hamstring was nothing more than a blip on the radar screen. And the bone spurs on my heels, well, that was a different story. They had to be removed.

Dr. Wagner performed the surgery on October 26. I was on crutches through the holidays. The 1984 season began with a surgery and ended with another surgery. I took an extra sip of champagne on New Year's Eve when the clock stuck 12:00, bidding good riddance to a lousy baseball season.

"Sorry, I Didn't Catch the Name"

During the season at Dodger Stadium on any given night, there could be a celebrity sighting in the clubhouse. Let me drop some names: Don Rickles, Burt Reynolds, Tom Selleck, Jonathan Winters, Jerry Vale, Ed McMahon—all visited Lasorda's office during the eight years I played for the Dodgers. Also, there were couples, Jane Fonda and her husband at that time, Tom Hayden, Ryan O'Neal and the late Farrah Fawcett, and the governor of Kentucky, John Y. Brown and his wife, Phyllis George, whom I met in the small lobby that connected the clubhouse, manager's office, video room, ramp to the dugout, and . . . the restroom. Had Phyllis, the former Miss America and CBS Sports broadcaster, walked into the lobby a few seconds sooner, she would have caught a few players standing at the urinal, doing their business in various stages of undress. That's just not the way one wanted to be remembered by this classy couple.

Once while returning to the clubhouse from the weight room (fully dressed, mind you), I opened the door and saw Lasorda and two guys my size wearing three-piece suits hovering around a smaller gentleman. As I tried to walk by, Lasorda grabbed my arm, swung me around, and said to the smaller guest, "And this is Jerry Reuss." When the suits parted, there was Frank Sinatra. He put his hand out and said, "Nice to meet you!" I shook his hand and said, "Sorry, I didn't catch the name." Instinctively, the suits reached for the bulge inside the breast pocket of their coats, as Lasorda held his breath after muttering something like, "Oh, shit."

Mr. Sinatra (in case the suits read this book) broke into a huge smile and said, "Schwartz, Heime Schwartz!" and laughed. The hands dropped to the sides of the suits, and Tom, who broke into a sweat, started laughing and told Mr. Sinatra, "This was the one I told you about." I went about my business after I said, "It was a pleasure to meet you as well. Thanks for stopping by!"

"Don't Look at the Horse's Balls!"

I was never one to embrace baseball superstitions. I never had a lucky piece of clothing or any kind of ritual that could turn the fortunes of a game to my personal advantage. Former teammate and broadcast partner Rick Monday once admitted on the air that he didn't believe in superstitions. "They're all bad luck," he said with a straight face.

It amused me to watch other players give in to this behavior. For example, when taking the field, many players jumped over the foul lines, as if they were avoiding a pile of dog shit. Or they would cross themselves, thinking the good Lord would bless this at bat. Never mind the fact that the pitcher could neutralize the effort by merely crossing himself!

One universal bad-luck omen in Chicago among players on all

the teams I played for had to do with viewing the statue of General Phillip Sheridan mounted on his anatomically correct horse. Located at the intersection of North Lakeshore Drive and West Belmont Avenue, it's along the route between the downtown hotel and Wrigley Field. Looking at the horse's balls guaranteed a prolonged slump, the legend went. The true believers were easy to spot, as their heads would turn the other way when the bus approached.

I made it a point to check out the good general and his steed because there were a number of times those brass balls were painted in the colors of the team that preceded us. I guess other clubs had their own way of dealing with perceived misfortune.

I didn't worry about a Chicago slump because I thought that had more to do with players challenging the bars on Rush Street at night with a day game a few hours away. Rush Street still owns a perfect record against every player who tried to challenge it.

The wind direction was more of a determining factor on days I pitched at Wrigley. When the wind blew in from the lake, I liked my chances. When it blew out, it could be a tough day. Overall, in the twenty-five games I pitched there, I was 4–9 with a 5.09 ERA. The wind had something to do with my numbers, but pitch location was a much bigger factor. Peeping at the horse's balls didn't figure in the outcome at all.[9]

I remembered the tale during my three-year tenure as a Dodger radio analyst. On the way to Wrigley for a game in 2006, I viewed the monument, thought about the superstition, and chuckled. "There's no way the legend can affect me now," I thought. "I'm immune."

Around the fourth inning I came down with a case of laryngitis and couldn't finish the game. Was it merely a coincidence? Or did the legend of the horse's balls finally catch up with me?

Rebounding from a Disappointing 1984

It was a new beginning for me in the spring of 1985. Because there were no aftereffects from either surgery, I could work as I did two springs ago. At the January winter workouts, I noticed that the spikes I wore in 1984 were a size too small. My feet expanded to a larger size because I no longer had to scrunch my toes to minimize the pain in my heels. That meant all new shoes.

It appeared the mojo had returned, as I won five games in spring training—the same total I had during the 1984 regular season. I noticed another subtle difference. My pitches lost a bit of the sharpness and velocity that I had a few years back. At the time I didn't know if it was because of the surgery or because I was thirty-five years old and time was catching up with me. With the normal aches and pains lasting a few days longer than they did in the past, I had my answer soon enough.

Four seasons removed from the world champs of 1981, this Dodger team had a different look, as Lopes, Smith, Monday, Garvey, Cey, and Baker were gone and Russell and Yeager were delegated to backup roles. Orel Hershiser was poised for a breakout year, as Fernando was the leader of the staff. The names in the lineup included Steve Sax, Mike Marshall, Dave Anderson, and Mike Scioscia. It was a talented group, but the team didn't jell until we obtained veterans Enos Cabell in mid-July and Bill Madlock at the trade deadline on August 31. We finished five and a half games ahead of the Reds to win the Western Division and redeem ourselves from a fourth-place finish in 1984. Our opponents in the playoffs would be the Cardinals.

I learned not to take a healthy season for granted. I finished with a record of 14–10, fourth best on this club.[10]

"We Will Not Pitch to Jack Clark with the Game on the Line"

When the Dodgers celebrated the twenty-fifth anniversary of the 1981 world championship in September 2006, they sponsored a luncheon in the Stadium Club and invited fans to participate in a Q&A session with the players, coaches, and manager. It didn't take long for one of the fans to ask Lasorda, "Why did you pitch to Jack

Clark in 1985?" Tom took the high road in his response and told the well-meaning fan, "If I'd known he was going to hit a home run, I would've walked him!" It brought the house down with laughter, then applause. Lasorda continued, "As manager, I'm entitled to the first guess. Everyone else gets to second-guess!" There was more applause as the program moved on.

What's hard for me to believe is how that one decision has, in many ways, defined Lasorda's managerial career in the minds of so many baseball fans. In his defense let's look at the numbers. He managed 1,599 wins (nineteenth best in Major League history), and his teams made it to the postseason seven times, the World Series four times, while winning it twice. He was elected to baseball's Hall of Fame in 1997. Off the field he's supported the military, numerous police and fire departments, and charities of all kinds as well as raised money for hospitals and schools. He also managed the gold medal—winning USA baseball team in the 2000 Olympics. Yet fans still want to know about Jack Clark. Tom probably doesn't discuss it anymore, but I was there and because this is my story, I'll tell you what I remember.[11]

Prior to the October 9 League Championship Series opener with St. Louis, Lasorda, the coaches, and Dodger advance scouts held a meeting in the Dodger clubhouse to discuss in detail the tendencies of each Cardinal player. When Lasorda got to Jack Clark, he told everyone in the room that "Clark is the only legitimate home run threat on their club, and he's especially tough in the clutch. We will not pitch to Jack Clark with the game on the line." Lasorda paused as he scoured the room, allowing his words to sink indelibly into the minds of all in attendance.

We won the first two games in Los Angeles, as the Cardinals took all three games in St. Louis. We had to win the next two games at home to advance to the World Series. We led the sixth game at the end of six innings by a score of 4–1.

In the top of the seventh, the Cardinals knocked Hershiser out of the game, scoring two runs on three singles and another run against Tom Niedenfuer when Ozzie Smith, whose home run beat Niedenfuer in Game Five in St. Louis, tripled in that extra run, as St. Louis tied the game at 4–4. With Smith on third base, Niedenfuer struck out Jack Clark and Andy Van Slyke to end the threat. Niedenfuer retired the Cardinals in order in the top of the eighth. Mike Marshall's homer gave us the lead again, 5–4, in our half of the eighth.

In the top of the ninth, Cedeño struck out, McGee singled and stole second base, Ozzie Smith walked, and Tommy Herr grounded out to first with the pitcher covering. On the play both McGee and Smith advanced, leaving first base open and Jack Clark coming to the plate. The career matchup between Clark and Niedenfuer showed a definite advantage to the pitcher (Clark versus Niedenfuer: 17 at bats, 4 hits, 0 homers, 1 walk, and 4 strikeouts).[12]

I was in the Dodger bullpen, warming up next to right-hander Kenny Howell. We were both ready to go into the game, as we looked at the scorecard with the lineups posted on the wall behind us. With first base open and Clark coming to the plate, we figured that Lasorda would walk Clark intentionally (Lasorda's words during the meeting were still ringing in our ears) and bring Van Slyke to the plate with the bases loaded and two outs. After walking Clark, Lasorda had to choose among three possible scenarios: let Niedenfuer face Van Slyke, replace Niedenfuer with Howell, or replace Niedenfuer with me. Chances are if Lasorda brought me in, Whitey Herzog would have countered with right-handed-hitting Brian Harper.[13]

Both Kenny and I waited to see what Lasorda would do. There was no visit to the mound, which was curious, but when we saw Niedenfuer go into his stretch, I looked at Kenny and said, "He's not going to pitch to him, is he?" Kenny responded, "I thought we weren't going to pitch to Clark with the game on the line." We watched Clark swing, and before we heard the crack of the bat, we knew the first pitch was heading deep into the left-field bleachers.

We watched left-fielder Pete Guerrero throw his glove to the ground and then looked at one another in silence. What could we say?

Clark's three-run homer gave the Cardinals a 7–5 lead and, after a 1–2–3 Dodger ninth inning, the ticket to the 1985 World Series. By the time our bullpen crew made their way to the clubhouse, everyone else was already there, removing their uniforms as a tearful Lasorda closed the door and made an impromptu speech. "I lost it for you guys. We worked so damn hard to get here, and we lost the game like that," he said, finally losing his composure. Hershiser stood up, put his arm around a weeping Lasorda, and told him, "We win as a team, and we lose as a team."

According to newspaper accounts, Lasorda handled the postgame interviews with class. He told Thomas Boswell of the *Washington Post*, "'I feel like jumping off the nearest bridge,' the Los Angeles manager said. 'If Jack Clark makes an out, I look good. But he hits a homer, and even my wife knows I should've walked him.'" Boswell continued, "Sure, it was a bonehead move to let Clark hit when Lasorda had the choice of forcing Andy Van Slyke (.091 in the playoffs) to face Niedenfuer, or else making Brian Harper (.000) win the pennant against left-hander Jerry Reuss."[14]

Lasorda told the Associated Press, "I decided to pitch to Clark because Niedenfuer had struck him out in the seventh. If he had hit a long fly ball for the final out, nobody would be talking about it," said a dejected Lasorda. "After he hit the home run, everybody in the world knows I should have walked him. If you second-guess anybody, second-guess me. I'm the guy who made the decision."[15]

Probably the most curious quote by Lasorda appeared in the *Los Angeles Times*. "The last three times Clark had come to the plate with a man in scoring position and first base open, Lasorda had ordered him walked. But this time, the left-handed Van Slyke was the next batter, not Cedeno. 'If I had a left-handed pitcher up, then it would have been a different story,' said Lasorda, who did have a left-hander ready—Jerry Reuss—but didn't use him."[16]

Did Lasorda forget that he had me warming up when Clark came to the plate, or, while sorting through the aftermath of his decision, did he forgot that I was ready in the bullpen when Gordon Edes was interviewing him?

Niedenfuer handled the postgame interview with the grace and class of a seasoned veteran. "I'm proud that I have the ability to be the person on the mound in that situation. . . . I wanted to succeed . . . but I failed. . . . [I]n about four days, I'll start working out, trying to improve for next year."[17]

I liked Lasorda's first guess on a possible Clark scenario during our preseries meeting. "Don't pitch to Clark with the game on the line." That was my opinion in that meeting, and it hasn't changed over the years. Lasorda second-guessed himself when he decided to pitch to Clark. However, though I didn't agree with Tom in choosing to pitch to Clark, I respected and supported his right as a manager to make that decision.

The World's Most Expensive Hot Dog

Lunch at one thirty or two just didn't always carry me through the rest of the day. The peanut butter and jelly or baloney in the food room at the ballpark just didn't satisfy my craving. I needed something more substantial. I needed a concession-stand delicacy, the spicy dog (otherwise known as a heart attack in a bun) with a huge squirt of mustard.

Of course, the best time to get them was around the second inning, when I was supposed to be on the bench. No problem. I gave Mitch Poole, who was a clubhouse attendant during my Dodger years and is the current Dodgers equipment manager, five dollars, which meant one for me and one more for him. I came into the clubhouse during the bottom of the second inning and found my treat under my jacket. I went to my hiding place on the stairs just outside the clubhouse and took my first bite. It was a little taste of heaven—at least it was until the clubhouse doors opened and Lasorda caught me.

"That's twenty-five dollars!" he says matter-of-factly as I chewed my spicy dog. "You know, you could buy a steak dinner at Chasen's for twenty-five dollars." I didn't say a word. I got caught. What could I say?

Tom headed to the food room, made a gigantic baloney sandwich, and came out talking while he's eating. I couldn't understand a word of it, but I knew it was more about the fine. Finally, he had to swallow. So I told him, "At least if I spent twenty-five dollars at Chasen's for a steak dinner, I could eat it in peace. I'll have the fine on your desk before I go home. I'll see you on the bench in five minutes . . . assuming you're finished by then." He looked at me, looked at his half-pound of baloney, and shook his head as I headed to the dugout.

After the game I went in his office to pay the fine. He told me, "Keep it. If I fine you, I have to fine me for doing the same thing." "Thanks," I told him, understanding that the rules applied to everybody. "Next time, find a better hiding place," he said with a smile as I walked away.

Where Else Could You Get a Dozen Pizzas for Fifty Dollars?

While waiting at the Montreal gate for our charter return to Los Angeles, Lasorda remarked that we would have to stop in Chicago to refuel. I could see he was annoyed, so I thought I'd stoke the fire. "So, what's the problem with Chicago? You're big there, aren't you?" I asked him. "I'm *big* everywhere," he shot back. "What's it to you?" I returned the volley, "How *big* are you?" He fired a verbal knockdown in a voice loud enough for everyone in our travel party to hear, "How *big* do I need to be?" He had everybody's attention and made a big deal out of it. "Are you big enough to have a dozen pizzas delivered to the plane when we land?" I asked, setting the hook. "That depends," he said. "How much you wanna bet?" I pulled out my wallet and saw a crisp, new fifty-dollar bill, the last remnant of the meal money passed out ten days ago. "I got this brand-new fifty-dollar bill if you think you can do it," I told him with a tone of challenge in my voice. He smirked and said, "I wouldn't think of doing this for less than a hundred dollars. But, because it's you, nothing would give me greater pleasure than taking that fifty dollars from you, you smartass!" So now the trip to Chicago had a real purpose.

When we landed at O'Hare and pulled up to the gate, I'll be damned if there wasn't a kid out on the tarmac with a mountain of pizza boxes in his arms, waiting for steps to be pushed to the plane's front door. Once the steps were in place, the door opened and the kid with the pizzas entered.

Lasorda greeted him, grabbed the microphone, and called me up front. "I bet Reuss fifty dollars that I could have a dozen pizzas delivered when we landed here. I want him to pay up in front of all of you!" he announced boldly. I happily gave him the fifty dollars, grabbed the mic, and told everybody, "Where else could you get twelve pizzas for fifty bucks? The food's on me, everybody. Enjoy!" To my surprise the cabin filled with applause. I shook Tom's hand, grabbed a few boxes, and distributed them to my appreciative teammates as I made my way to my seat, accepting high-fives the whole way. It took Tom a few minutes to realize he had just been had.

"I Can Start or Pitch Out of the Bullpen"

In spring training of 1986 with many of my contemporaries from the 1981 world championship club playing elsewhere, I knew instinctively my days as a Dodger were numbered. With Valenzuela, Hershiser, Welch, Honeycutt, and Pena all younger (Honeycutt, at thirty-two, was the only starter, besides me at thirty-seven, who was over thirty years old), I heard the whispers of the Los Angeles media.

At first the questions were subtle. "Do you see your role as changing now that you're the elder statesman?" "Do younger players ask you for advice more than ever before?" I tried a simple "No, not really" answer to both questions, and it may have appeared in print as "As the elder statesman of this club, I don't see my role changing," or "Young players aren't asking me for advice any more this year than in other years." It was more of the same old shit. I didn't make a big deal out of the manufactured quotes because I learned by this time to pick and choose my battles.

However, when the questions pointed to a possible trade, I decided to have some fun with it. "Did you know there were scouts watching you pitch today?" was a question asked on a daily basis from a number of different writers. "Really?" I asked in mock amazement. "I hope they liked what they saw. By the way, who was here?" And they gave me a list from their notes. So I kept a list for myself.

If I remember correctly, nearly every team saw me pitch that spring. In fact, I met the writers in the pressroom after a game (something players weren't allowed to do) with a notepad and pen to record the names of the teams and the scouts. I commented about a team or a scout, "Hey, he's their top guy. I'm flattered!" or "How much would it cost the Dodgers to have them take me?" The writers liked the exchange because (1) they didn't have to walk in the locker room, ask a question, and wait for a response and (2) it was better than the yes and no answers.

I told Gordon Edes of the *Los Angeles Times* that I suspected the Dodgers were actively trying to trade me. "There are three signs you're about to be traded," I said. "One, Al [Campanis] says there's no trade in the making; two, Lasorda says he loves you like a son; and three, you get your meal money one day at a time!" At least these quotes were my own.[18]

This kind of exchange continued into the season. Writers from across the country read what their counterparts were writing, and when the team came to town they were ready with their own questions. "Do you feel as if you're auditioning for your next job?" was one question I heard. "Would you waive your no-trade clause for a deal with [name the club]?" was another. Mind you, I didn't mind the attention. It's just that nobody wants to deal with this kind of attention. It forced its presence in the clubhouse and made everybody uncomfortable.

My way of handling a situation like this was to do something so off the wall that it would remove the tension and make life fun for me, as well as my teammates. Timing was essential. The baseball gods presented me with the perfect opportunity on May 6, 1986, in Chicago. Both the Cubs and the White Sox had home games scheduled with the Dodgers and Yankees, respectively. It was one of those rare occasions when the true Chicago baseball fan could enjoy an afternoon game at Wrigley and a night game at Comiskey. It was also a chance for me to pull off one of my best pranks in front of baseball writers from three major markets.

After we lost a tough game to the Cubs on a Leon Durham walk-off homer in the ninth, I sat at my locker and answered questions from the Chicago writers about trade rumors. Someone brought up the Yankees as a possible trade partner and that they were playing the Sox tonight, and suddenly I thought this was the perfect stage.

Rick Honeycutt had the locker right next to mine. So I asked him, "How far is Comiskey from here?" Rick had spent his first four years in the majors with Seattle and the next three with Texas before he joined the Dodgers in 1983. He said, "It's not that far, maybe a half hour by cab. Why?" "I think I'm going to trade myself to the Yankees," I told him.

"You what?" Rick asked. "Yeah, I'll pack my bag with towels and walk right into the Yankees' clubhouse and tell Piniella I'm now a Yankee," I boldly told a confused Honeycutt. "You think you can just walk into the Yankees' clubhouse and pull this off?" he asked as his interest was piqued. "I can . . . and I will!" I answered, as the idea now became a personal challenge. "Mind if I come along?" he asked, as he started laughing. "I gotta see this!" "I insist on it,"

I told him. "After all, I need someone to point me to the visitors' locker room at Comiskey," I answered matter-of-factly.

In a *where no man has gone before* scenario like this, it's prudent to do one's homework. Not knowing Lou, except by reputation, I wanted to get an idea of how he might handle it. Lou was in his first year as a manager, and he had just been suspended for two games. And it was only May. So I went to the best source I knew, Tom Lasorda!

I walked into Lasorda's office while he was eating, which meant every man for himself. "Hey, Tom," I asked while keeping a distance from his fork. "What do you want?" he growled with his mouth full. "How well do you know Piniella?" I asked. "He's Italian [actually, he isn't], ain't he? He's gotta be a good guy!" Tom answered, spewing with every word. "Why all this interest in him?" Lasorda asked.

I told Lasorda my plan. He stopped eating and started laughing. "You're one crazy son of a bitch! It's not enough that you torment me every day, now you want to *bleep* with a manager from another team," he said. "What the hell! Go for it. If I tell you not to do it, you're gonna do it anyway!" he said shaking his head. "Now, get your ass out of here," he said as he shoveled another bite in his mouth. Because this was the way most of my visits to his office ended, I figured I had his blessing.

I went back to my locker and packed my travel bag with towels. Honeycutt asked me what Lasorda said. "He told me to go for it! And he thinks it's a great idea! Personally, I think he hopes Lou will keep me," I told Rick. We made our way through the Wrigley faithful, bag full of towels in tow, and jumped into a cab.

Rick's directions to the visitors' clubhouse at Comiskey Park were on the mark. As we got out of the cab and I grabbed my overstuffed bag, he told me, "I can't believe you're going to do this! This is going to be great," he said with the excitement of a kid anticipating Christmas morning. I took a deep breath and said, "Show time!"

We walked to the clubhouse door, and I told the guard, "Hi, I'm

Jerry Reuss, and I just got traded to the Yankees." He looked at the Dodger bag draped over my shoulder and said, "Welcome to the American League!"

Rick and I entered the Yankee clubhouse that was full of players, coaches, and reporters, as the team had just come off the field after batting practice. The players were in various stages of undress as I walked in, and I asked in a voice loud enough for all to hear, "Which way is Lou's office?" As I walked ten to twenty steps to the manager's office, I saw the looks on the players' faces that seemed to ask, "Now what the hell is going on? Who the *bleep* is he and [most important!] who's gone?" I heard a voice from the coaches' area, say, "Goddammit! George [Steinbrenner] told me he'd let me know when he made a deal! Look at this shit! No *bleepin'* respect!"

Lou's door was closed. I knocked, and a voice from behind it told me to come in. There was Lou, putting on his underwear, as he was suspended and wouldn't be dressing for tonight's game. I approached his desk, held out my free hand, and introduced myself. "Hi, Lou. I'm Jerry Reuss. I can start or pitch relief for you. I'm proud to join the Yankee organization," I said with such complete earnestness that even I believed it. He shook my hand and said with a puzzled look on his face, "I know who you are. What the hell is this about?" I threw my bag on his desk as papers started flying in every direction. "Well, the Dodgers were in town playing the Cubs, and they told me after the game that the deal was made," I told him, absolutely loving the exchange.

Lou was getting annoyed. "What the *bleep* are you talking about? Nobody told me about a deal with the Dodgers!" "Lou, I'm just going by what I was told. I'm shocked that you, the manager of the Yankees, knew nothing about this," I responded sincerely. "Oh, I'll find out what this is about, you can bet on that!" he muttered as he continued to dress.

He turned his back and muttered something that sounded like "Bullshit!" and "Dammit!" One look in his eyes as he turned to face me, and I knew that slow burn was turning to a boil. It was time to come clean.

I opened my bag to expose the towels. He looked at me rather confused. So I told him the story, beginning with the trade rumors. When I finished he looked at me, smiled, and shook his head just like Lasorda did.

"You went through all of this as a joke?" he asked. He laughed and said, "You know, you would fit in here." "I appreciate your sense of humor," I told him as I stood up and zipped the bag. "You have a game. I better get out of here." I grabbed the bag and made my way to the door. "Like hell you will!" he barked. "This is the first laugh I had in a while. Sit down. I'm suspended. I'm not going anywhere. I'll let you know when you can leave," he told me. (What is this "stay-leave" power trip with managers and umpires?)

When I finally left Lou's office, there was Honeycutt laughing his ass off. "You wouldn't believe what happened while you were in there," he told me with a glimmer in his eye. "I told them what you were doing with Lou, but only after I told them about the deal. You wouldn't believe the reaction. I couldn't keep a straight face," he told me. "Let me tell you about what happened with Lou," I said with a big smile on my face.

We exchanged our stories as we walked out of the clubhouse, through the gates, and to the curb. We looked at each other and started laughing again as we waited for a cab to take us back to our hotel. I asked Rick, "Are you hungry? Let's get something to eat." I paused. "I thought that went well!"

1986: The Beginning of the End of My Dodger Days

As I approached my thirty-seventh birthday, my body was in the process of betraying me. Muscle soreness stuck around a few days longer, and I had to back off my training. Because of knee problems, I missed my first start in spring training. I missed another start because of a sore throat.

Probably what mattered most was that I couldn't fully straighten my left elbow because of a bone spur that developed after the bone-chip surgery of 1984. That caused a lack of feel in my fingertips when I released a pitch, which affected the movement and command of my pitches. Although I pitched some good games, I struggled through the All-Star break. I tried everything to get the finish on my pitches, but nothing seemed to work. So Dr. Jobe and I decided the bone spur had to go. I had surgery on July 22. The estimated time for return to action was five weeks. As that five-week period came to an end, my elbow still wouldn't straighten, and I was nowhere near ready to return.

I was in the training room before a night game at Dodger Stadium when Al Campanis called and wanted to talk to me. This was the only time I can remember Al wanting to talk to a player in the training room. If Al wanted to meet with a player, coach, or manager, he would hold the meeting in the manager's office.

He got right to the point. "Jobe told me you'd be ready in five weeks, and the trainers tell me that won't happen. What gives?" Calmly, I told Al, "I've been in the training room every day since I was released from the hospital doing everything the trainers tell me to do. But you already know that, Al, because you read their daily reports." That's not what he wanted to hear. Al, with frustration in his voice, said, "This is what I know! Jobe said five weeks. The trainers said they're doing everything they can possibly do, and you're still not ready." He paused as if to carefully measure what he wanted to say next. I wouldn't let him speak because I knew where he was going. He wanted to pin the blame on me.

Choosing my words carefully, I responded to Al, "I'm here every day before any of the other players get here and begin the work prescribed for me by the trainers. I precisely complete every set of exercises while they watch. I ask every day if there's any more that I can do, and every day they tell me not to overdo it. When I finish my work in the training room, I'm on the field, keeping my legs in shape. Now, if you have anything in mind that would get me back into action any quicker, I'd like to hear it." With his frustration turning to anger, Al told me, "I'll get to the bottom of this!" And with that he hung up.

When Dr. Jobe arrived at the park before the game, I gave him a heads-up regarding my conversation with Al. With the patience of Job, he explained that the five-week recovery period was just an estimate and he would tell that to Al later that evening. I never heard from Campanis again on the matter.

I had two more appearances in 1986. One was in relief on September 12, and the other was a start against San Diego on the twenty-fifth. I took myself out of the game after giving up just a run in four innings because of the pain in my left elbow. It was a fitting end to a most disappointing season. At the start of the year, I envisioned winning fifteen to eighteen games. By the end of the season, my concern was if my elbow would heal well enough to continue pitching. I would get my answer in the spring of 1987.

Cast from the Garden of Eden

After my first tosses during the Dodgers' winter workouts in January 1987, I knew the inflammation was absent from my left elbow. After elbow pain in 1984 and 1986, I renewed my appreciation of throwing without pain. There were still adjustments to be made in my workout regimen. Running on hard surfaces caused lower-back stiffness and pulled calf muscles. The Dodgers purchased a device called a Versa-Climber that was featured in one of the *Rocky* movies. Using the climber, I could control my cardio output at varying resistance without stressing my legs and lower back. I liked it so much I bought one for my personal use.

On December 10, 1986, the Dodgers traded first baseman du jour Greg Brock to Milwaukee for Tim Leary and Tim Crews. Leary, who would turn twenty-eight years old in March, was 12–12 in thirty starts in 1986 and was immediately plugged in as the Dodgers' fifth starter going into 1987. Returning from shoulder surgery after nearly two years of rehab was Alejandro Pena, who would turn twenty-eight in June. Pena was also being considered for that fifth starter spot. That put me, at age thirty-seven and coming off a disappointing 1986, into the position of fighting for a spot on the roster.

That wasn't a problem for me. After eighteen years in the Majors, I knew that one day I would be in this situation, so I was prepared for it. Heading to Vero Beach, my concern was the same as always, getting ready for the season. I had no control over the decision-making process. Determining the roster was the job of both Campanis and Lasorda. Keeping this focus also kept me from looking over my shoulder at both Leary and Pena. I never wanted to be in a position of wishing ill will on a teammate to improve my status. I wanted the job because I earned it.

The sportswriters who followed the club on a daily basis didn't quite see it that way. The competition for the fifth starter job became a subplot for the spring of 1987, and Leary, Pena, and myself had to answer questions about it on a daily basis. I explained to everyone who asked that my performance spoke for itself. After a good outing I told reporters that everything was heading in the right direction. After a struggle I told them it was part of spring training. When speculation of a possible trade was brought up or the possibility of pitching in relief, I said that decision was above my pay grade. I said, "I'm not going to deal with what-ifs. I'd rather deal with what is."[19]

All spring both Campanis and Lasorda were noncommittal about the fifth starter spot. If believing what one read in the sports section carried any weight, consider what Al said in early March. "When the club acquired Leary from Milwaukee, Al said that Leary and Pena would battle for the final spot. What about Reuss? Campanis now says he considered Reuss a candidate all along. And Campanis said Reuss is looking the best he has seen him in more than a year."[20]

With two weeks remaining in spring training, Campanis was

quoted again: "Right now, we're disappointed in Reuss. His stock is pretty low. There has been little trade interest, but it'll probably cost us some money if we make a deal." The story, reported in the *Los Angeles Times*, went on to mention Al's trip to the pressroom at Dodgertown to deny the quotes. "Why would I say this?" an angry Campanis said. "I've been in the game too long to do that. That would be a ridiculous statement to make, especially if we're trying to trade him." Responded Matt McHale, the *Star-News* reporter who wrote the original story, "I had my pen out and was writing down every word." Later in the article, both Lasorda and Campanis agreed that I was pitching well, allowing just four earned runs in eleven innings.[21]

After pitching the equivalent of eight innings in a loosely constructed intrasquad game due to a rainout of the scheduled game, I was asked to evaluate my performance. "It's a good question—but to the wrong person," I said. "It doesn't matter what I think. Ask Al or Tom—their opinions are the ones that matter."

When pressed with a follow-up question of what I thought they thought, I responded, "I can't read their [Lasorda's and Campanis's] minds. Ask them." So the reporters did just that. Al, still stinging from his remarks of the previous week, simply stated, "He threw better today." Lasorda told them, "I thought he pitched good."

Continuing the he said, she said drama, I was asked what I wished for (more of the same old shit, asked a different way), I told them, growing weary of this game for the past six weeks, "I tell you what I wish: I wish I could go out there and pitch without worrying about my job or the supposed competition with my teammates. But it hasn't been that way. I'm not thinking about my situation out on the mound or in the clubhouse. I only think about it when somebody brings it up." I built up a nice head of controlled steam. "You have to keep in mind that spring training is preparing yourself for the season," I said. "It shouldn't be for me to pass judgment. The way it's been presented to me—and the way you guys [reporters] see it—is that every time I put on a uniform I have to prove myself. All of that [evaluation] is subjective [and others will determine] whatever decision will be made. It's not my decision."[22]

As was the custom during my days with the Dodgers, spring training ended with the Freeway Series against the crosstown Angels back in Southern California. The Dodgers usually waited until the completion of these exhibition games before announcing the opening-day roster. As the script of this drama would have it, both Leary and I pitched against the Angels on that final Sunday, April 5. Tim pitched quite well, allowing no runs and no hits in four innings of work. I gave up a run on two hits in four innings.

As a result, the Dodgers optioned outfielder Reggie Williams to Albuquerque and kept all three of us (Leary, Pena, and myself) and a rookie pitcher by the name of Brian Holton. Eleven pitchers on a roster of twenty-four players (from 1986 to 1989 teams had the option of keeping a roster of twenty-four or twenty-five players) meant little room for maneuvering by a manager who loved to make numerous changes. The opening-day roster was a temporary solution. A permanent solution would come only after a bombshell interview would cost a respected member of the Dodger front office his job and his career.

The *Nightline* Interview and My Release from the Dodgers

On April 6 Al Campanis appeared on ABC's *Nightline*. The club opened in Houston, and Al, who had been traveling all day, agreed to appear on the show, coinciding with the fortieth anniversary of Jackie Robinson's debut with the Dodgers. It was the exchange with show host Ted Koppel regarding the lack of blacks in significant positions in baseball that led to Al's ultimate dismissal. Once the story of Al's comments reached the newspapers, it became evident that he would be asked to resign his position of general manager.

Peter O'Malley asked Fred Claire, then the club's executive vice president, to take over the duties of the general manager. Fred wanted full authority of the baseball operations, and Peter gave it to him. Fred immediately made his presence known. First he addressed the players to let us know that he was in charge. Then he met with the press for the first time as GM.

Now it was time for business. Because the Dodgers were carrying eleven pitchers, they found themselves short a position player. After the Thursday afternoon home opener in which third baseman Bill Madlock injured his shoulder, Fred had to make a move. He was aware that Mickey Hatcher, who had come up through the Dodger system and played all outfield positions as well as first and third bases, had just been released by the Minnesota Twins. It made perfect sense to sign Hatcher to replace Madlock.

Fred called me at home around ten that Friday morning and asked me to meet with him before I went to the clubhouse. Instinctively, I knew that this wasn't a social call. He was ready to make a roster change that involved me. So I asked Fred, "Rather than have me wait for four or five hours wondering what this call is about, would you mind if you told me over the phone?" He hesitated a bit and then said, "Okay, I can understand that. Jerry, we decided to give you your release."

After Fred got those words out, my reaction was much like that of a death in the family. I still heard Fred talking through the receiver, but my heart raced and my mind wandered as the reality set in. I heard him say, "If you want, we will be more than happy to arrange a press conference for you . . ." My mind was still elsewhere.

During the past winter, through the winter workouts at the ballpark, continuing through spring training, I prepared myself for the moment my days as a Dodger were done. I considered the possibility of a trade (I had a no-trade clause—remember how that worked in Pittsburgh?), perhaps a release, which gave me control over choosing my next team, or retirement, which gave me control over the rest of my life. During those moments I could take the probability only so far.

Until that day of reckoning arrived, I didn't really know how I'd react. I just didn't imagine that the reality over my release after all the time I spent considering the various options would hit me like this.

"Jerry, would you like me to have Steve Brener [the Dodgers' publicity director] call you?" Fred was still on the line. "Fred," I said, as I kept my composure and snapped back to the moment, "if you could have Steve call me in a hour or so, I'd appreciate that." I continued, "Also, thanks for telling me now." Fred, making his first roster change since becoming general manager, continued, "Jerry, you earned the right to make that choice. If I don't see you today, I still want to say thank you for all that you've done for the Dodgers in the eight years you were part of this club. And I wish you the best in whatever your future holds for you."

I hung up the phone and told my wife what had transpired on the other end of the line. We sat quietly for a few minutes as we allowed the news to sink in. Then we got down to business on my first day as an ex-Dodger, calling family members and close friends and telling them what had transpired before they read about it in the newspaper or heard it mentioned on TV.

When Brener called I told him I'd pass on the press conference. I also told Steve that I wouldn't come to the park that day. I remembered the three previous times I was traded and how awkward it was walking into the clubhouse, gathering my equipment, and saying the good-byes. I also remembered how painful the interviews were, and I didn't want a comment made at an emotional time destroying eight great years with the Dodger organization.

For me, going to the park that day would have been baseball's equivalent of the corporate ritual of an employee at work called into a superior's office, fired, told to clean out his office or desk, and then escorted from the premises. No one should ever have to face that indignity. Instead, I told him, "Steve, thanks for your willingness to handle this, but I prefer to take some time to determine my future privately."

I called David Wright, the Dodgers' equipment manager, and asked if I could come into the clubhouse on Saturday morning to clean out my locker and write him a check for his services. I was there before noon, before anyone else showed up. I cleaned out the locker that I used for eight years, grabbed some of my bats and some baseballs, and paused a moment to look around one more time. I couldn't leave without saying good-bye to everybody, so I erased the chalkboard near the coaches' offices and wrote,

Guys,
Thanks for the memories!
JR

It was simple, direct, and definitely not awkward. I put everything into a shopping cart and made my way through the tunnel that took me past the bullpen to the parking lot. I returned the cart to a spot near the batting cage, per David's request.

Eventually, I spoke to all of the media members who were interested in a conference call on April 22 after I agreed to terms on a Minor League deal with Cincinnati. The first question came from Gordon Verrell of the *Long Beach Press-Telegram*. "I speak for all of us in this room when I ask you why you didn't return any of our phone calls since your release," he said. I responded, "Gordie, in fairness to all of you, I couldn't return one phone call and not speak to the rest of you. Besides, I needed time to determine my future. I chose not to have a press conference on the day the release was announced because I wanted to forego a media circus." It was the truth, and I believe they understood.

Asked if I was disappointed, I answered, "I have no anger, no malice toward the Dodgers whatsoever," I told them. "It was a great eight years." To the Los Angeles media, I said, "I consider you guys friends, at least to the extent that I can do so."[23]

CHAPTER TEN

Hits, Misses, and Whistle-Stops

To this day, I consider Fred Claire a good friend. You might be asking, "Why? Isn't he the guy who released you?" That's true. But it's what he gave me in the process that's had a huge impact on my life.

In the early 1990s while working as an analyst for ESPN, I was assigned a Friday-night game with Chris Berman featuring the Dodgers in Atlanta. The next morning I upgraded to a first-class seat on the first flight back to Los Angeles. Stepping onto the plane with just a few minutes to spare, I placed my carry-on in the overhead section, and while looking at my assigned window seat I spotted a familiar face in the seat that was next to mine. It was Fred.

With newspapers and books spread neatly across his lap, he was jotting notes on a legal pad when he saw me. We exchanged hellos as I got settled. The jet taxied to the takeoff position while Fred continued his work. As I sat there I thought, "This can be a miserable five-hour trip, or I can make it a trip to remember." So I looked at Fred and said, "I owe you a huge thank-you!" That got his attention.

He put his pen down, turned to me with a smile on his face, and a perplexed look in his eyes. "How so?" he asked. I told him, "For years after I joined the club, I would introduce myself as Jerry Reuss, pitcher for the Los Angeles Dodgers. After my release, I introduced myself as Jerry Reuss . . . with no qualifier! It dawned on me that I was Jerry Reuss before I ever played a game of baseball, and I'm still Jerry Reuss now that my playing days are over." Fred was still with me as I continued, "In effect, when you gave me my release, you also gave me something that I was missing for years. Fred, you gave me . . . ME!"

Fred had a smile that was wider than that of the Chesire cat from *Alice in Wonderland*. He looked at me and said, "Then I guess it really was a good deal!" We both laughed. Fred put away his books, turned to me, and said, "So, bring me up to date." It turned out to be the best trip ever from Atlanta to Los Angeles.

Whistle-Stops

April 18, 1987: Signed as a Free Agent with the Cincinnati Reds
The Reds were willing to give me a shot, but they wanted me to pitch in Triple A Nashville to show if I still had anything left. I pitched well enough at Nashville to warrant a start against the Tigers in Detroit during an exhibition game. I gave up a run in six innings, and the Reds added me to their roster.

June 14, 1987: Released by the Cincinnati Reds
The game against the Tigers was the highlight of my time with the Reds. I was 0–5 with an ERA of 7.79 before the Reds released me. When Pete Rose, who managed the Reds that year, called me into his office to tell me the news, he told me he didn't want to release me. He thought I needed some time, but the Reds were struggling and needed help with their rotation.

Back to California

June 19, 1987: Signed as a Free Agent with the California Angels
While my wife and I packed our Cincinnati apartment, I got a call from Mike Port, the general manager of the Angels. Mike asked me if I was still interested in playing. After being released twice in two months with a trip to the Minors, I was grateful for any opportunity.

So, after I threw in the bullpen for manager Gene Mauch a few days after my release from the Reds, he was satisfied with what he saw, and I signed with the Angels.

I shut out the Royals on eight hits on June 21 in front of an Old-Timers Day crowd of 47,797 for my first American League win. It was my first complete game since September 21, 1985, and the first shutout since August 11, 1985, against the Reds. It was also my biggest highlight that season.

I won my next two starts against the White Sox and Cleveland, but it was a struggle after that. My elbow was slow responding to the 1986 elbow surgery, and the arm strength just wasn't there. I ended up 4–5 with a 5.25 ERA at thirty-eight years old. The Angels were 75–87 and looked to move in a different direction without a number of veteran players. I was one of them.

How miserable was 1987? Let's see. I was released twice, spent time in the Minor Leagues for the first time since 1970, told no thanks by the Angels after the season, and, for good measure, released by Adidas, the shoe manufacturer with whom I had an exclusive contract since 1979, because I missed time on a Major League roster. My confidence took a beating, but I believed I could help some team if my arm strength returned.

Retooling

November 9, 1987: Granted Free Agency

During the off-season I contacted Ken Ravizza, a sports psychologist at Cal State—Fullerton, to help rebuild my mental approach. I met Ken during my time with the Angels, and we went to work immediately. I drove to Fullerton once a week for sessions that began in his office and, later in the winter, ended on the ball field. Gradually, my confidence returned, and I was able to focus on my work, specifically on the part that I could control, locating my pitches. Between the time on campus, pitching a few innings in Sunday league games for the Pasadena Redbirds, and altering my off-season workouts (I was no longer able to work out in the winter at Dodger Stadium as I had since 1980), once again I was a man on a mission. All that remained was to find a team that would give me a shot.

Another Change in Status

*March 29, 1988: Signed as a Free Agent
with the Chicago White Sox*
In early February my agent, Jack Sands, was able to secure an invitation for me to attend the Chicago White Sox spring-training camp. My status was nonroster invitee. That simply meant there were no promises made and I could be released at any time without any financial consideration. All that concerned me was a chance to show I could still pitch.

It took some work on Jack's part because Sox owner Jerry Reinsdorf was a force in the ongoing battle with the Major League Players Association and was aware of my involvement with the association over the years. Once Jerry was convinced those days were over, he had a plan in mind that could benefit both of us . . . if I could still pitch.

Jerry, my wife, and I discussed my future with the White Sox in the early part of spring training during dinner at a Sox function. Anytime a person came to our table with a bottle of champagne, it definitely got our attention. This was how he laid out the Sox future. "We're rebuilding here. Our plan is to sign the best amateur players we can through the draft and scouting in Latin America and bring them through our system. If and when they make it to our Major League club, we'll build a club around them with players from other organizations until we find a winning combination. A few years ago we picked up Tom Seaver,[1] who was in a situation much like yours," Jerry explained.

Seaver was 5–13 with a 5.50 ERA in 1982 with the Reds and 9–14, 3.55, with an encore stop with the Mets in 1983. At that point in his career, he had 266 wins. After a pair of unimpressive seasons, he was made available in the free-agent compensation draft. The Sox believed he still had something to offer and picked him up.[2]

"Before Seaver signed with us, I told him what I'm about to tell you. We're not going to win with you or without you. We're rebuilding, and I believe that having a veteran presence with your stature would be invaluable to the development of our younger players," Jerry said.

Jerry turned his focus on me. "My people tell me you have a makeup similar to Seaver, and we're willing to repeat this scenario with you." Jerry waited for my response. "Jerry, I've been in this game for over twenty years, and no general manager, or owner, for that matter, ever laid it out as honestly as you just did. Thank you for your candor, and I accept," I answered. "Good. I hope it works out," Jerry said. "Because if you make the club and do well, I plan to trade you to a contender for more prospects. It's win-win, as you'll have another chance to play in the postseason." After Jerry said good-bye, I told my wife, "That's a class act. If I make this club, this will be a fun year."

I had to sacrifice salary arbitration, a hard-fought right negotiated during my years as a player representative, for a chance to play. Had I pressed the issue with Reinsdorf or notified the Players Association about losing the right, my career would have been over then.

Also, I could have a single room on the road, but I had to pay the difference from the double-room rate. I asked Jerry why he insisted on players sharing a room on the road. He was willing to give me bonuses that were in the six-figure range but wouldn't pay a few thousand a year for a single room. Reinsdorf answered this way: "It's not about the money. I believe it's beneficial for players to room together." I thought for a second and asked, "Okay. How about if we do this? Let's rewrite that clause and say, if you trade me, that the receiving club will give me a single room on the road." He paused, looked to the ceiling, and said, "Yeah, I like that. We can do that. In fact, I'll use that for other contracts," he said with a smile.

I Tell Ya, I Get No Respect!

As spring training approached the last week, my status was undetermined when I was scheduled to pitch against Toronto in Dunedin on March 27. While standing behind the protective screen in the outfield and talking to catcher Carlton Fisk, a ball thrown in from right field smoked me in the back. Fisk saw who threw the ball and yelled out to right field, where Ken Patterson, a rookie left-hander who came over from the Yankees in a trade in August 1987, stood by himself.

"Watch where you throw the ball!" Fisk yelled. Patterson answered, "Tell that white-haired asshole to get out of the way!" Fisk and I looked at one another in disbelief. "Did he just call me an asshole?" I asked. "That's what I heard. That's no respect," the future Hall of Famer replied. "You know, I got more years in the big leagues than he has days. I earned that respect," I said with a laugh. So we called out to Patterson and asked him to join us for some veteran advice. Once he arrived Fisk told him, "Hey, you can't call another player an asshole unless you're prepared to fight. More important than that, you can't ever talk to a veteran player with that lack of respect." Patterson, nodding his head during Fisk's lecture, finally spoke. "You're right. That definitely was a lack of respect. What I should have said was, 'Watch out, Mr. Asshole!'" He then ran back to his spot in right field as Fisk and I stood there in disbelief.

Even with the exchange with Patterson, I did pitch well that day. I went six innings, allowing a run on four hits. My performance convinced the White Sox to sign me to a Major League contract the next day.

The manager, a former teammate from Pittsburgh, Jim Fregosi, called me into his office the next morning to tell me I made the club. "Congratulations and welcome to the club!" he said with a smile. "At this point, you're the fifth starter, so when I skip your turn when we have an off day in the schedule, I can use you in relief." I didn't care how he used me. I made the club, and I had the chance to purge 1987 from my life.

Get Off My Mound

Not many people are aware that Jim Fregosi was a six-time All-Star from 1964 to 1970 before he was traded in December 1971 to the Mets for four players, one of whom happened to be a pitcher by the name of Nolan Ryan. After two and a half years in New York, he was sold to the Rangers. The Pirates picked him up in June 1977 for Ed Kirkpatrick. That's where I first met him.

The Pirates used him to spell an aging Willie Stargell at first base and to pinch-hit. Jim saw a lot of action after joining the club, as the Pirates played seven doubleheaders from June 19 to July 17. I started the game versus the Cardinals' left-hander, Pete Falcone, as did Jim on July 6 in Pittsburgh.

I was struggling early that season, losing my first five decisions, and was 3-9 with a 4.13 ERA going into this game. Add my antisocial disposition on days I pitched to my season-long frustration, and you know something was going to spill over.

I had a 6-1 lead going into the seventh inning. A ground out, two singles, and two walks preceded my exit.[3] Somewhere between the hits and walks Jim, who was playing first base, came over to the mound and tried to be the calming veteran influence and help me get through the inning. I was in no mood to hear common sense. I looked at him and said, "Get the hell off my mound! If I wanted to hear your shit, I'd invite you here. Besides, have I ever called time out during one of your at bats, come out of the dugout, and talked to you? Hell, no!" Jim looked at me and, with his calm demeanor, said, "Seems like you got everything under control," and went back to his position.

Surprisingly, we were still on speaking terms after the game. He told me to forget about it when I later apologized for my behavior. He was the bigger man, as I forgot about it. He didn't.

Jim retired as an active player on June 1, 1978, as the Angels offered him the manager's job. He managed the Angels until 1981. After a five-year absence from the field, he managed the White Sox from 1986 to 1988. Once I made the club I was looking forward to the opportunity to play for him.

I made two starts to begin the season. Because the schedule had some off-days, I made my next appearance in relief against Oakland on April 22 in Chicago. Starter Jack McDowell allowed a leadoff double and a walk, as the A's led 4–3 in the eighth inning. With lefty Dave Parker the next batter, Jim came to the mound and called me into the game. I retired Parker on a weak grounder back to the mound. With Mark McGwire the next hitter and a right-hander warming up in the bullpen, Fregosi came out to make a pitching change.

When he got to the mound, I handed him the ball. He looked at me and said, "Now it's my mound!" I looked at him and said somewhat befuddled, "What?" "You heard me. Now it's my *bleepin'* mound!" he said defiantly. Suddenly, I remembered our Pittsburgh blowup and started laughing. Catcher Mark Salas looked at both of us like we were nuts. "What the hell," I said. "Jim, that happened eleven years ago. You told me to forget about it," I reminded him. "Yeah, I told you to forget it, but I didn't," he responded.

Because Jim hadn't signaled for the righty, Larry Barnett, the home-plate umpire, came to the mound and asked him what he wanted to do. "I want the right-hander, Larry," Fregosi told him. Larry called in the reliever from our bullpen located in center field. Now it was a party of four. Salas asked Fregosi, "What's this about?"

As we had some time, Jim told him the story. "We played together in Pittsburgh, and one game, I came in from first base to talk to him while he's struggling, and he tells me to get off his *bleepin'* mound."

So Barnett asked me, "Did you really say that?" I answered him somewhat sheepishly, "Yeah, I did." Wanting this meeting to end, I looked at Fregosi and asked if I could leave. Fregosi looked at me and said, "Oh, no, I waited all this time, so you just wait here until I tell you to go." So, there I stood, as Jim paused to relish the moment. "You can't believe how I prayed that you had something left and could make the club. I dreamed of having to make this pitching change. If nothing else happens this season, at least I'll have the satisfaction of finally getting your ass!" he said.

By this time Salas and Barnett were laughing their asses off. John Pawlowski, the right-handed reliever who arrived from the bullpen, stood right beside me and wondered what the hell was going on. Fregosi gave the ball to Pawlowski, looked at me, and said, only as a man who finally got his revenge could, "Now, you can leave." I swear I remember Barnett, who couldn't resist, adding, "Will ya get off his *bleepin'* mound, for chrissakes! We got a game to finish!"

I went 13-9 with a 3.44 ERA for a Fregosi-led team that had a record of 71-90 and finished fifth, thirty-two and a half games behind the division-winning Oakland A's. Considering all that happened in 1987 and what I had to do to get this job, 1988 was one of the most satisfying years in my career.[4]

Where's the Sammy Doll?

The Sox didn't rehire Fregosi, and Jeff Torborg took over as manager in 1989. Jeff had spent the previous ten years with the Yankees, and our paths crossed briefly during the 1981 World Series. Jeff told Jerome Holtzman of the *Chicago Tribune* one of the reasons he wanted to join the Sox is because of "the focus on the young arms. I'm intrigued by the young pitching staff and by the direction Larry Himes has taken the club. It's not an easy course, building from the bottom, but that's the way you have to do it."[5]

Jeff was right about the course not being easy. At the All-Star break, the Sox were 32-56, in last place, twenty-one and a half games out of first place, and we just lost our last six games. We opened the second half of the season at Comiskey against the Brewers. On my way to the clubhouse, I spotted a concessionaire setting up a display of bobblehead dolls. When the heads moved, it reminded me of the neck twitches of our pitching coach, Sammy Ellis.

So I bought one of them, but it wasn't ready for the clubhouse. I had one of the clubhouse attendants purchase some white paint and proceeded to match the hair color of Sammy. Of course, the pitchers loved it! Sammy sneered when he saw it and said, "You oughtta be concerned with getting opposing hitters out!"

I brought it to the bench before the game with the Brewers and placed it between Jeff and me on the dugout steps during the national anthem. The doll had its place of honor on the bench, as we beat the Brewers to end the losing streak.

As luck would have it, we swept the four-game series against Milwaukee and won the two games against the Yankees for a sweep of the home stand and a six-game winning streak. Standing between Jeff and me during the anthem and observing from his dugout perch during the six games was the Sammy doll.

I packed the doll carefully for the three-game series in Boston, but a piece broken from the head needed repair. We won the first game against the Red Sox on a brilliant effort by Melido Perez and Bobby Thigpen to run our winning streak to seven games. Sammy watched from the bench, as a Band-Aid held the broken piece in place. I bought some glue the next day and repaired the broken doll, but kept it in the clubhouse as the game started.

Boston was leading 6–4 at the end of six innings when Jeff, standing at the home-plate side of dugout, suddenly turned and scanned the dugout. He immediately stood in front of me and asked, "Where's the doll?" Surprised, I answered, "It's in my locker." Jeff looked at me and said, "It doesn't belong there. That doll belongs here during the game. Go get it!"

There's a long tunnel that separates the dugouts from the

clubhouse at Fenway. I was on my way when Jeff shouted into the tunnel, "Hurry up!" So I ran to my locker, grabbed Sammy, and returned to the bench just as the seventh inning began. As soon as the doll was in its place, Dave Gallagher singled, Steve Lyons doubled him to third, and after a strikeout by Harold Baines, Ivan Calderon homered to give us the lead. We scored three more runs in the eighth and eventually won the game 10–6.

Walking off the field after I congratulated my teammates, Jeff grabbed my arm and told me, "The doll stands between us during the anthem and stays on the bench until I say it goes." I started laughing. "I'm serious. You're responsible for it," Jeff said sternly.

Jeff knew a good thing when he saw it. With the Sammy doll becoming a part of the team, we won eleven of twelve games. It was our best run of the 1989 season. But all good things must come to an end. We lost four of our next five games, and on July 31 I was traded to Milwaukee.[6]

Déjà Vu All Over Again

*July 31, 1989: Traded by the White Sox
to the Brewers for Brian Drahman*

I didn't pitch anywhere near as well in 1989 as I did in 1988. After winning opening day in Anaheim, the wheels again fell off the wagon. By the end of May, I was 3–2 with a 6.94 ERA.

After a four-game stint in the bullpen, I came back to the starting rotation and sported a 5–3 record with a respectable ERA of 3.53. It was good enough for the Brewers, whom I'd beaten earlier in the year, to pick me up in a deal for Minor Leaguer Brian Drahman, who eventually pitched parts of four years in the Majors.

November 8, 1989: Released by the Milwaukee Brewers

I couldn't get on track with the Brewers. I pitched well in a game at Detroit but was removed because I pulled my right hamstring. While rehabbing the injury in Milwaukee, I pulled the other hamstring.

I came back too early and had to be removed from a game twelve days later in the first inning. Then there was an eighteen-day trip to the disabled list.

When the smoke cleared, I ended up 1–4 for the Brewers. My time in Milwaukee was like Cincinnati and Anaheim two years earlier: it showed some promise but ended in disaster.[7]

Sarasota Stopover

*March 1, 1990: Signed as a Free Agent
with the Chicago White Sox*
With another bad taste in my mouth, I still wanted to finish my career on my terms. I still believed there was something in the tank and I could help somebody. Now that I was forty years old with injuries that led to trips on the disabled list and a poor 1989, Jack called the White Sox, who issued another invitation as a nonroster player. The agreement was that I was an insurance policy for any of their five starters (Melido Perez, Eric King, Jack McDowell, Greg Hibbard, and Jerry Kutzler) if they couldn't start the season, and I would be given enough innings to land a job elsewhere if their starters were healthy.

I pitched well in one start and stunk up the place in my next start. With teams trying to pare their rosters and an unimpressive showing, no one was interested, However, I heard there was an opening with Houston in their bullpen.

Two More Minor League Stops

April 3, 1990: Released by the Chicago White Sox
April 14, 1990: Signed as a Free Agent with the Houston Astros
I met the Astros before a game in Lakeland, Florida, and threw in the bullpen. Art Howe, the manager and a former roommate with the Pirates, and Bob Cluck, the pitching coach, watched the session. They liked what they saw well enough to recommend signing me to a Minor League contract. Because there were no open

spots in Triple AAA Tucson, they asked me to go to Double A ball in Columbus, Georgia. I made the commitment over the winter to give this one last chance all I had.

May 14, 1990: Released by the Houston Astros
I did well in Columbus, so the Astros sent me to Tucson. Instead of kids in their early twenties and a manager and pitching coach younger than I was, I joined a team of veteran guys like myself, who were just looking for one last chance. I wouldn't find it in Tucson. I was released after ten days.

One Last Chance

July 7, 1990: Signed as a Free Agent with the Pittsburgh Pirates
Still determined to find a spot, I returned home and continued workouts. I did my weight work at the La Canada YMCA, played catch and threw off the mound at Glendale City College, and did my cardio work on the Versa-Climber I had at home. Also, I played first base on Wednesdays and pitched on Sundays for the Pasadena Redbirds.

Ed Roebuck, a former Dodger reliever and then a scout for the Pirates, watched me work one Sunday and sent in a recommendation to sign me. I threw in the bullpen for Pirates general manager Larry Doughty and Pirates manager Jim Leyland when they were in Los Angeles in early July. Once again, an impressive effort in a bullpen session got me signed to a Minor League contract. This time, my destination was Buffalo, New York.

The Pirates were in the process of winning the National League East when I joined Buffalo in mid-July. Once again, I was an insurance policy if the Pirates needed a pitcher and no one in the farm system was ready. Healthwise, I was in great shape. My arm was 100 percent, and the leg injuries from 1989 were gone. It showed when I arrived in Buffalo.

I pitched in ten games for the Bison and had a 4–4 record with a respectable ERA of 3.52. There was also a streak of twenty-four consecutive scoreless innings,[8] and there was a start in which I went seven innings using seventy-four pitches, sixty-two of which were strikes. The command that was absent since 1988 finally returned.[9] While pitching this well, I knew there would be an opportunity for a call-up to Pittsburgh. It came on August 6. The Pirates needed a starter for a game in Philadelphia. I pitched eight innings two days earlier, so the timing wasn't right. The Pirates called up Randy Tomlin from Double A Harrisburg. Tomlin, in his Major League debut, threw a complete game, giving up a run on five hits. This game earned him a spot in the Pirates' rotation for the rest of the year.

On August 8 the Pirates traded for left-hander Zane Smith in a four-player deal with Montreal. The reason they went after Smith was because of his record against the Mets, who were battling the Pirates for the National League East championship. It turned out to be a great deal for the Bucs, as Smith was 6–2 with a 1.30 ERA in eleven games during the stretch run.

The next chance was August 17 in Cincinnati for a split double-header. The Pirates' plan was to call up a pitcher and send him back the next day. They chose another rookie, Mike York, who pitched seven shutout innings in this game, his Major League debut. York was on the Major League roster, which made the move routine. If Pittsburgh had called me up, someone would've been removed from the roster, and I would've had to clear waivers to return to Buffalo.[10]

Touching the Brass Ring One More Time

There wasn't a need for another pitcher in Pittsburgh as the season in Buffalo came to an end. Chuck LaMar, the Pirates' farm director, was in town to see the club and make selections for the September call-ups. Initially, I wasn't on the list. So I had a meeting with Chuck to find out why. "Chuck, when I signed with the club, I was told I would get a chance at the Majors if I could still do the job. Well, I did the job. There were two times that I could've been called up to pitch in a doubleheader but wasn't. I can accept that. I can understand why the club dealt for Smith. What I can't understand is why I won't be given a shot during the stretch run."

Chuck was willing to look at my situation. He called Terry Collins (yep, the same Terry Collins from my years with the Dodgers), then the Buffalo manager, into the office and asked for his opinion. "He did the job here and earned a call-up," Terry said frankly.

Chuck called general manager Larry Doughty and went to bat for me. "I want to ask you about Reuss. He's done a helluva job here," Chuck told him. Sitting next to Chuck and not hearing Larry's side of the conversation, I can only assume the questions he asked by hearing Chuck's answers. "Yes, sir, Terry thinks he can help us," Chuck said. There was a pause for Larry's question. "Based on our reports, I think he can help us," Chuck replied. There was another pause, and this one would determine if my baseball career was over or if it would continue in Pittsburgh. "Yes, sir, I'll tell him," Chuck said and hung up. "Larry said to add your name to the list of call-ups. Congratulations!"

With a smile on my face, I told Chuck, "We only met for the first time today, yet you went the extra mile for me. I can't begin to tell you how much I appreciate it!" I turned to Collins and said, "Thanks for everything." Terry looked at me and said, "Hell, you deserve it with the way you worked and performed here." I gave Terry a hug and a few back slaps before heading for the locker room to pack my equipment.

I was part of a group of six or seven players who made the one-hour flight from Buffalo to Pittsburgh the next morning, September 7, to join the Pirates in Pittsburgh. It rained the whole trip, and when we landed in Pittsburgh I had doubts if we would play that night, the series opener against Montreal.

We went from the airport to the Pittsburgh Hilton to check into our rooms. I had a quick lunch and walked to the ballpark. I worked my ass off to get back to the big leagues, and I didn't want to miss a minute of it.

Walking from the opening in center field toward the dugout, I noticed the turf had been updated and the walls were painted a blue color, as the park looked the best I'd ever seen it. When I arrived in the home clubhouse, I noticed some of my Buffalo teammates were already there, unpacking their gear and hanging their clothes on laundry racks in the middle of the clubhouse as space was at a premium. I guess I wasn't the only one who wanted that taste of the big leagues.

I didn't see my name above any of the lockers, and as I grabbed my equipment bag a voice from the past approached from behind me. "Jerry, step into my office!" It was Hoolie, who was still handling the chores as the clubhouse manager.

We walked into the laundry room, and I told him, "Hoolie, always good to see you." "How long has it been since you've been in this clubhouse?" Hoolie asked. "Spring of '79. That was a lifetime ago," I answered. "Look, I don't want you dressing in the middle of the clubhouse with the kids. There's a spot in the corner to hang your stuff, if you don't have a lot of it," Hoolie said. "Hey, I'm glad to be here. And I appreciate the thought. I'll take the spot. Just point me to it," I said. "It's right there," he said as we walked out of the laundry room. "Right there between Bonds and Bonilla!" he pointed. It was a pie-shaped area, with the opening maybe a foot wide. I looked at him as he looked at me. We both started laughing. "I'm gonna love this. Hope they have a sense of humor!" I said. His face suddenly was serious. "They don't," he said with some resignation as he lit a cigarette and walked away.

I grabbed my bag and walked across the locker room to my hole in the wall, while Barry and Bobby were having a deep conversation. They looked up as I approached. "Guys, I'm Jerry Reuss. The space between your lockers will be my home for the next month," I said as I held my hand out. They had a confused look on their faces and broke out in big smiles as they put their hands out. We shook the handshake of players who never met but had a mutual respect for one another.

"We were just talking about you. We thought you were with ESPN. We had no idea you were still playing!" Barry laughed. They couldn't have been nicer. They cleared the area, and Bobby said, "If you need anything, let me know." I imagined many different scenarios for this moment, but I would've never dreamed that two of the game's biggest stars would welcome me to their corner!

There was no batting practice because of the rainy weather, but the pitchers still had their work to do. I changed clothes, put on a Major League uniform once again, and made my way down a path that was familiar territory more than eleven years ago. Just walking down the same hallway to the field brought back a number of memories. This time, they were all good. I even passed the spot I kicked that damn bucket. I would have never guessed back in 1979 that I'd make this walk in 1990.

A Four-Decade Player

A sidelight to finishing my career on my terms was adding my name to the list of players playing in four decades. Four contemporaries of mine accomplished the feat earlier in 1990: Carlton Fisk, Nolan Ryan, Rick Dempsey, and Bill Buckner. It's an asterisk beside our names that said we played at the Major League level for at least twenty-two years.[11]

I got my asterisk that night, September 7, 1990. It was in the eighth inning, and Stan Belinda was pitching in relief of John Smiley. Belinda gave up a leadoff single to Marquis Grissom, and the phone in the bullpen rang. Tommy Sandt, the bullpen coach, answered it, looked at me, and said, "Get ready!"

I thought, "Get ready? I've been dreaming about this all year long. I am ready!" A single and a strikeout later, the phone rang again, and Tommy asked, "You ready?" "Yep," I answered.

Jim Leyland, the Pirates' manager, made his way to the mound and signaled for me. I grabbed my jacket and started running to the mound. That voice of wisdom inside me said, "What's the hurry? They'll wait for you. Besides, you need a moment to shift your focus from the moment to the job at hand." The voice, as always, was right. It was a very nice ovation from the twenty-two-thousand-plus on hand, but my concern was Larry Walker of the Expos, waiting for his turn at bat after I finished my warmups.

Walker took the first pitch for a ball and then tried to pull an outside fastball and slapped what should have been an inning-ending double-play grounder to second. We got the out at second, but Gary Redus, an outfielder most of his career and a first baseman this night, missed tagging the bag at first. A stolen base and an intentional walk loaded the bases, but I got out of the inning on a grounder to short.

After the game I walked across the field through the gate in center field on my way back to the hotel. I thought about all that I went through just to get there. There was spring training with the White Sox, a couple of weeks in Georgia, a few more in Tucson, a month of Sunday-league ball in Pasadena, and six or seven weeks in Buffalo before the September call-up.

Mentally, it was a lot more difficult. There was the doubt about my ability that would creep into my mind after disappointing games in spring training and again in Tucson. There was another kind of doubt after pitching in the Sunday-league games, wondering if the scouts who attended saw enough to give me a recommendation. I stopped in the middle of center field, looked around the ballpark in the dim light, and asked myself, "Was it worth it?" You bet your ass it was!

Know When to Hold 'Em, Know When to Fold 'Em

Knowing that I would retire at the end of the 1990 season, I had my camera by my side everywhere I went. On road trips I arrived at each ballpark early in the afternoon and took pictures from every angle possible. On more than one occasion, teammates would join me as we made our way around the ballparks of the National League East, each of us with camera in tow, talking baseball, ballparks, and photography as we bonded. It was a trip in a time machine reviewing some of these pictures before I posted them recently on Flickr. The ballparks that no longer exist and the players who were Pirates in 1990 are alive and well (and young!) on the Internet.

On our final road trip in St. Louis, I mentioned to Jim Leyland (in the bathroom, no less) that this was my last season. I was retiring, and I wanted him to know before I mentioned it to the sportswriters. I thanked him for everything, knowing that I might not have the chance during the last few days. We shook hands (yes, we had both washed with soap). He appreciated the consideration and later mentioned our conversation on his daily radio show.

The Pirates clinched the Division Championship in St. Louis on September 30. The postgame celebration on the field spilled into the clubhouse. I stayed on the field and visited with friends for about fifteen minutes. Somehow, it seemed to me that the celebration was about the guys who were there the whole year, and I wanted to give them some space. I did get in the spirit of things when I joined them later. I grabbed a bottle of bubbly and wrapped it in a towel, as I wanted to share it with my wife, who was waiting for me in Pittsburgh. Just like the Pirates, I wanted to celebrate the moment with the person who was with me the whole year.

Once the Pirates' charter arrived in Pittsburgh, I could see that the fans who waited for the arrival of the plane had started their celebration without us. They were yelling and screaming as the team made their way through the police lines in the terminal to the buses that would return us to the ballpark. I enjoyed the moment, not for myself, but for the guys who earned it with their performance during the season. It was their time. I remembered similar celebrations with the Pirates of the seventies and the Dodgers of the eighties. That was my time.

There was also another reality. For many of the players on this bus, this moment was as good as it was going to get. They weren't thinking of the ups and downs of baseball while watching the crowd like I was. For many of them, the downs would come soon enough and definitely much faster than they hoped. For me, I got to touch the brass ring one more time. And the best was yet to come.

Better than a Gold Watch

Because of the lockout during spring training, the regular season had to be pushed back three days to complete the full 162-game season. That meant there were three games to play at home against the Mets. Because the games didn't mean anything in the standings, the next three games gave Jim Leyland a chance to rest some regulars, give some bench guys a chance to play, and set up his pitching staff for the playoffs against the Reds, who won the NL West.

I settled into a routine while pitching out of the bullpen. If I didn't get up the day before, I waited until the fifth inning the next day before asking Tommy Sandt if I could throw. He would then call Ray Miller, the pitching coach, and ask for permission. That's what happened on Monday, October 1.

Ray gave the okay, and I started my work. But the phone in the bullpen rang a few minutes after I started throwing. It was Ray, who wanted to talk to me. This was a first. I grabbed the phone and asked Ray, "What's up?" "Jimmy [Leyland] heard my conversation with Tommy about you getting your work in. He asked me to ask you if you want to start Wednesday afternoon," Ray told me. I stood motionless with phone in hand, mouth wide open, before I answered. "Ray . . ." I was speechless. "Absolutely! Thank you, thank you . . . and thank Jim for considering me," I managed to say. Ray told me before he hung up, "Well, I guess you know more than me what you need to do to get ready."

Tommy, who treated the bullpen phone like it was his personal domain, wanted to know what the conversation was about. I told him, "Ray told me Jim wanted to know if I wanted to start Wednesday's game." There was a pause. "Well, what did you tell him?" Tommy asked. "Are you shittin' me? I told him, 'Absolutely!'"

As was Jim's daily regimen, he toured the outfield and talked to as many of his players as possible. There were some players with whom he'd share a laugh. Other times it was a teaching moment. Much of the time it was a chance to pat a player on the back while he was down. Jim paid me a visit on Tuesday.

"Hey, we haven't had much time to visit, have we?" he said. "No, with all the players here, the upcoming playoffs, and the time you give the media, you have your hands full," I replied. He paused a few moments, scanning the field, turned to me, and said, "You're gonna be all right tomorrow, aren't you?" he said, not asking a question but making a statement. I turned and looked at him and said, "Jim, I can't thank you enough for the opportunity. This month has been better than anything I could've dreamed of. As far as tomorrow, I'll be fine. Still, I don't want to embarrass myself or the Pirates, so, if you sense the game getting out of control, do what you have to do. I'll understand." He nodded his head, smiled, and said, "Good luck!" and continued his tour of the outfield.

I decided to walk to the ballpark Wednesday morning. There wasn't a cloud in the sky, with a hint of fall in the air and a warm sun . . . the kind of day you pay full retail for. I tried to keep my perspective and focus on the game, and I was okay until I walked on the field through the center field gate. I started 547 games in my Major League career, and it hit me, you have only one first start and one last start. (For some guys, it's one and the same!) So I took a moment to gather it all in.

Standing alone in the middle of the outfield, I looked all around the ballpark and acknowledged that this would be the last time I would do this as a player. The voice inside my head told me, "You're ready now."

Once inside the clubhouse I saw the new uniform in my locker. I asked Hoolie to change my number from 47 to 49. I was a September call-up in 1969 with the Cardinals and again with the Pirates in 1990. It just seemed right to wear the same number from 1969 to complete the full circle.

For a Wednesday afternoon game that had no bearing on the standings, there was a crowd of more than twenty-seven thousand on hand. For the Mets starter, Frank Viola, the game had a special meaning. He was going after his twentieth win.

Well, Frank had a two-run lead before he threw a pitch, as I gave up a pair of runs on three hits in the top of the first. We got one of them back in the third, as José Lind doubled, I sacrificed him to third, and he scored on an infield out.

With just two hits over the next four innings, the score was 2–1 after five innings. Tim Teufel led off the Mets' sixth with a home run to left to make the score 3–1. The next batter, Tom O'Malley, grounded out to first. Out of the Pirates' dugout came Leyland. I recognized the walk. He wanted to make a pitching change.

It was only fitting in my final Major League game that I'd hear another manager say, "Bring in the right-hander." But it would be the last time. When Jim got to the mound, he didn't say a word as he put his hand out for the ball. Instead of giving it to him, I shook his hand and simply said, "Thanks." There was a short pause. "Mind if I keep the ball?" I asked. He smiled and said, "I don't give a shit about the ball. I'm proud to shake the hand of a man who pitched twenty-two years in the big leagues."

Once reliever Mike York got to the mound, I walked off the last time to a standing ovation. After shaking hands and exchanging hugs from teammates of just a month, I got to the bench, dropped my glove, grabbed my jacket, and put it on. At the urging of the

Pirate players, I took a deep breath and walked a few steps onto the field to acknowledge the appreciative Pirate faithful.

I took off my hat, and, looking down the right-field line, moving my way to behind home plate, where my wife was sitting, I paused and said thanks to all of them. As I looked at the fans on the left-field side of the park, I saw the entire Mets team on their feet in front of the dugout applauding. I pointed with my left hand to each of them, thanking them for the show of respect. As I continued from left field to the fans in center, I saw the message on the scoreboard that read, *Thanks for the Memories, Jerry!*

That was the only curtain call I took in my twenty-two-year career. Hall of Famer Ralph Kiner, who announced the game for the Mets on TV, remarked that the ovation "was better than a gold watch!" You're right about that, Ralph!

By the way, the Pirates scored two in the sixth to tie the game, which meant I spit the hook one more time and finished my career with a no-decision. The Mets broke the tie, as they scored a run in each of the last three innings to win the game 6–3. Frank Viola pitched seven innings and won his twentieth game, the second time in his career he accomplished the feat.

I sat on the bench for the seventh inning and then walked to the clubhouse. No sooner had I arrived when there was a call from White Sox trainer Herm Schneider. "Lefty, you did it just as you hoped you would. Congratulations!" I smiled and answered, "Hermie, it was a long, strange trip, but it sure got the job done. Thanks for thinking of me."

On an emotional day, I wasn't surprised that the feeling of relief overwhelmed me. I just knew when to say when. All year, I wanted to end my career on my terms. With the help of the Pirates who gave me another chance, a quirk in the schedule, and the class of Jim Leyland, I walked off the field in my final game with my head held high to a standing ovation. Very few players were given the opportunity to say good-bye in style. I'm humbled to be among those few.

After the game, I said my good-byes to all the players and coaches, thanked them, and wished them the best in the postseason. As I did with every club later in my career, I put my uniform in my equipment bag before leaving for home. I saw the uniform top every day that I worked on this book, as it's displayed in its frame just to the right of my computer.

Maybe Pete Peterson knew something back in 1977 when he told me he hoped I would finish my career with the Pirates. However, I don't think Pete had this career path in mind. Maybe Willie Stargell was right when he said, "What goes around comes around." I was the luckiest twenty-year-old in St. Louis on my first day in the big leagues and had a fairy-tale ending on my final day some twenty-two years later. On October 3, 1990, I had come full circle with the Pirates and with baseball, and I was ready to begin the rest of my life.

November 5, 1990: Granted Free Agency

As one door of opportunity closed, another one opened. While I was a member of the White Sox in 1989, Jeff Torborg sent me to the radio booth to work the game that afternoon with Sox announcer Wayne Hagin. WMAQ in Chicago, which carried the Sox games, gave me an audiocassette of the broadcast. I sent a copy to ESPN in the winter of 1990 that led to an in-studio audition for the cable network in its second year of broadcasting Major League Baseball. I signed a three-year contract as an analyst for their Tuesday- and Friday-night games beginning in 1991. My playing career was in the past, and a broadcasting career was under way.

Epilogue

With a variety of jobs as an on-air analyst on both radio and television, I've been involved in the game of baseball since my retirement as an active player. After three years at ESPN, I worked on Major League Baseball's *Baseball Night in America* in 1994–95. I split the California Angels TV duties with Hall of Fame manager Sparky Anderson from 1996 to 1998 and partnered with former teammate Rick Monday on Dodger radio broadcasts from 2006 to 2008. From 2000 to 2004 I was back in uniform as a Minor League pitching coach for the Expos, Cubs, and Mets.

Over those years I've been asked by a number of different sportswriters about a collaborative effort on a book. I took those conversations seriously, but for one reason or another, nothing ever came from them. Over the years, however, the dynamics changed.

After my dad passed away in 1998, followed by my mom in 2000, my brothers and our families sorted through the belongings and pictures of unknown people and places that passed through Mom's and Dad's lives. Because of today's technology, the families have been able to piece together some of the facts about our legacy. We're still making discoveries today.

I learned many lessons from their passing. One was cataloging my baseball memorabilia and the numerous photos I had taken over the years so that those who are interested in my life can get their questions answered directly from me. During my rehab for a knee replacement in 2005, I learned everything I could about Photoshop. Eventually, the resulting photos were good enough to place in an album for our ever-growing family. Instead of printing them, I posted them online through Flickr. A thought occurred to me while uploading the images . . . why not make them available for anyone in the world to view? And that's where I am today! To see much of my baseball career (as well as some of my other work) in pictures, you can find them online at http://www.flickr.com/photos/jerryreuss/.

Over the years I've read or heard about my career in numerous books, articles, and interviews. The stories being printed or mentioned weren't the way I remembered them. Because my broadcasting jobs allowed me flexible hours, I wanted to set my story straight, or at least the way I remembered it. Still, I wasn't certain how I wanted to present it.

The solution came during a Dodgers Fantasy Camp in Vero Beach in 2008 when longtime friend and former Dodger Carl Erskine gave me a copy of his book, *What I Learned from Jackie Robinson*. The book contains 160 pages and was written as a vignette of first-person stories. I read it on the flight back home, and it dawned on me that if I ever wrote a book, I would use Carl's book as a template.

In August 2010 my wife I watched comedian Tom Dreesen being interviewed on David Letterman's *The Late Show*. The conversation turned to baseball, and to our surprise Letterman asked Tom if my story about umpire Frank Pulli and the signed baseball I slipped into the game was true. Tom didn't remember the story, but the fact that Letterman recalled it put the thought in my mind that perhaps it was time to write that book.

I contacted Tom through his website, and within a few hours he called me, and we shared some laughs about a few other stories he did remember from my playing days. When I told my wife, Chantal, about the call from Dreesen, she suggested I write the Pulli story as I remembered it.

From my upstairs office, I did just that. When I finished I sent her the story via e-mail (the story was much too long for a tweet or a text). After a few minutes she laughed out loud! I walked downstairs for the full reaction. "Loved it . . . Got any more?"

I wrote and sent her another recollection. Same reaction. That's how this book came to life. It took hours, days, months, and a few years of my time. But it was worth it. The story of my baseball life is here for all to share. My thanks to all of you who took the time to read it.

Notes

3. LIFE IN THE MINORS

1. http://en.wikipedia.org/wiki/George_Kissell.
2. http://www.retrosheet.org/boxesetc/R/MU1_reusj001.htm.
3. http://www.ballparktour.com/Former_San_Diego.html.
4. http://www.baseball-reference.com/minors/player.cgi?id=reuss-001jer.
5. http://www.baseball-reference.com/minors/team.cgi?id=0e7b5034.
6. http://en.wikipedia.org/wiki/1969_Major_League_Baseball_season.
7. John Helyer, *Lords of the Realm: The Real History of Baseball* (New York: Villard, 1994), 84–85.
8. Helyer, *Lords of the Realm*, 95.
9. Helyer, *Lords of the Realm*, 96.
10. Helyer, *Lords of the Realm*, 98.
11. Stuart L. Weiss, *The Curt Flood Story: The Man behind the Myth* (Columbia: University of Missouri Press, 2007), 96.
12. Helyer, *Lords of the Realm*, 99.
13. Weiss, *Curt Flood Story*, 119.
14. Weiss, *Curt Flood Story*, 100.
15. Peter Golenbock, *The Spirit of St. Louis: A History of the St. Louis Cardinals and Browns* (New York: Spike, 2000), 502–3.
16. Weiss, *Curt Flood Story*, 117–18.
17. http://www.americanassociationbaseball.com/office-history.php.

4. TWENTY-FOUR HOURS FROM TULSA

1. http://www.retrosheet.org/boxesetc/1969/B09240NYN1969.htm.
2. http://www.retrosheet.org/boxesetc/1969/B09270MON1969.htm.

5. MEET ME IN ST. LOUIS

1. "Stoneman Might Have Used Slingshot," *Montreal Gazette*, August 11, 1970, 9.

2. Golenbock, *Spirit of St. Louis*, 520.

3. Rob Neyer, *Rob Neyer's Big Book of Baseball Blunders: A Complete Guide to the Worst Decisions and Stupidest Moments in Baseball History* (New York: Fireside, 2006), 169–73.

4. Bob Gibson with Lonnie Wheeler, *Stranger to the Game* (New York: Viking, 1994), 233–34.

5. The win totals and the names of the traded players came from http://retrosheet.org.

6. Neyer, *Neyer's Big Book of Baseball Blunders*, 169–76.

7. Golenbock, *Spirit of St. Louis*, 318–19.

8. Helyer, *Lords of the Realm*, 112–13.

9. Helyer, *Lords of the Realm*, 122.

10. http://www.retrosheet.org/boxesetc/1972/VSLN01972.htm.

11. Dick Kaegel, "Cards Trade Reuss," *St. Louis Post-Dispatch*, April 16, 1972, Sports, 1.

12. Jack Herman, "Reuss Claims Principal Led to Astros Trade," *St. Louis Globe-Democrat*, April 16, 1972, Sports, C1.

13. MLBPA, Decision 11, Reuss-STL 72-2, e-mailed by Steve Rogers.

14. Neil Russo, "Redbirds Trim Fat Off Budget, Deal Dissident Reuss," *Sporting News*, April 29, 1972.

6. HOUSTON, I'M COMIN' TO SEE YA

1. http://www.astrosdaily.com/history/worsttrades.html.

2. Home runs: Lee May 29, Jimmy Wynn 24, Doug Rader and César Cedeño, 22. RBI: May 98, Wynn and Rader 90, Bob Watson 86, Cedeño 82. http://www.retrosheet.org/boxesetc/1972/UHOU01972.htm.

3. All statistics and play of the game courtesy of retrosheet.org.

4. http://www.retrosheet.org/boxesetc/A/Paloum101.htm.

5. Jimmy Wynn with Bill McCurdy, *Toy Cannon: The Autobiography of Jimmy Wynn* (Jefferson NC: McFarland, 2010), 145–46. Here's the list of six reasons Wynn believes Harry was fired:

   1. By August 1972 Spec knew very well that the club's black players had no respect for Harry and his racist attitudes

   2. Spec also knew by then that Harry was terrible in general in handling people and that several of his team talks had led to near riots in the clubhouse

3. Spec and his management team also knew that the team was winning on their own and in spite of Harry's presence at the helm

4. The club needed an action that would further help take the fans' minds off the Morgan, Staub, and Cueller trades as the reasons the Astros still would not win a pennant in 1972

5. Spec wanted a manager who could inspire hope and sell a few more tickets during the last dog days of another lost season

6. And, finally, an available manager was out there, and he was the kind guy who could pump a gate with curiosity seekers in spite of the fact that the club wasn't going anywhere

6. Leo Durocher with Ed Linn, *Nice Guys Finish Last* (New York: Pocket, 1976), 380.

7. Durocher with Linn, *Nice Guys Finish Last*, 380.

8. Numbers provided by retrosheet.org.

9. Neil J. Sullivan, *The Dodgers Move West* (New York: Oxford University Press, 1987), 210.

10. http://www.retrosheet.org/boxesetc/1973/B07061MON1973.htm.

11. http://www.755homeruns.com/1973.shtml. Hank hit number 662 against me on August 9, 1972, in Atlanta and number 684 on May 16, 1973, in the Astrodome before connecting for number 713 on September 29, 1973, in Atlanta.

12. Game information courtesy of retrosheet.org.

13. "Pirates Ready for Concessions," *Pittsburgh Post-Gazette*, September 12, 1977.

14. Lee May hit 28, Jimmy Wynn had 20, Doug Rader hit 21, and César Cedeño ended with 25 home runs. May had 105 RBI, Rader 89, and Watson 94. All statistics courtesy of retrosheet.org.

15. Dierker was 15-8 in '72. Don Wilson went from a 15-10 in '72 to an 11-16 record in '73. Dave Roberts enjoyed the best season of his career in '73 with a 17-11 mark after posting a 12-7 record in '72, while I had my first winning season with 16 wins. All statistics courtesy of retrosheet.org.

16. Charley Feeney, "Pirates-Astros Slated to Put Together Trade," *Pittsburgh Post-Gazette*, October 31, 1973, 29.

17. All statistics courtesy of retrosheet.org.

18. Jack Herman, "Ex-Astro Reuss Claims Pirates Got Bargain; Blasts Durocher," *St. Louis Globe-Democrat*, November 2, 1973.

19. Durocher with Linn, *Nice Guys Finish Last*, 381.

7. MAKIN' MY WAY TO THE STEEL CITY

1. Charley Feeney, "Brett, Reuss to Fight 50-Year Pirate Jinx," *Sporting News*, December 1, 1973.
2. http://en.wikipedia.org/wiki/Danny_Murtaugh.
3. David Cantaneo, *Baseball Legends and Lore: A Crackerjack Collection of Stories & Anecdotes about the Game* (New York: Barnes and Noble, 1997), 125–26.
4. http://www.johnfmurray.com.
5. http://www.retrosheet.org/boxesetc/1974/VPIT01974.htm.
6. http://www.baseballreliquary.org/ellis.htm.
7. Andrew O'Toole and Al Oliver, *Baseball's Best Kept Secret: Al Oliver and His Time in Baseball* (Pittsburgh: City of Champions, 1997), 107.
8. All statistics courtesy of retrosheet.org.
9. Willie Stargell and Tom Bird, *Willie Stargell: An Autobiography* (New York: Harper and Row, 1984), 152–227.
10. Derek A. Reveron, "Dave Parker: Big Man, Big Bat, and Baseball's Biggest Salary," *Ebony*, October 1979.
11. All statistics courtesy of retrosheet.org.
12. Hebner batted .249 with 8 HR, 51 RBI, 60 runs scored, and 1 stolen base in 4 attempts. In 1977 Garner batted .261 with 17 HR, 77 RBI, 99 runs scored, and 32 stolen bases in 41 attempts. All statistics are courtesy of retrosheet .org.

8. CALIFORNIA, HERE I COME!

1. To read the complete story click, http://tommy.mlblogs.com/?s=tom+lasorda+tombstone.
2. All statistics courtesy of retrosheet.org.
3. To write the details about the game, I sat down one afternoon and watched the entire game. It was just the second time in more than thirty years that I watched it.
4. Bruce Jenkins, "Reuss No-Hits Giants: One Batter from Perfect," *San Francisco Chronicle*, Sporting Green, 43.
5. Leonard Koppett, "The Case for Reuss: Better than Perfect," *Sporting News*, July 26, 1980.
6. Jenkins, "Reuss No-Hits Giants," 43.
7. All statistics courtesy of retrosheet.org.
8. Rick Monday with Ken Gurnick, *Rick Monday's Tales from the Dodgers Dugout* (Champaign IL: Sports Publishing, 2006), 75.
9. Attendance figures courtesy of retrosheet.org.
10. Monthly records courtesy of retrosheet.org.

11. Marvin Miller, *A Whole Different Ballgame* (New York: Birch Lane Press, 1991), 286.

12. Miller, *A Whole Different Ballgame*, 298.

13. Miller, *A Whole Different Ballgame*, 298–319.

14. Tommy Lasorda with David Fisher, *The Artful Dodger* (New York: Arbor House, 1985), 215.

15. Jay Johnstone with Rick Talley, *Temporary Insanity: The Uncensored Adventures of Baseball's Craziest Player* (Chicago: Contemporary, 1985), 20.

16. Mark Langill, *Game of My Life: Dodgers Memorable Stories of Dodgers Baseball* (Champaign IL: Sports Publishing, 2007), 135.

17. http://www.retrosheet.org/boxesetc/1981/B10060HOU1981.htm.

18. http://www.retrosheet.org/boxesetc/1981/B10070HOU1981.htm.

19. http://www.retrosheet.org/boxesetc/1981/B10090LAN1981.htm.

20. http://www.retrosheet.org/boxesetc/1981/B10100LAN1981.htm.

21. http://www.retrosheet.org/boxesetc/1981/B10110LAN1981.htm.

22. http://www.retrosheet.org/boxesetc/1981/B10130LAN1981.htm.

23. http://www.retrosheet.org/boxesetc/1981/B10140LAN1981.htm.

24. http://www.retrosheet.org/boxesetc/1981/B10160MON1981.htm.

25. http://en.wikipedia.org/wiki/The_Happy_Wanderer.

26. http://www.retrosheet.org/boxesetc/1981/B10190MON1981.htm.

27. http://www.retrosheet.org/boxesetc/R/MU1_roges001.htm.

28. Monday with Gurnick, *Monday's Tales from the Dodgers Dugout*, 136.

29. All game information courtesy of retrosheet.org.

30. http://www.retrosheet.org/boxesetc/1981/B10200NYA1981.htm.

31. http://www.retrosheet.org/boxesetc/1981/B10210NYA1981.htm.

32. *Los Angeles Times*, October 24, 1981, Series Notes, D11.

33. *Reading (PA) Eagle*, October 23, 1981, 20.

34. Tony Jackson, "Valenzuela Pitched Best Game in 1981 World Series," ESPN LA, June 24, 2010.

35. Dick Kaegel, "Fernando Saluted for Gritty Job," *Sporting News*, November 7, 1981, 16.

36. Kaegel, "Fernando Saluted for Gritty Job," 16.

37. Kaegel, "Fernando Saluted for Gritty Job," 16.

38. Dick Kaegel, "Dodgers 'Skyhigh' after Mad Scramble," *Sporting News*, November 7, 1981, 17.

39. Scott Ostler, "Reggie Can't Beat the Dodgers If He's One of Them," *Los Angeles Times*, October 25, 1981, D21.

40. *Sporting News*, November 7, 1981, Game Four Notes, 17.

41. "Jackson Gets Something Off His Chest," *Los Angeles Times*, October 25, 1981, D1.

42. Play-by-play courtesy of retrosheet.org.

43. "Jackson Gets Something Off His Chest," D1.

44. "Jackson Gets Something Off His Chest," D1.

45. "Even Stephen for LA," *Daytona Beach Sunday News Journal*, October 25, 1981, D9.

46. Kaegel, *Sporting News*, November 7, 1981, 17.

47. http://www.retrosheet.org/boxesetc/1973/B06190SDN1973.htm.

48. AP, "Dodger Power Sweeps LA into Series Lead," *Palm Beach Post*, October 26, 1981, D1.

49. UPI, "Guerrero, Yeager Join Elite Tandems," *St. Petersburg Times*, October 26, 1981, C4.

50. AP, "Dodger Power Sweeps LA into Series Lead," D1.

51. AP, "Reuss Shows Winning Strategy . . . ," *St. Joseph (MO) Gazette*, October 26, 1981, C1.

52. Monday with Gurnick, *Monday's Tales from the Dodgers Dugout*, 135–56.

53. http://www.retrosheet.org/boxesetc/R/MU1_reusj001.htm.

54. Ross Newhan, "If Yanks Fall Flat, Steinbrenner Won't Wait till Next Year," *Los Angeles Times*, October 26, 1981, D3.

55. Newhan, "If Yanks Fall Flat," D3.

56. Newhan, "If Yanks Fall Flat," D3.

57. Mike Littwin, "Lasorda Sure Had That Fella Yeager Rested for Series," *Los Angeles Times*, October 26, 1981, D13.

58. Littwin, "Lasorda Sure Had That Fella Yeager Rested," D13.

59. Mike Littwin, "Dodgers Save Lopes' Life," *Los Angeles Times*, October 26, 1981, D14.

60. Mark Heisler, "It's Champagne with a Twist of Lemon," *Los Angeles Times*, October 29, 1981, G1.

61. Mike Littwin, "The Dodgers Win before That Old Gang Is Broken Up," *Los Angeles Times*, October 29, 1981, G1.

62. Littwin, "Dodgers Win," G1.

63. "3 Dodgers Declared MVP's," *Kingman (AZ) Daily Miner*, October 29, 1981, Sports, 8.

64. All postseason statistics courtesy of retrosheet.org.

65. "75,000 Fans Salute L.A.'s World Champs," *Inland Empire Press-Enterprise* (Riverside CA), October 31, 1981, Sports.

66. "75,000 Fans Salute L.A.'s World Champs."

67. http://en.wikipedia.org/wiki/Bigger_Than_Both_of_Us.

68. *Record World*, November 21, 1981.

69. *Los Angeles Times*, November 3, 1981, Morning Briefing, D2.

9. LIFE AFTER THE WORLD SERIES...

1. All game information courtesy of retrosheet.org.

2. My 1983 numbers are courtesy of retrosheet.org.

3. James Lipton, *An Exultation of Larks; or, The Venereal Game* (New York: Penguin, 1977), 108. The term *slant* in Lipton's book refers to journalists. It works just as well for sportswriters!

4. "Reuss' Elbow Surgery Is a Success," *Los Angeles Times*, January 25, 1984, Newswire, D1.

5. Gordon Edes, "Dodgers, Minus Landreaux and Guerrero, Beat Astros," *Los Angeles Times*, April 24, 1984, Dodger Notes, sec. OC_B1, 4.

6. Gordon Edes, "Koosman Gets a 3-1 Win with Holland's Help," *Los Angeles Times*, May 23, 1984, Dodger Notes, sec. OC_B1, 16.

7. Gordon Edes, "Reuss Struggles; Dodgers Lose, 5-2," *Los Angeles Times*, July 19, 1984, sec. F1, 16.

8. Numbers courtesy of retrosheet.org.

9. Wrigley Field numbers courtesy of retrosheet.org.

10. I finished at 14-10 in 33 starts with a 2.92 ERA. On many clubs those are the numbers of a second or third starter. Not on the 1985 Dodgers. Hershiser was 19-3 in 34 starts with a 2.03 ERA, Fernando checked in at 17-10, with 35 starts and a 2.45 ERA, and Bob Welch in just 23 starts was 14-4 with a 2.31 ERA. Numbers courtesy of retrosheet.org.

11. http://en.wikipedia.org/wiki/Tom_Lasorda.

12. Matchups courtesy of David W. Smith, retrosheet.org.

13. Van Slyke versus Niedenfuer: 5 at bats, 3 hits, 1 homer, 1 walk, 2 strikeouts; Van Slyke versus Howell: 3 at bats, 0 hits, 0 walks, 2 strikeouts; Van Slyke versus Reuss: 3 at bats, 0 hits, 0 walks, 0 strikeouts. Harper versus Reuss: 10 at bats, 3 hits, 1 homer, 0 walks, 0 strikeouts. Matchups courtesy of David W. Smith, retrosheet.org.

14. Thomas Boswell, "Baseball: If You Don't Bend, It'll Break You," *Deseret News*, October 18, 1985, sec. 8B.

15. "LA Knows How Close It Was," *Nashville (TN) Daily News*, October 17, 1985.

16. Gordon Edes, "Dodgers Pitch to Clark . . . It's His Pitch," *Los Angeles Times*, October 17, 1985, sec. C1, 15.

17. Boswell, "Baseball: If You Don't Bend, It'll Break You."

18. Gordon Edes, "Padres Defeat Dodgers in Extra Innings Again and by Run Again, 2-1," *Los Angeles Times*, April 16, 1986, Dodger Notes, sec. C1, 6.

19. Sam McManis, "Reuss, 37, Won't Give Up without a Fight," *Los Angeles Times*, March 4, 1987, sec. E4.

20. McManis, "Reuss, 37, Won't Give Up without a Fight."

21. Sam McManis, "Odd Man Will Be Out, but Talented Pitchers Make Decisions Tough," *Los Angeles Times*, March 24, 1987, sec. E4.

22. Sam McManis, "Reuss, Hoping to Make Club, Goes Eight against Teammates," *Los Angeles Times*, March 31, 1987, sec. E4.

23. Sam McManis, "This Time Trevino Gets Even, Gives Dodgers 5–3 Win," *Los Angeles Times*, April 23, 1987, sec. E1, 8.

10. HITS, MISSES, AND WHISTLE-STOPS

1. Seaver's contract was assigned to the White Sox, as he was selected from the Mets in the player-compensation pool draft on January 20, 1984.

2. Statistics compiled from retrosheet.org.

3. Statistics compiled from retrosheet.org.

4. Game information and statistics courtesy of retrosheet.org.

5. Jerome Holtzman, "Sox Pick Torborg as Manager," *Chicago Tribune*, November 4, 1988, Sports.

6. Game information and statistics courtesy of retrosheet.org.

7. Statistics courtesy of retrosheet.org.

8. Karen Anderson, "At 41, Reuss Makes Pitch for Return to Majors," *Chicago Tribune*, August 18, 1990, sec. 3, 8.

9. Bob Dicesare, "Reuss Sizzles as Herd Trims Indians, 4–2," *Buffalo (NY) News*, July 31, 1990.

10. Dates for Tomlin's and York's games and the statistics on Zane Smith courtesy of retrosheet.org.

11. http://www.baseball-reference.com/bullpen/Category:Played_in _Four_Decades.